THE CANALS OF THE
EAST MIDLANDS
(including part of London)

THE CANALS OF THE BRITISH ISLES

EDITED BY CHARLES HADFIELD

Other Books by Charles Hadfield

Canals of the World

Holiday Cruising on Inland Waterways (with Michael Streat)

The Canal Age

Atmospheric Railways

THE CANALS OF THE
EAST MIDLANDS

(including part of London)

by

Charles Hadfield

WITH PLATES AND MAPS

SECOND EDITION

DAVID & CHARLES: NEWTON ABBOT

7153 4871 X

1st edition 1966
2nd edition 1970

© *Charles Hadfield* 1966, 1970

Printed in Great Britain by
Latimer Trend & Company Limited Whitstable
for David & Charles (Publishers) Limited
South Devon House Newton Abbot
Devon

THIS BOOK
IS RESPECTFULLY DEDICATED
TO THE MEMORY OF

William Jessop

PRINCIPAL ENGINEER

of the Cromford, Ellesmere, Grand Junction,
Leicester and Nottingham Canals, and of the
Trent Navigation

AND OF

Benjamin Outram

CANAL AND TRAMROAD ENGINEER

CONTENTS

ILLUSTRATIONS

PLATES

TEXT ILLUSTRATIONS AND MAPS

PREFACE

I HAD originally planned to write a single book on the Midland waterways to follow my three earlier studies of canal history. The first, *British Canals*, gave a general account of British canal navigation from the beginning of the canal age to the passing of the Transport Act of 1947. In *The Canals of Southern England* I described in more detail the waterways south of a line from Gloucester to the Thames, and in *The Canals of South Wales and the Border* those of South Wales, Monmouthshire, Herefordshire and the Forest of Dean. But when it came to be written, it seemed more convenient for the pocket and the hand to divide a long book into two.

The two Midland volumes are concerned with the navigations between and near the Thames and the Trent. On the east, I have drawn a line from the Trent to London that includes the Grantham Canal and the schemes to join the Grand Junction to the Great Ouse at Bedford, but excludes those waterways that look towards the North Sea, as well as the Lee and Stort. I apologize for including London in the Midlands, though I do not regret an arrangement which brings the whole of the Grand Union system within a single volume.

The Midlands saw the rise and fall of a busy and extensive canal system. I have found it impossible satisfactorily to arrange the text so that the reader can simultaneously read the complete history of a waterway in one place, and understand how that history was affected by what was happening elsewhere. I have compromised by dividing it into three parts, the first telling of the building of the earlier canals, the success of which led men greatly to expand the system; the second of the period when canals flourished; and the third of competition with railways and, later, road transport, and of their decline. He who wishes to read the story of a single canal straight through can do so by using the page references given in the text, or the bold figures of the index.

Very few detailed historical studies of any part of the Midland canal system exist. This book and its companion, *The Canals of the West Midlands*, for that reason based almost entirely on original sources, can therefore be no more than an introduction. I shall feel the spare-time labour of a dozen years to have been worth while if they encourage others to write full-length accounts of such important concerns as the Trent Navigation, the Grand Junction or the Oxford Canal.

One thing remains to be said. There is almost nothing here about the years since 1948. They are too close, and I have been too personally involved in what has happened, to be able to write about them in perspective. I therefore leave them to historians yet unknown.

CHARLES HADFIELD

PART ONE—TO 1790

CHAPTER I

The Line to Oxford

++++++++++++++++++++++++++++++++++++++◆++++++++++++++++++++++++++++++++++++++

'WE have several Navigation schemes in embryo,' Josiah Wedgwood wrote in March 1767. 'One from the GRAND TRUNK to
Coventry, Banbury & I don't know where. The money was sub-
scrib'd for surveying, &c. & Mr. Brindley applied to, but he told
them they were too precipitate (for they wo^d have been in Parliament this Session), he wo^d look over the Country in a year or two
if he could.'[1] In spite of this discouragement, a meeting at Warwick
on 18 August considered a canal from the Trent & Mersey to
Coventry* and an extension to Oxford. It endorsed that to
Coventry, but temporarily shelved the Oxford extension pending
examination of a line through Warwick to Stratford to join the
Avon Navigation.[2] On 3 September another meeting at Coventry
endorsed a canal connection by way of Lichfield to the Trent &
Mersey, and £17,000 was subscribed.[3] A bill was immediately
introduced. One of the canal's strong supporters was Richard
Parrott, who with his partner owned a colliery at Bedworth and
a tramroad and small private canal which ran for about ⅜ mile
from Bedworth hill to near Hawkesbury, which was to be absorbed into the new line.

There was some opposition from members of the Trent &
Mersey's committee, who 'had been made to believe that the
Coventry Navigation wo^d injure ours'[4] and from the Staffs &
Worcs, who hoped themselves to be part of a through canal line
to London. 'The Coventry People have had a narrow escape of
losing their Bill', wrote Wedgwood, 'by precipitateing it too quick
through a *select* Ctee, without acquainting or sending Cards to any
of the other Members, or even to Mr. Gilbert who was appointed

---

* Henry Bradford, who in 1758 had proposed to make the Tame navigable, had
in 1766 and 1767 surveyed for a canal from Coventry to Tamworth, with a river
extension thence to Fazeley; and in 1759 there had been a bill for a canal from
Lichfield to the River Trent at King's Mills.

to report what the Ctee had done, to the House, at which he was greatly disgusted; however, the storm is blown out, & I believe they are in a way of doing very well.'[5]

The Act[6] was passed on 29 January 1768 for a line from the Grand Trunk at Fradley by Huddlesford not far from Lichfield, Fazeley, Atherstone and Nuneaton to Coventry, where, at the *White Bear*, the first meeting of the company took place, and where the main shareholdings were centred. Thus Lichfield's hope of getting a canal by supporting the Trent & Mersey was partially rewarded. The authorized capital was £50,000 in £100 shares, and £30,000 more if necessary. James Brindley was appointed engineer and surveyor at £150 p.a., 'he undertaking to give at least two months' attendance in the whole in every year upon the Design',[7] while Joseph Parker, appointed Clerk of Works, was sent to Hugh Henshall for a month's training.

The first object of the company was to improve the supply of coal to Coventry. Construction began on 25 April 1768, and the first two boatloads of coal were brought from Bedworth to Coventry on 10 August 1769,[8] though the basin at Bishopgate (Bishop Street) was not completed till towards the end of that year. By April 1770 the Company was itself selling coal at Coventry, a practice that continued for many years, and later it took for a time to hiring boats to those engaged in the coal trade. Meanwhile, in April 1769, the Oxford Canal company had obtained an Act to join the Coventry's line at Longford near that city and build a waterway to Oxford.

The pace of canal cutting led to some 'improvident Issuing and Expenditure of Money on account of Labourage'.[9] This, together with hooliganism at the works, construction difficulties at Bedworth 'hill' and, one suspects, his failure to put in his agreed two months in the year on their affairs caused the proprietors in September 1769 to dismiss Brindley and give the inexperienced Parker a severe warning. Most canal companies that had employed Brindley had recorded their exasperation with him, but only the Coventry ever nerved themselves to dismiss him. Both sides must have been equally surprised. The elderly engineer Thomas Yeoman, who had worked on the Lee and Stort Navigation works and elsewhere, was called in. He advised the company for some months and then, Parker also having left, a new man, Edmund Lingard, was appointed, with Samuel Bull, later engineer of the Birmingham Canal, as his assistant, and cutting went on towards Atherstone.

The shareholders were now most annoyed to learn that, at a meeting in Lichfield on 18 August 1770 to discuss a possible canal from Walsall to Fradley, Samuel Garbett had announced 'that he was Authorized by Mr. Brindley to Declare they had no Intention of Executing the Coventry Canal so as to communicate with the Staffordshire Navigation upon ffradley Heath And that Mr. Brindley . . . had repeatedly heard from them Declarations to that Effect'.[10] They issued a contradiction to the press, but later agreed with the Birmingham Canal company that their two engineers should jointly survey a possible junction between the Coventry Canal at Fazeley or elsewhere and the Birmingham Canal,* which they did in 1771. Brindley, on the other hand, stuck to his guns and authorized a counter press statement.[11]

In June 1771 the canal was open from Coventry as far as Nuneaton, and by the end of the year to Atherstone, by which time the whole of the £50,000 authorized capital seems to have been used. Beyond Atherstone the committee was not happy about the Parliamentary line, and again called in Thomas Yeoman, who recommended a new route to Polesworth and a level crossing over the River Tame instead of an aqueduct. Discouraged by this, by lack of money, and by their quarrel with the Oxford company, they did nothing, and for many years the Coventry Canal consisted of an isolated stretch of water from Atherstone to Coventry, carrying enough local traffic to enable a first dividend of £2 per £100 share to be paid in September 1774, and similar sums in most years afterwards.

In *England's Improvement by Land and Sea*, published in 1677, Andrew Yarranton had proposed to make the River Cherwell navigable from Oxford to Banbury for £10,000, so that corn from the neighbourhood could be carried to London. The project for a canal from the Coventry line to Oxford derived partly from this impetus to join the Thames and so gain access to London, but perhaps more from Banbury's and Oxford's need for coal. The main promotion meeting was held at the *Three Tuns Inn*, Banbury, on 25 October 1768 to receive Brindley's report and survey. The gathering was enthusiastic, and subscribed over £50,000 there and then, the town clerks of Oxford and Coventry being deputed to draw up the bill.[12] The canal had impressive support, for

'The Dukes of Marlborough and Buccleugh, the Lords Spencer, Guildford, and North, the Vice Chancellor, and several of the Heads of Houses, the two Members for the University, with

---

* For the Birmingham & Fazeley Canal see Chapter V.

B

many other Gentlemen of great weight and consequence, as well as the Corporations of Oxford, Woodstock, Banbury, and Coventry, communicated . . . their most sanguine wishes for the success of the undertaking'.[13]

After opposition from those who feared for the Newcastle coastal coal trade and the nursery for seamen it provided, from landowners and from road carriers, the Act[14] was passed in April 1769. It authorized a capital of £150,000 in £100 shares, and £50,000 more if necessary from old or new subscribers. The supporters of the coasting trade had won their point, however, for a clause prohibited the carriage of any coal beyond Oxford down river, on pain of forfeiture of the vessel and cargo, and a fine of £50. A meeting on 12 May reported that all the money had been subscribed, the final entry being by James Brindley for £3,000 worth of shares. The principal shareholders included the Duke of Marlborough (50 shares, and another 40 in his family), Sir Roger Newdigate (20), Dr Wetherell, Vice-Chancellor of the University (20), James Brindley (20, soon increased to 30 and then 45), Richard Parrott (10) and Francis Page, owner of the Kennet Navigation.[15] Newdigate and Parrott represented colliery interests round Coventry, and Page the hope of traffic, but most of the weight behind the company came from the Oxford colleges. The reverend gentlemen proved good businessmen and provided their well-managed canal with an ordained chairman till 1885.

Brindley was appointed Engineer and General Surveyor at £200 p.a., with James King as his Clerk of Works and Samuel Simcock as assistant. Bricklayers and a carpenter were sent to canal works in Staffordshire 'for their Improvement',[16] it was decided that 'the Accounts of the Company shall be kept in a Merchantile Manner by Double Entry',[17] and notices of calls were to be put not only in newspapers, but on church doors, where absent-minded clergymen shareholders would presumably be likely to see them.

In its early days the committee had to struggle with Brindley. They began efficiently by observing that the Act only broadly laid down the canal line; they therefore instructed him to make a detailed survey and estimate. Two months later he wrote from Coventry to tell King to make the survey; as for the estimate, 'I will not attempt making any Estimate of the Works because I know the great Difficulty as well as very great Expence of making them to any Degree of Certainty'.[18] The committee minuted: 'James Brindley hath in no Degree complied with the Orders of the Committee', but recorded no further action. They had another

crisis with him a year later. It could have resulted from a minute
that: 'the Engineer Surveyor and Clerks of this Company do not
associate or drink with any of the Inferior Officers or Workmen'.[19]
Six weeks later they received Brindley's resignation, without explanation. They wrote hurriedly: 'We are very sorry that anything
has happened that has given you Offence and shall always be
willing to place the greatest Confidence in you, as we consider the
Assistance of your Abilities and Experience essential to the carrying this Navigation effectually into Execution.' A meeting was
suggested. This must have soothed him, for no more was heard of
resignation.

The development of both canals was hampered by a quarrel
over making the junction between them. The cause was a stipulation in the Oxford Act that the Coventry company were to take
the toll on coal (not to exceed 1d per mile) on the Oxford Canal for
the first two miles from the junction at Longford, whether or not
the coal had been navigated on the Coventry Canal itself. On the
other hand, the Oxford company was to have the tolls on all
articles *except* coal which came from their canal and were navigated
for up to 3½ miles on the Coventry Canal towards Coventry.
According to a Coventry Canal document,[20] the original Oxford
Canal bill provided for a junction at Gosford Green near Coventry.
During its passage through Parliament Brindley changed his mind
and recommended Bedworth, which would have meant that coal
from Bedworth colliery going on to the Oxford would not also
pay tolls on the Coventry. Longford, two miles nearer Coventry
than Bedworth, was therefore chosen as the junction, even though
it necessitated building two lines of canal parallel to each other,
and the compensation clause inserted to give the Coventry company the same financial return as they would have had from
Gosford.

Almost immediately the Oxford company sought to get rid of
its liability and to negotiate for Bedworth instead of Longford as
the point of junction. First they offered £1,500 to commute the
compensation payments; then they sought an amending Act,
which the Coventry's supporters helped to defeat; and then in late
1773 or early 1774 they tried to by-pass the junction by discussing
with the Birmingham Canal company and other Birmingham interests, schemes for a link between their two lines by way of
Napton, Bedworth, Atherstone or Fazeley.[21] Surveys were made,
and a group of supporters of a Birmingham & Napton canal was
gathered. When these plans failed, they did nothing, drawing their

own coal supplies from Hawkesbury and Wyken collieries on their own line, or by road from Bedworth and the Coventry Canal.

The Oxford again tried to break the deadlock in early 1776 by suggesting that if the Coventry completed their canal to Fradley within five years, they would no longer object to the compensation tolls. The Coventry replied that if the Oxford made the junction at Longford at once and undertook that 'no Coals or other commodities shall with their Knowledge, Permission or Connivance pass out of one canal into the other but by the Point of such Junction',[22] they would complete to Fradley as soon as possible. If they had not done so within seven years, they would drop their compensation claim till they had. In fact, at this time the Coventry were more interested in making a connection with the Staffordshire collieries than with the Trent & Mersey, and were quite willing to waive their rights if they could do so.

The Oxford then suggested they should help the Coventry to build a canal to the collieries, an unwelcome proposal. At this, the Coventry stopped negotiating and sought a mandamus to compel the Oxford to make the junction. The treatment worked. The Court of King's Bench made an order, and on 15 April 1777 the junction was made at Longford, two lines of canal running parallel for over a mile. Both companies got their tolls, the owners of goods carried paid for unnecessary mileage, and boatmen wasted time on the doubled length and lost temper on the half-circle bend at Longford. Brindley or King had made a mistake and instead of the stop-lock controlling a level junction, the Oxford Canal was 6⅞ in. higher. Sir Roger Newdigate described it as 'a very troublesome contrivance to conceal the want of taking a right level at first',[23] 'which is a most egregious error where a Canal is so distress'd for Water', as old Samuel Weston said in 1778,[24] for it meant a continual loss of water to the Coventry.

By March 1771 ten miles of the Oxford had been opened, and during the summer the first tolls on coal were taken. When Brindley died in 1772 Samuel Simcock succeeded him as engineer at £200 p.a. By the middle of 1774 £30,000 more was needed, and the company asked the shareholders to subscribe this sum by extra calls on their shares. Those who were willing were told that they would be preferred in future subscriptions 'when the Stock bears a Premium as there is no Doubt but it will as soon as the Canal is compleated to Banbury'.[25] All the same, outside shareholders had to complete the subscription. By August 1774 the canal had reached Napton. An Act[26] of 1775 then enabled them to raise

£70,000 by mortgage, and with this support the company got
their line to Banbury on 30 March 1778,[27] a distance of 63¾ miles,
at a cost of £199,304, of which about £140,000 had been raised in
shares and the balance in loans. The principal engineering works
were the great aqueduct at Brinklow, from the beginning known
as Brinklow Arches, with its twelve arches each of 22 ft span, and
the tunnels at Fenny Compton, 336 yd and 452 yd, separated by an
opening of 155 yd, 9 ft 4 in. wide, which was particularly troublesome to build, Newbold, 125 yd long,[28] 12½ ft wide with a towpath, and Wolfhampcote near Braunston, 33 yd, of which Samuel
Weston in his report of December 1778 said: 'a Bridge wou'd have
answered the purpose'.[29] At Banbury the work stopped for the
time being. The financial position of the company was difficult,
the Coventry was making no progress with their canal, and the
American War had begun.

There is no obvious explanation for the very winding original
line of the Oxford Canal north of Cropredy, for canals set out
earlier by Brindley, such as the Bridgewater, Trent & Mersey and
Coventry, do not cling so exaggeratedly to the contours. Indeed,
in June 1769 King and Simcock were told to set out the canal from
Longford 'in as Strait a Line as the Ground will permit,[30] and
chose to build a canal 26½ miles long from Longford to Hillmorton, 12¾ miles between Claydon and Napton, and 91 miles in
all to the Thames. Yet a survey[31] of 1768 by Robert Whitworth
shows two lines from the Coventry Canal to Hillmorton, the
shorter of which, from Gosford Green, is 15¾ miles and level, the
length of the whole canal being 77⅜ miles. Curiously, also, in the
Gentlemen's Magazine for April 1771, nearly two years after construction began, a map appeared showing an 82-mile line, the
distance from Longford to Hillmorton being 20 miles, and from
Claydon to Napton 12¾ miles. One naturally assumes that the
responsibility was Brindley's. When he died, however, construction had only reached Brinklow, and contracts for the land required for most of the curves down to Braunston had not yet been
signed. The long loop at Wormleighton was definitely set out by
Simcock;[32] he also set out the old Birmingham Canal, also very
circuitous (though Brindley defended it), and I tend to think the
main responsibility was his. There had been difficulty at Wormleighton with the landowner, Earl Spencer, and one argument for
Simcock's line was that it had no lock; therefore 'the navigators
will have no business to stop for any purpose, so that the apprehended Danger from the inroads of the Bargemen will be less'.[33]

Much later, in 1829, the company itself said: 'in consequence of opposition on the part of the Land Owners . . . and from the art of making Canals not being so well understood then as it now is, and also from the necessity of saving expense . . . the Canal in its Northern part was made in a direction too circuitous'.[34] In so far as this statement can be relied upon, the second reason given seems to apply better to Simcock than to Brindley.

In 1779 the committee recommended that the canal should be completed to Oxford, where they thought there should be a good sale of coal and lime for building, and Simcock and Robert Whitworth surveyed it. This possibility in turn interested a group at Birmingham in the possibility of a junction, and late in 1780 the Oxford company opened talks. They found that the Birmingham Canal company were again considering a connection by Warwick and Napton. It was an unwelcome idea, for whereas a connection by way of Fazeley on the yet unbuilt section of the Coventry, such as had been considered in 1771, or by Atherstone, as had been discussed in 1773,[35] would enable the Oxford to collect tolls over its whole length, a line from Birmingham to Napton would be far less productive. The Oxford company therefore discouraged the Napton idea, though it acquired some momentum of its own at meetings held in Birmingham and Warwick in October and November 1781, at which sufficient interest was shown for money to be raised for preliminary expenses, and was therefore a help in putting pressure on the Coventry.

In April 1781 the Oxford and Coventry companies met to discuss plans, 'particularly a Plan from Faseley to the Birmingham Canal',[36] and agreed to make a joint survey to the Wednesbury collieries. At this point action was taken by an independent group, which called a meeting at Warwick in August 1781 to propose a canal from Wednesbury by Fazeley to Atherstone, the present termination of the Coventry. This suited the latter, but a further meeting on 4 October altered the proposed end to Fazeley, upon which the Coventry offered to give up its right to build the Atherstone–Fazeley section if Atherstone could be reinstated. They considered that it would cost over £28,000 to extend their line to Fazeley, not counting the cost of a Tame aqueduct should one prove necessary, and that 'a sufficient Sum is not likely to be raised to carry the same into Execution'.[37]

The Trent & Mersey was meanwhile promoting a bill to compel the Coventry to complete their line. This was defeated, and their action was then overtaken by the growth of the Birmingham &

Fazeley project. Within Birmingham a battle was raging between
its promoters and the Birmingham Canal company, jealous of its
monopoly position; outside, however, there was arranged the
Coleshill agreement, made at that town on 20 June 1782 between
the Birmingham & Fazeley promoters and the Oxford, Coventry
and Trent & Mersey companies, to come into force as soon as the
Birmingham & Fazeley had got its Act. It was agreed that the
Oxford company would complete their line to Oxford, and the
Coventry theirs as far as Fazeley by raising £30,000. The Birming-
ham & Fazeley would build half the rest of the Coventry's line to
Whittington Brook, and the Trent & Mersey the other half to
Fradley, the Coventry having an option to repurchase the Trent &
Mersey's half within two months of completion at cost plus
interest.

As we shall see, the Birmingham Canal company and not the
new promoters were authorized to make the Birmingham &
Fazeley, the two concerns being amalgamated in 1784 as the Birmingham & Birmingham & Fazeley Canal company. The amalgamation took over the original promoters' obligations under the
Coleshill agreement. Robert Whitworth then surveyed the extension to Fazeley, and Thomas Dadford senior, engineer of the
Trent & Mersey, and his colleague from the Birmingham Canal,
advised on the proposed Tame aqueduct. But the Coventry's heart
was still not in getting their line built, for in 1785, while the Trent
& Mersey were actually cutting the Fradley–Whittington Brook
section, the Coventry opposed the bill to legalize the agreement of
1783, and tried to substitute an independent proposal to extend
the Trent (Burton) Navigation upwards and make navigable the
Tame and Anker rivers to Atherstone, which 'will effect the purposes intended more advantageously to the Publick'.[38] The Trent
& Mersey company were clear that the predominant group in the
Coventry concern were the coalowners of the Atherstone region,
who did not want the canal completed and their favoured position
eliminated, even though the shareholders generally might greatly
benefit.[39]

However, the Act[40] passed, and after the Court of King's Bench,
at the instance of the Trent & Mersey, had granted a Rule for the
company to show why a mandamus should not issue compelling
them to complete their canal, they agreed in June 1785 to continue
to Fazeley, and engaged Thomas Sheasby, senior, to build the
extension. An agreement was now reached between the Oxford
and Coventry companies to have a more sensible junction at

Hawkesbury instead of Longford, eliminating most of the parallel lines, and this was cut about the end of September. By the end of 1787 the Trent & Mersey had completed their Fradley–Whittington Brook section, under the supervision of Thomas Dadford sen., and soon afterwards the Coventry exercised their right of repurchase and took it over at a cost of £10,541, the Whittington–Fazeley section becoming part of the Birmingham & Fazeley line. By May 1788 the Coventry committee were given a glimpse of the possibilities of the through route when Matthew Pickford the carrier made proposals for the carriage of Manchester goods even before the canal was completed. They now set themselves to a general improvement of their line and basin at Coventry, and offered capital to those willing to trade in coal from the Staffordshire collieries to Coventry and the Oxford Canal.

The Birmingham & Fazeley itself was finished on 11 August 1789, and on 13 July 1790,[41] the Tame aqueduct having been completed, the extension from Atherstone to Fazeley was opened at a cost of £30,000. The canal line from Manchester, Liverpool and the Potteries was complete, and immediately traffic began to flow from the Trent & Mersey and from the Birmingham & Fazeley. So good did the prospects now look to the formerly reluctant Coventry committee that in September 1791 they ordered 'that a Pipe of the best Port Wine be provided by our Clerks at the Expence of the Company for the Use of the General Meeting and Committees'.[42] The annual dividends, which had been 3 per cent in 1789, were 8 per cent in 1791, 12 per cent in 1793, 14 per cent in 1795 and 18 per cent in 1797; such profits could easily pay for best port wine.

Once the Coventry company had finally decided, in June 1785, to go ahead, the Oxford commissioned Samuel Weston to survey the Cherwell from Banbury to Oxford to see whether it could be made navigable.* Apparently he thought it could, but all the same a canal was decided upon in 1786. A curious proposition was now embodied in a bill; that a syndicate of Weston, Simcock and four other men connected with the company should build the extension for £29,000 on condition that the company gave them exclusive carrying rights and two-thirds of the profits. This Parliament refused to agree to.

Whitworth now surveyed the final line, and decided that the canal should not cross the Cherwell twice on aqueducts, as had been considered earlier, but should make use of a mile of the river

* Also, incidentally, the Swift from Cosford to Lutterworth.

bed.* James Barnes was engaged as resident engineer and cutting
began. An Act[43] of 1786 authorized a further £60,000 on mortgage, and repealed the earlier prohibition on coal exports down
the Thames to allow coal to move as far as Reading.

While construction was proceeding, thought was given to
water supply. In 1786 a plan to use windmills to pump water into
the canal was approved, and the first was ordered to be built at
Hardwick lock after Simcock had been sent to Cambridgeshire to
study their use. A second was ordered for Hillmorton locks in
1789; later a steam engine was installed. In 1787 a second reservoir
at Wormleighton and the enlargement of Clattercote was approved, to make four with Byfield, already built, but only the
work at Clattercote was done. Barnes also pressed for side ponds[44]
to be made at the locks, and was authorized to try them at Hillmorton, while water from the Cherwell was obtained through the
enlarged Aynho Weir and Shipton Weir locks.

The section from Banbury to Oxford was opened on New
Year's Day 1790[45] by the arrival of boats with over 200 tons of
corn, coal and other goods, the first boat showing the Union flag
and having on board the band of the Oxford militia. It was $27\frac{1}{2}$
miles long, and had cost about £56,350, which had been raised in
loans. At the end of 1790 the company had raised £177,148 in
1,771$\frac{48}{100}$ shares of £100, and £130,000 on mortgage, or £307,148
in all.

Trade was waiting. At the end of 1789, even before the canal
was finished, the company wrote to Bedworth asking the mines to
'give the Boats to Oxford one Day's preference in a Week in
Loading, to Others; as the call for Coals at Oxford are very
great'.[46] In July 1790 the junction was completed at Fazeley, and
the Hawkesbury toll-collector had 'a sudden and expected Increase
of Business at his Station',[47] so much so that he was provided with
firearms to defend himself. By December he had to have an
assistant. The company now did all they could to extend trade by
judicious toll reductions and drawbacks[48] made where openings
appeared for an increase of traffic, especially that passing the whole
length of the canal, such as iron, copper, chemicals, cotton and
Irish linens. A newspaper report of September 1792[49] said that
'last Wednesday at a Meeting, in Banbury, of the Proprietors of
the Oxford Canal, One hundred pound shares, which some years

* Between Baker's Lock and Shipton Weir Lock. There is also a river crossing on
the level between Nell Bridge Lock and Aynho Weir Lock, that pound therefore
being at river height.

ago were as low as fifty-three pounds, fetched one hundred and seventy-five'. Anyone who bought them at that price had a bargain; by 1798 the company was paying 6 per cent and 11 per cent by 1801.

Development up the Thames was helped by the Duke of Marlborough, who in 1789 built and opened the Duke's Cut,[50] ¼ mile long, from near Wolvercote to a side-channel from the Thames, apparently quite independently of the canal company. In the following year the Thames Commissioners rebuilt the lock at Godstow to help traffic from the cut going to Oxford or below. The Duke then tried to sell his canal to the company. They, however, thought its use might injure them, and in 1792 it was conveyed in trust to the Vice-Chancellor of the University and the Mayor of the city for the time being. Finally, in 1798 it was leased for 200 years at £6 p.a. to the canal company.

The canal had been completed to New Road basin, and the accounts of St Thomas's church note: '1790, Jan. 7. Ringing Day at Mr. Blenhan's for rejoicing at ye coals coming to Oxford to ye New Cannal Wharf.'[51] Later, a second basin was built.

Connection between the canal and the Thames was also made in 1796 through Isis lock and the Sheepwash channel. This was originally a wide lock, built to allow Thames barges to reach the wharves, though narrow boats soon became used to going some way down-river. It was narrowed between 1850 and 1876, probably in the sixties when the river trade collapsed.

So, in 1790 through the Duke's Cut or in 1796 at Oxford, Mersey, Trent and Severn were linked to the Thames for the second time. A roundabout connection had been made on 17 November 1789, when a barge had passed through the Thames & Severn Canal,[52] but this was now superseded for most of the through traffic from the North and Midlands to Oxford and places down to London. Both the routes foreseen by Wedgwood twenty-five years before had been completed. (*To continue the history of the Coventry Canal turn to p. 142; of the Oxford Canal to p. 156.*)

The Newdigate Canals

Arbury,[53] the seat of the Newdigates, stands near Nuneaton in a large park crossed by several streams that drain eastwards into the Wem brook. East of the house lie the collieries of Griff, where one of Newcomen's earliest engines was built in 1711[54] to supplement existing water power. Even before 1711, at least three 'boatways'

had been built to carry coal in small craft to the nearest tramroad.*
These probably survived to be absorbed into the Arbury canals;
traces of one can still be seen.

Sir Roger Newdigate became interested in canal navigation,
especially perhaps after acting as Counsel in connection with the
Bridgewater Canal's extension to the Mersey. Between 1764 and
1795 he built about 5½ miles of private canals, mainly to carry away
coal, but also to serve as a means of communication for goods and
pleasure craft moving about the estate.

Beginning at the junction the system consisted of:

(a) the *Communication Canal*, from the Coventry Canal at Griff
    under the Coventry–Nuneaton turnpike to a wharf below a
    worsted factory. Completed at the end of 1773 though channel
    and junction made in 1771; length 1,078 yd; stop-lock at the
    junction.

(b) *Arbury Lower Level or Griff Canal*. Originally a boatway in use
    in 1771, it was linked to the Communication Canal by a flight
    of six locks (staircases of four and two) finished about 1794,
    and to the Coventry Wood Canal by a single lock. A branch
    was built from above the six locks to a new wharf (itself
    connected to the pits by tramroad) on the road from Arbury to
    the turnpike in 1793, and carried back over the locks by an
    aqueduct to the worsted factory. A feeder ran to Kenilworth
    Pool. Length, 1,540 yd.

(c) *Coventry Wood Canal*. Used in 1771, the locks at either end
    being completed in 1772. Length, 528 yd.

(d) *Arbury Upper (or High) Level*, from the head of the Coventry
    Wood Canal to the tail of Garden lock in Swanland. Boating
    had been done on this line at an early date, and in 1764 it was
    surveyed to see how it could be incorporated into a system.
    Garden lock was built in 1773 and gave a connection to the
    Garden Pool for estate traffic. A line out of Garden Pool led
    through a double (staircase) lock and a single to Hall Pool.
    Probably built in 1775; total length, 2,505 yd.

(e) *Seeswood Canal*. Originally the feeder from Seeswood lake for
    the lower canals, this was made navigable in 1777, and the lock
    at the junction with the lake built in 1784. Length, 1,980 yd.

(f) *Coton Lawn Canal*, which ran from the Arbury Higher Level
    just below Garden lock on one level across Coton Lawn,

---

* As in former books, I use the word 'tramroad' to mean a horse-drawn railway,
whatever the type of rail laid, to simplify indexing and avoid confusion with later
locomotive lines.

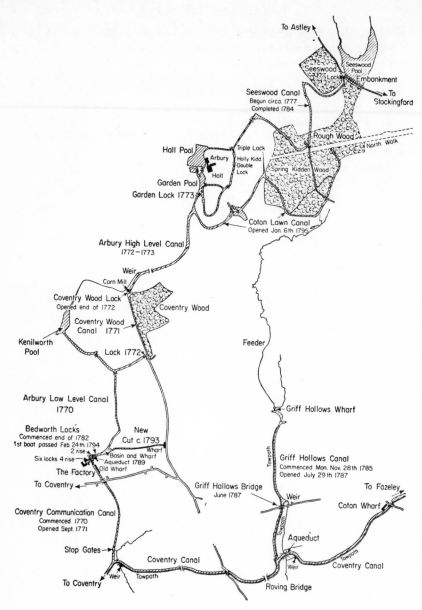

1. The Newdigate Canals

through Spring Kidden Wood to a landing stage on North Walk. It was opened in 1795. Length, 2,112 yd.

The system's thirteen locks lifted it 93 ft 6 in. from the Coventry Canal to Seeswood Pool; each was 40 ft by 6 ft. The single lock at the top of Arbury Upper Level was known as the 'triple' because it was shaped like a Y, having two separate sets of top gates, one to the Hall Pool branch and one to the Seeswood Canal, both on the same level. Most of the system's engineering was undertaken by William Bean of Derbyshire and John Morris, the estate mason and bricklayer.

Sadly, one must record a total lack of evidence for the story that Sir Roger Newdigate, when M.P., travelled in the same boat from Arbury to the Houses of Parliament. He died in 1806, aged 88; for six or seven years the canals continued in use, and then decayed. By 1819 all navigation had ended except upon the Communication Canal.

Separately from the Arbury system, Newdigate started work in 1785 upon a private canal from the 'Hollows' on the Coventry's line, which was to run for 1,320 yd westwards to a wharf to which coal was brought from the collieries by a tramroad. It was opened on 29 July 1787, and was in constant use for 174 years until 1961.

CHAPTER II

The Trent and its Tributaries

+++++++++++++++++++++++++++++++++++◆+++++++++++++++++++++++++++++++++++

BEFORE the canal age, the natural River Trent had two navigable tributaries, the Idle and the Derwent, both of which were provided with improvement Acts on the same day in 1720.

Idle River

When, early in the eighteenth century, Defoe saw the River Idle,[1] he described it as 'full and quick, though not rapid and unsafe . . . with a deep channel, which carries hoys, lighters, barges, or flat-bottom'd vessels' and the riverhead port, Bawtry, as 'famous all over the south part of the West Riding of Yorkshire, for it is the place whither all their heavy goods are carried'.[2]

In the sixteenth century iron from Sweden was imported at Hull to be carried by water up the Humber, Trent and Idle, and then by road to Sheffield, cutlery and finished goods returned, together with cast and wrought iron wares from furnaces in Derbyshire and Nottinghamshire.[3] During the seventeenth century mill-stones and lead brought by pack-horses through Worksop, Blyth or East Retford, together with timber and coal from the Handsworth pits, were also sent down the ten miles of the river to be transhipped at Stockwith (to which 200 ton craft could come), or elsewhere.[4]

The lead came mostly from Derbyshire, and therefore the inhabitants of Bawtry opposed the making navigable of the Derwent in case it might divert this trade, while in 1720 those of East Retford obtained an Act[5] to extend the navigation upwards from Bawtry to that town, the corporation being empowered to undertake the work and to levy toll. Nothing seems to have been done, though the plan was still being considered in 1757.[6] The river lost most of its Sheffield trade in the years between 1724 and 1750 as a result of the improvement of the River Dun.

At some time before 1764 Misterton Soss* was built on the Idle about ¼ mile from Stockwith by the Hatfield Chase company, which had been established in 1626 by Vermuyden when he re-aligned the River Idle as part of his drainage works. This sluice was also a lock with gates 17 ft 8 in. wide. Thereafter the shallow-draft craft working on the river were about 48 ft long and 13 to 14 ft wide, carrying from 12 to 24 tons.

In 1767 the river carried 4,415 tons of goods, over a quarter of which was lead;[7] it was then said that 'the business at the Wharf has been gradually decreasing for a number of Years'. A year or two later, when the Chesterfield Canal was being promoted partly by lead interests who wanted better transport, there was a sub-sidiary proposal for a part-canalization of the Idle and a cut 12 miles long from Bawtry to the Trent at Gainsborough, and also an alternative suggested line for the canal itself that would have taken it past Bawtry. However, neither were adopted, and the canal ran south of the Idle from Stockwith to Retford and onwards. Once the canal was opened, the river had little trade, and in 1828 the historian of Retford described it as 'idle, as far as navigation goes, and in all probability will so remain'.[8]

Derwent River

King John's charter to Derby in 1204 gave the townsmen the right to use the 'Darent, navigable from ancient times'. In 1268 and 1270 Simon, abbot of Dale, built mills near Borrowash and blocked the river with weirs, and in 1281 so obstructed the channel that no boat could pass.[9] Edward I seems to have ended this interference, but later the river became once more unnavigable, because in April 1638 Charles I wrote to Derby corporation asking them to accommodate Sir Cornelius Vermuyden 'Who, with his partners, has undertaken a work very acceptable to the King about the lead works at Wirksworth, and to make the river of Derwent to be navigable till it fall into the Trent'.[10] Presumably the Civil War interfered with this project, but in Charles II's reign three bills were introduced, all of which failed to pass.

John Houghton, writing in 1693, says: 'Great endeavours have been made to bring the navigation to Derby, and as far above as Darley in the peak. And whoever stood for parliament man, and gave hopes for effecting of this, has commonly been chosen, al-

* Maybe from the word 'sos' used in Iceland for the outlet of a lake, in this case Lake Humber.

though Nottingham for their own interest always opposes.'[11] Further bills were introduced in 1695, 1698 and 1702. Those in favour wanted better transport than the roads could give for Derbyshire's lead, iron and mill-stones, and a wider market for grain, butter and cheese. At the beginning of the eighteenth century it was said that the land carriage from Derby to Wilne cost twice as much as the water carriage thence to Gainsborough. Opposition came from Nottingham, anxious not to lose its importance as a port, and from Bawtry. The case for improvement was now strengthened as the hosiery industry spread to the Derby district, Wirksworth lead again found a market in the town, and a silk industry was planned.

A bill was introduced at the end of 1719. Opposed by Lord Chesterfield, the Wilmot family, and others, it[12] passed in April 1720, and empowered Samuel Fox, Abraham Crompton and eight other undertakers to make the river navigable for ten* miles from Derby to the Trent, the maximum toll to be 1s. The ten made a covenant together in June, with a penalty of £500 for not carrying out the work.[13] The first boat reached Derby on 17 January 1721. The local newspaper reported:

> 'Yesterday arrived here a Boat laden with Dale-Boards, Tobacco, Fish and other Merchandize, &c., which . . . was received with Ringing of Bells, and other Demonstrations of Joy . . . it must be acknowledged there were never any Rejoycings in which the Inhabitants were so unanimous . . . however, it cann't be expected that our Trading will be so advantageous, as when the River is wholly fitted for that purpose, which will be in a few Months Time if the Weather favours.'[14]

In the same issue appeared a bad poem on the subject entitled 'A Choak-Pear for Nottingham' who, however, continued to charge tolls on up-river traffic at Trent Bridge.

The plans accompanying the bill of 1702 had been prepared by George Sorocold, a well-known water supply engineer who in 1692–3 had provided Derby with water. They showed four new cuts and nine locks to overcome the 50 ft fall. However, Sorocold died in 1717, and it does not appear that any major works were built; there may have been flash-locks at Borrowash and Little Wilne. In 1752 two partners at Derby and Wilne Ferry advertised that they intended to carry by road to Wilne and then by water, a method which 'will not be subject so frequently to the inconveniences so detrimental to navigation up the River Derwent viz:—too much or too little water'.[15] However, in 1755 there was a shortage

---

* Rees says nine or ten; Priestley says thirteen.

I. The engineer, William Jessop (*left*), and the chairman, William Praed (*right*), of the Grand Junction Canal company

II. Oxford Canal: (*above*) the basin at Oxford about 1890; (*below*) Brinklow arches

of corn at Derby, and 'large quantities have been bought in Lincoln and elsewhere and sent loose by boat up the River Derwent'.[16] From this date references appear in the press to the Derby Boat Company trading on the river.

In early 1758, however, an earlier proposal to bridge the Trent at Wilden Ferry was revived, an Act was passed in June, and the toll-bridge* was probably opened in the following year. It then became part of a main road from Derby to Nottingham, and by making road transport easier seems to have reduced the river trade. In 1771 a proposal by Brindley for a canal from Chesterfield to the Trent & Mersey at Swarkestone, which with the Chesterfield Canal itself, would have by-passed both Trent and Derwent, was opposed at a meeting in Derby on 27 June, the river interests pointing to the mounting costs of the Trent & Mersey, then building, to show that river navigations were much cheaper.[17]

In January 1783 the Derby Boat Co advertised the sale of six craft, two of 30 tons, two of 20 tons, and two lighters, five-eighths of the tolls and wharfage of the river, several cheese and other warehouses,[18] and five-eighths of the profits of the lease of Borrowash corn mill. Probably these six craft had done most of the trade to Derby, and the sale was occasioned by the competition of the Trent & Mersey Canal, which now ran within 5½ miles of the city. In 1787 W. Stretton advertised that he had taken over the warehouses and carried goods by water,[19] and in 1791 there seem to have been about 5,000 tons of traffic,[20] towing, as always, being done by men.

In 1788 the precursor of the Cromford Canal had envisaged the making navigable of the Derwent and Amber rivers upwards from Derby, but by the end of the year the project had shifted to an extension upwards of the Erewash Canal.[21] When the Derby Canal was promoted, therefore, the owners of the river navigation were glad to sell their rights, wharves and warehouses for £3,996. This amount was included in the Derby Canal company's Act of 1793, and the property was transferred on 24 March 1794.

Chesterfield Canal

This ambitious tributary of the Trent seems to have been promoted partly by the London Lead Company, who wanted a more accessible shipping place for the lead from their smelt mill at Ashover than Bawtry, partly by the Cavendishes as owners of the

* Cavendish Bridge.

C

furnace and forge at Staveley, and partly by other landowners with
potential coal resources. In 1769 James Brindley was called in to
make a survey; his plans and estimates were produced to a meeting
at Worksop on 24 August 1769.[22] He proposed a line from Chesterfield to Norwood, where there would be a long summit tunnel,
and thence past Shireoaks and Worksop to East Retford and the
Trent at Stockwith, a small boat-building and repair centre and
transhipment point at the mouth of the Idle a little below Gainsborough. He estimated the cost of a narrow canal at £100,000,
thought that coal brought down the canal would undersell River
Dun coal at Gainsborough, and estimated a gross revenue of
£16,400 p.a. and an annual tonnage of 110,000.[23] An alternative
route from Retford direct to Gainsborough was rejected.

The promoters seem then to have obtained the views of another
engineer, John Grundy, who proposed a line 5½ miles shorter and
£23,430 cheaper from Stockwith* via Bawtry, Blyth and Carlton
to join Brindley's line at Shireoaks. However, the advantages of
including Worksop and Retford in the canal line were great, and
Brindley's proposal was adopted. The canal Act[24] was passed on
28 March 1771 after opposition from the River Dun company;
when the news reached Chesterfield bells were rung, fireworks
were let off in the market-place, and 'the utmost Joy and Satisfaction appeared on every Countenance'.[25] It authorized a Company of Proprietors of the Canal Navigation from Chesterfield to
the River of Trent, the company's official title, with power to raise
£100,000 in £100 shares, and £50,000 more if necessary, cutting
not to begin until the full sum had been raised. Among the promoters were the Dukes of Devonshire and Newcastle, Lord Scarsdale and Sir Cecil Wray. Other substantial shareholders were God-
frey Clarke, William Milnes, William Kirk, Lindley Simpson,
Phillips Glover, Charles White and James Brindley himself, who
held 15 shares. Anthony Lax of Chesterfield was appointed Clerk,
and there were Treasurers at Chesterfield and Retford. Power was
granted to take the comparatively low tolls of 1½d a mile on coal,
lead, timber, etc., and 1d on lime, and to make toll-free roads up
to one mile long from the canal.

Subscriptions were sought locally and in London, and by mid-
July the full capital had been found. Brindley was engaged for
'superintending the Execution of the Works . . . until the same
shall be completed',[26] and work began on the cutting of Norwood

* So Priestley, but I think Gainsborough, for the company later refunded money
subscribed for a Chesterfield-Gainsborough canal.

tunnel, 8 ft 10 in. wide, 12 ft high from invert, and 2,850 yd long.*
In May 1772 a proposition to make the canal a broad waterway
was considered but rejected; towards the end of 1774, however, it
was agreed to do so downwards from Retford, towards the cost of
which nine shareholders contributed £500, as did also the corporation. This section included the short Drakeholes tunnel,
which would take craft 15 ft 6 in. wide.

In the autumn of 1772 Brindley died. John Varley, Clerk of
Works, then became resident engineer with Hugh Henshall,
Brindley's brother-in-law, who was working on the Trent &
Mersey, who engaged to make a complete survey of the works
every three months and to be available for consultation when
needed. In the latter part of 1773 trouble occurred at the tunnel,
where one of the contractors was Thomas, Varley's brother. The
committee first found John Varley's books to be in a muddle, and
then that the tunnel contracts 'have been improvidently made and
at prices greatly exceeding the real value thereof and in a collusive
manner'.[27] After this Henshall was appointed chief engineer,
though Varley was kept on, unlike Thomas and two other Varleys
on the works, who were all discharged.

By 6 April 1774 the canal was navigable from Shireoaks to
below Worksop, by 3 August to East Retford, which reduced the
price of coal in that town from 15s 6d to 10s 6d a ton,[28] and by
22 February 1775 to Hayton. On 9 May the great tunnel at Norwood was opened

'when three vessels sailed through the same with no less than
300 people on board, attended with a band of music. They
performed their subterraneous voyage in one hour and one
minute. . . . The range of the tunnel is so truly directed, that a
person, standing at one end thereof, may see out of the other'.[29]

Completed before Harecastle, it was a credit to Henshall and, in
spite of his financial manœuvres, Varley.

In late 1775 it was decided to make a branch about a mile long
from the canal between Renishaw and Staveley to the turnpike
road at Norbriggs, probably to speed up transport to Chesterfield
itself till the main line was open. In 1777, however, the company
took a lease of a colliery at Norbriggs and began to work it under
Henshall's supervision, the object being 'not to profit by trading
in Coal but by commanding the Sale of such Quantity of Coal into
the Trent as to raise a considerable sum of money by Tunnage

* In *Bradshaw* and other modern sources the length is given as 3,102 yd, but no
alteration seems to have been made to the tunnel at any time.

which would not be received by the Company if such scheme had not been adopted'.[30] Late in 1778 a 'Newcastle Rail Road' with wooden rails was built from the colliery to the branch canal. In 1797 the colliery, which till then had been worked by the company, was advertised as to let.

By 2 April 1776 the canal was open from Stockwith (though the river lock had not been begun) to Killamarsh on the Chesterfield side of Norwood, and by 16 August to Norbriggs, by which time the company had advertised that they themselves would act as carriers. The whole line appears to have been opened on 4 June 1777, though it seems likely that the Trent tidal lock was not completed until the autumn. Almost immediately, other carriers announced services. Excluding the branch, the canal was 46 miles long. From Chesterfield it fell by five locks to Staveley, rose by 14 to Norwood tunnel, then fell by 46 more to the Trent, the last six, including the river lock, being broad. Reservoirs were built at Pebley, and later at Harthill, Woodall and Killamarsh. The private Lady Lee branch canal near Worksop, ¾ mile long, ran to a quarry, and another branch near Netherthorpe joined the East Inkersall tramroad which ran to pits near the Adelphi Canal. At Hollingwood there was an underground level belonging to the Duke of Devonshire, and worked for him by George Dickens of Staveley, which ran southwards for 1¾ miles to end under West Wood, where a brick shaft remains. It was one foot lower than the canal and not physically connected with it. The tunnel was 6 ft high, 5 ft 9 in. wide, and took 20 ft tub-boats each holding seven tubs of coal, which at Hollingwood were hoisted by crane and tipped into canal boats. A number of tramroads also served the waterway.

To finish the canal the company had raised considerable sums by mortgage as well as calls on shares. By 1789 £152,400 had been spent on the works, and for that year the gross income was £8,320 and the net profit £2,780 after payment of interest; a 1 per cent dividend, probably the first, was paid at a cost of £990. The traffic was 74,312 tons, of which 42,379½ tons was coal, 3,862¼ tons lead, 1,554½ tons iron, 7,569¾ tons stone, and the rest corn, lime, timber and sundries. Within a few years the canal was to prove a satisfactory investment. (*To continue the history of the Chesterfield Canal,* *turn to p.* 73.)

Loughborough Navigation

On the same day as the Trent & Mersey and the Staffs & Worcs Canals were authorized, and a little earlier in the numerical se-

quence, an Act[31] was passed to make the Soar navigable to Loughborough, with a cut from the river to the town. As early as 1634
Thomas Skipwith had been granted letters patent to enable him to
make the river navigable to Leicester on condition that he took
reasonable tolls and paid Charles I a share of his profits. He is said
to have executed five or six miles before his funds ran out.[32] In
1736 another attempt was made, this time to get a bill, but it
failed, and now powers had been granted to a body of Commissioners—the method that Wedgwood had rejected—to make a
navigation as far as Loughborough, with no limit on their
borrowing powers.

The first meeting of Commissioners on 24 June, at which
twenty-nine were present, resolved that 'Brindley or his Agent or
some other able Surveyor be employed to Survey the said River
and Design'd Canals' and to make an estimate.[33] It was a precaution they might have taken earlier, for when Brindley came on
13 September 1766 he recommended against making the river
navigable at all from Kegworth mill downwards to the Trent
because of its many shallows and frequent floods, and in favour of
a canal. The Commissioners sadly concluded that their Act did not
empower them to do this, and the project rested till 1775.

It was revived by William Douglass and William Cradock, the
latter a local solicitor. They had in mind a waterway for Trent
barges that would bring necessities to Loughborough and the
river villages, and carry away the local produce, notably wool; so
modest were their ideas of what was to become the most profitable
canal in Britain that in September 1776 they minuted[34] that instead
of a swing bridge at Kegworth for all traffic, there should be a
ford for carriages and a small swing bridge for sheep and foot
passengers. An Act[35] was obtained in April 1776, authorizing a
company to make the river navigable or to build cuts to Bishop's
Meadow, and a canal thence to the Rushes at Loughborough, the
termination that Brindley had originally recommended. They were
empowered to raise £7,000 in £100 shares and £3,000 more if
needed, and were granted substantial tolls, including 2s 6d a ton
for the 9¼ miles of the navigation for coal and everything not
agricultural produce. The money was almost all subscribed either
by the Earl of Huntingdon (£1,000) or by Loughborough people.
Cradock was appointed both Clerk and Treasurer, John Smith as
engineer to build the navigation by contract, and the bill of John
Watkinson, solicitor to the 1766 project, was at last paid.

At Redhill, near the junction with the Trent, a staunch and not a lock was built, with a windlass to haul craft through, and another at Thorpe Field near Loughborough. By August 1777 some boats were passing up to Kegworth after struggling with the Redhill staunch, which was clearly going to prove a nuisance. By this time the ideas of the shareholders had widened, for they had been closely concerned with the successful launching of the Erewash Canal, which had been authorized in the previous April and promised a useful coal trade into Leicestershire. They therefore called William Jessop, then a young man and with his reputation not yet made, to report.

He recommended a lock at Redhill, the widening and deepening of certain cuts, and the extra deepening of the upper canal to act as a reservoir. With his usual charm and gentleness he wrote:

'one cannot avoid the reflection—what Pity it is that Ideas of Frugality should have been so busy at the Conception of this Design . . . I believe there never was a work Executed upon which a review would not exhibit some Errors that might have been avoided; and I can readily suppose that if Mr. Smith had this work to do over again he would alter the cituation of his Locks, and would remember that Millers are some times found to be a Mischievous set of People'.[36]

Smith had not yet finished work on the original contract; being thought too slow, John May was put in general charge, he in turn employing contractors.

Tolls were approved at the shareholders' meeting on 16 April 1778 (coal being charged 1s for the whole length) and navigation probably began about this time. In April 1779 Redhill lock was reported built, together with passing places on the cuts, and Thorpe Field staunch taken up, having been replaced by Loughborough lock. By April 1780 all the improvements had been made. The navigation had six broad locks;* the cost of construction was about £9,200, and the nominal value of the £100 shares, £120. In February 1779 coal was selling at Loughborough at 8¼d cwt instead of 1s, and by the summer it was down to 6d[37] presumably after the Erewash had opened about July. Barges could now make the through and convenient trip from the Erewash collieries, across the Trent, and up the Loughborough Navigation; they were hauled across the Trent by a rope, men and horses being ferried over. When Cranfleet lock was built under the Trent improvements of the 1790s, the crossing was greatly improved, for

---

* A seventh, Kegworth Flood lock, was added later.

barges now kept above the weir, moving upstream a short distance from the Soar mouth before entering the Erewash.

Trade expanded, and new wharves and warehouses were built at Loughborough. One immediate problem facing the company was control over its water. By 1780 Dishley mill was being rented; then in 1783 the miller at Zouch was reported to be deliberately running down the water and obstructing boats, and it was agreed to buy a half-share in the mill, and that at Kegworth also if possible.† Another was the attitude of the Derbyshire coalowners. The Loughborough company maintained that when the Erewash Canal had been planned, the owners had promised to sell coal on its banks at 4s 2d a ton, but that when the Act had been obtained they had raised this to 4s 8d, and that it had subsequently risen further to 5s 4d, at which price it was sold at 6½d cwt retail. In April 1784 the company therefore introduced a sliding scale of tolls which varied with the sale price of coal, from 1s on coal sold at 5½d cwt to 2s 6d for coal sold at over 6½d. This action got the price down to 6d till 1789, when it rose to 7½d and 8d. They then explained in public that this rise was not their fault, but as in 1792 all cargoes were in fact paying the 2s 6d toll, this was reduced to 1s 6d as a flat rate, the sliding scale being abandoned.

The company paid its first dividend, of 5 per cent, at the end of 1780, and by 1790 had raised it to 20 per cent. Prospects looked good for a further rise, for proposals were being discussed for an extension of navigation upwards to Leicester and along the Wreak river to Melton Mowbray. (*To continue the history of the Loughborough Navigation, turn to p. 82.*)

Erewash Canal

Not long after work on the Loughborough Navigation had begun, some of its supporters joined certain colliery owners, business men and landowners of Nottinghamshire and Derbyshire to promote the Erewash Canal to carry to the Trent coal which would then cross the river, enter the Navigation and be carried to Loughborough and then by road to Leicester and elsewhere. John Smith surveyed a line from the Trent below Sawley and just above Soar mouth past Long Eaton and up the west bank of the Erewash river to a crossing above Ilkeston. It then followed the east bank

† Half of Zouch was bought, and the other half in 1800. Kegworth not till 1838, when it cost £4,000.

to end at Langley Mill, the survey showing a total rise of 108 ft 8½ in.[38]

A public meeting was held at Heanor on 4 November 1776 to hear proposals[39] and another in Nottingham on 27 December to explain its utility, and to take measures to execute it immediately.[40] The Act,[41] which had been vigorously supported by Leicester and opposed by Nottingham, was carried on Second Reading in the Commons by 79 to 56 votes,[42] and passed on 30 April 1777. It authorized the company to raise £15,400 in £100 shares and £7,700 more if necessary. Of the original subscriptions, 57 shares were from Loughborough, 28 from elsewhere in Leicestershire & Rutland, 48 4/5 from Nottinghamshire, 17 1/5 from Derbyshire and three from Birmingham. A useful clause in the Act exempted the company from rates and taxes; it was taken by a rating authority to the Queens Bench in 1856, but upheld. Another provided for roadstone to be carried free, under which an enterprising carrier later tried to carry railway ballast without payment.

At the first meeting William Cradock, already Clerk and Treasurer of the Loughborough, was also appointed to the combined offices in the Erewash company. They remained so combined in one man from the same firm of solicitors throughout the canal age. An advantage of linking the offices was that one means of paying him as Clerk was the interest earned on the balances he kept as Treasurer, till a separate bank account was opened in 1879. The managing committee was a small and stable one of seven, that of 1777 containing two members of the Loughborough's committee and two others connected with the navigation, the other three being from Nottinghamshire. The committee always had one or two clergymen on it, and from 1825 to 1841 clerics were in a majority at the time the canal was at its most prosperous; there were still three in 1860.

John Varley of the Chesterfield Canal was appointed engineer at £220 p.a., with John and James Pinkerton as joint contractors, and work began. By 30 May 1778, not much more than a year after the passing of the Act, water was let into part of the canal, and on 24 October tolls began to be collected. By 30 April 1779 the canal was navigable for nine miles from the Trent to Ilkeston Common, and about July for its full length of 11¾ miles as built to Langley Mill, though the newspaper did not describe it as completed till 9 December.[43] It had fourteen broad locks. Again Varley was to be in trouble. He seems to have failed to keep proper accounts for land and damage compensation payments, and also to have made a mistake in the levels for the uppermost lock. He was dismissed in May 1780, and in August the lock had to be taken down and rebuilt, Varley being ordered to pay the cost of £78 less the value of the bricks. I do not know whether he did.

The canal had cost about £21,000. By the autumn of 1782 it was coal that was lacking, and a notice was put in the paper

'to such Gentlemen as have Colliery's near the Line of the . . . Canal, that there is, and has been cause of Complaint of the great Scarcity of Coals, to supply the Consumption wanted upon the said Canal; they earnestly recommend to such Gentlemen as have Coals upon the Line of the said Canal to open Pits, and the . . . Proprietors engage to allow every Conveniency'.[44]

The need was urgent, for the company was exporting down the Trent as well as to the Soar, and was at the time also actively supporting the improvement of the main river. Pits were opened, receipts rose quickly, and a first dividend of 2½ per cent for the year ending 6 April 1783 had by 1787 become 20 per cent and 1794, 30 per cent.

A new phase began when at a meeting on 1 May 1787, two letters were read about a possible extension upwards of the canal. (To continue the history of the Erewash Canal, turn to p. 64.)

Cromford Canal

This, which later became the Cromford Canal, was at first promoted by landowners in the valley as an extension of the Erewash Canal upwards to Pinxton, 'as a six mile stretch of coal on the Erewash is unworked, owing to lack of a communication'.[45] In July a group that included Outram* and Hodgkinson† met the Erewash proprietors, but could not agree with them. In the following year Sir Richard Arkwright of Cromford took a hand. In July a meeting at Matlock supported 'a Navigation from Derby to Cromford, and up the River Amber';[46] another a month later substituted a course from Langley Mill to Cromford, with a branch to Pinxton mill.[47] In December 1788 a meeting at Alfreton heard William Jessop present his estimate of £42,697. Half this sum was raised on the spot and the rest within a fortnight.

The main obstacle to success was the conviction of the Erewash company that they had an exclusive right to the water of the river.

---

* I assume Benjamin Outram; the minute book says 'Altram'.
† I assume John Hodgkinson, Outram's associate.

They therefore opposed the bill in Parliament, to such effect that it passed Second Reading in the Lords by one vote. At this point the promoters agreed to bring in a bill in the following session to give force to the agreement that had by then been arrived at, on which condition the bill was allowed to pass in 1789.[48]

The line had great possibilities. Apart from many mines, it was intended to serve iron furnaces at Butterley and Somercotes, limestone quarries at Crich, lead-works at Alderwasley, Cromford where Sir Richard Arkwright had established large-scale cotton mills, and towns such as Matlock, Belper, Wirksworth, Alfreton and Mansfield not far away. Among its supporters were Arkwright, who that year bought the manor of Cromford, the Gell and Beresford families, and the Outrams, Jessops and Hodgkinsons, all of whom were connected with industry and mining. Three of them, Benjamin Outram, William Jessop and Francis Beresford, were to join a fourth, John Wright, in 1790 to form the Butterley company; Wright became a canal shareholder a year or two later.

Each new development meant the prospect of more traffic carried on the Trent, upon which some improvements had been made, though more radical ones were needed. (*To continue the history of the Cromford Canal, turn to p. 50.*)

Trent River*

As sections of the Trent & Mersey Canal were opened upwards from Wilden Ferry, so trade was brought to the river below. On the upper Trent, the lessees who had taken over in 1762 worked hard to repair the damage done by the misconduct of their predecessors; they said in 1766 that they 'have been the Instrument of restoring the Lock, which their predecessors had destroyed; they have enlarged their Wharfs and Warehouses; encreased the Number of their Boats . . .'.[49] They must, however, have lost much of their Burton trade to the new canal's wharves and warehouses at Horninglow, and seen that their only hope of survival was as the terminus of another canal. From 1781 onwards we find proposals for a line from Burton to the Coventry Canal at Marston, which in another form became part of the Ashby Canal; for another junction with the Coventry at Atherstone by way of the rivers Tame and

* For a short account of the earlier history of the river, see *The Canals of the West Midlands*, p. 15.

Anker; and for a canal and railway to the Breedon limeworks. None succeeded.

The first Act[50] to improve the lower river was passed in December 1772. The Trent has two channels near Newark, one by the town itself, and the other past Kelham, which then carried most of the traffic. The inhabitants of Newark wanted to bring their trade closer to the town without obstructing the other line. Newark Navigation Commissioners were therefore appointed, given power to build two barge locks at Newark Town and Newark Nether, to borrow money, and to levy a toll of 2d a ton on goods passing the locks, or 4d on those landed. Barges were to be bow-hauled, a limitation that was removed eleven years later. These works were completed in October 1773: 'Friday, the 22nd, past, the Navigation was finished at Newark, on which account great Rejoicings were made, such as firing Cannon upon the River, ringing of Bells, and Bonfires,'[51] which were only slightly marred when a cannon burst without much damage. By the Trent Act of 1783 the 2d transit toll was abolished, being replaced by a charge of 1s per boat using either channel of the river.

The traffic using the river from the Trent & Mersey, Loughborough and Erewash Canals required a more radical improvement. The initiative came from the Trent & Mersey company, who approached the Erewash and others to ask that they should join in having the river to Gainsborough surveyed. Locks and side cuts, dredging and a horse towing-path were all essential, and were recommended by the Dadfords, engineers to the Trent & Mersey, at a cost of £20,000.[52] The bill was opposed by all the vested interests; horse towing 'would deprive near five hundred higging men, who plied upon the river to drag vessels up the river, of bread';[53] the landowners did not want side-cuts built on their land; merchants did not want to pay tolls; others preferred a public trust to a company that might make excessive profits.

Agreement was not possible. The bill was withdrawn, and William Jessop was asked to re-survey the river to see what could be done without making locks. He listed 67 shoals between Cavendish Bridge and Torksey, but considered that he could get a minimum of 2 ft depth by dredging, deepening where there was hard bottom, and contracting the river's width by piles and faggots. Nevertheless, he recommended cuts at such notorious spots as Holme, Nottingham bridge and Wilford.

In 1783 a compromise Act[54] was passed to establish a company with powers to improve the river from Wilden Ferry to Gains-

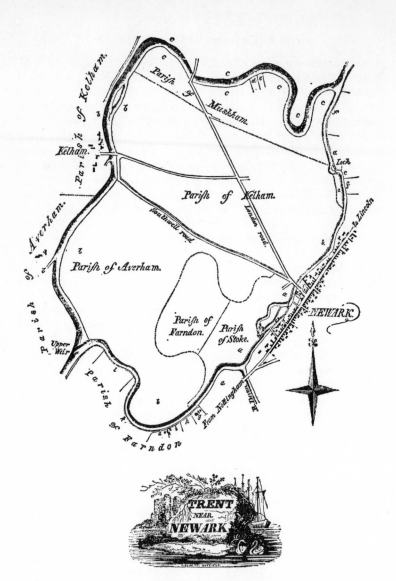

LANDS ADJOINING.

a Duke of Newcastle.	e Foster.	i Darcy.
b J. M. Sutton, Esq.	f Sir J. W. Gordon, Bart.	k Tomlinson.
c Lord Middleton.	g Spafford, &c.	l Steward.
d Fletcher.	h Lamb.	

2. The Newark Navigation in 1774: the old course of the navigation was by way of Kelham. The map does not show Newark Town lock

borough with a minimum depth of 2 ft over the fords at Sawley, Wilford, Holme and Gunthorpe, and 27 in. elsewhere, to allow a loading of about 35 tons. Horse towing was authorized (as on the Burton Navigation by a separate Act) and the company was empowered to build a towpath. The capital was £13,000 in £50 shares with power to raise £7,000 more, and dividends were limited to a maximum of 7 per cent on the precedent of the Calder & Hebble Act of 1769. Tolls varied from 3d to a maximum of 9d for Wilden Ferry to Gainsborough or return; no toll was, however, to be charged for the crossing between the Erewash Canal and the Loughborough, but instead each company was to pay £2 10s od p.a.

The company first met at the *Blackamoor's Head* at Nottingham on 24 June 1783, with Lord Middleton in the chair, Job Brough of Newark being appointed Clerk and John and Thomas Wright of Nottingham Treasurers. Jessop was the engineer, to be paid £675 by instalments to complete the authorized works. He began to make the path and improve the river at Wilden Ferry, and worked down. As each section was completed, tolls were then taken; to Trent Bridge, Nottingham, on 1 January 1784, to Newark on 12 May and to Gainsborough on 29 September.[55] The Newark section under the Commissioners' control probably got its path and other improvements during 1785, the cost being shared between them and the company. Various obstructions still needed attending to, and it was not till 4 September 1787 that the General Assembly minuted that it considered the navigation complete. Jessop was then paid his balance, and engaged as the company's permanent engineer at £100 p.a. Already, however, a first dividend of 5 per cent had been paid for 1786; the same amount was paid for 1787, and thereafter the maximum of 7 per cent.

The company occupied itself in sharing with riparian owners the cost of necessary bank protection to prevent erosion, in considering in 1784 a proposal from a Nottingham group for bypassing Trent Bridge,* and in trying to catch enterprising boatmen who evaded the payment of tolls, or whose bills of lading did not agree with their cargoes, evasion being easier than on a canal because of the absence of locks at which craft could be inspected. Then in July 1789 Jessop was asked to survey the river at Sawley to estimate the cost of a side-cut. He reported that it was necessary; the landowner agreed to a lock and cut being made if no additional toll were charged; the company agreed and bought the land; and

* The first for what later became the Beeston cut.

the cut was made before 1793, the lock having a fall of 3 ft. The decision to build it was taken against a background of many happenings: the Cromford Act, the plans for new canals round Leicester, talk everywhere about how necessary new waterways were if the country was to progress. The acceptance of Jessop's report was the first step in the complicated story that led to the canalization of the Trent between Sawley and Holme under the Act of 1794, nearly fifty years before a similar Act was passed for the Severn. (*To continue the history of the River Trent, turn to p. 74.*)

PART TWO—1790–1845

II. (*above*) King's Mills lock on the Trent (Burton) Navigation in 1745; (*below*) a caricature of the packet boat on the Grand Junction Canal between Paddington and Uxbridge

IV. (*above*) The bottom lock and turnover bridge of the Nutbrook Canal in 1956; (*below*) Little Eaton wharf on the Derby Canal, showing containers of coal being transferred from the horse tramroad to a canal boat

CHAPTER III

Derby, Nottingham and the Trent

++◆++++++++++++++++++++++++++++++++++++++

UNTIL 1794 the collieries and other heavy industries of Derbyshire and Nottinghamshire were served only by the Erewash Canal and the River Trent, the latter with a towpath and one lock above Newark, but having also the dangerous passage of Trent bridge and only two feet of water over some of its shallows.

The first new project, an extension of the Erewash upwards to Cromford and Pinxton, was authorized in 1789. Between 1794 and 1797 five canals were opened, the Cromford (August 1794), Nutbrook (Autumn 1795), Nottingham (April 1796), Derby (June 1796) and Grantham (Summer 1797), at a cost of about £400,000. They provided the collieries, ironstone mines, ironworks and stone quarries of the Derwent and upper Erewash valleys, the areas round Denby and Pinxton, Wollaton and Bilborough, with carriage by water to the growing cities of Nottingham and Derby and onwards to the Trent and Grantham, or on to the Trent & Mersey. Production rapidly increased, and the coal carried found ready markets towards Leicester, along the canal line to Grantham, or down the river. A considerable secondary traffic also developed in road and other stone from quarries on the Cromford and Nottingham Canals. By September 1801 the Trent also had been improved at a cost of about £20,000 by dredging to a minimum depth of 30 in. to take 40 ton craft and by the building of further locks and a by-pass to Trent bridge.

Enterprise was its own reward. The Nottingham, Derby and Trent companies were statutorily limited in the dividends they could pay, and by 1814 the Trent and Nottingham had reached their limits and the Derby nearly so. The Cromford was paying

10 per cent, and the shareholders of the old-established Erewash happily cashed dividend warrants for 42 per cent. Only the Grantham lagged with its 4 per cent, but by 1821 even this had passed 5, and soon settled to a respectable 6⅔.

The coal trade down the Trent and into the Fossdyke grew steadily, limited only by competition from River Dun coal on one side and that imported at Boston on the other. That to the Leicester line of canals increased sharply when the opening of the Grand Union in 1814 gave access to the Grand Junction and Oxford lines, then fell away again before the competition it had aroused. The coming of the Leicester & Swannington Railway in 1832 gave the Leicestershire coalowners their chance, and Derbyshire and Nottinghamshire trade was driven backwards down the Soar, and forced to seek other markets. The opening of the Grand Union also affected Trent traffic, for such goods as pottery to London now preferred it to the coastal route by Gainsborough. Trade was so buoyant, however, that by 1818 the temporary effect had ended.

The canals of our group had supported the various schemes to link them to the Peak Forest or the Sheffield Canals. The only result was the Cromford & High Peak Railway of 1831, which did affect the trading pattern. Though intended as part of a through canal-rail route from London to Manchester via the Grand Junction, Leicester canals, Erewash, Cromford, Peak Forest and Ashton, its main effect was upon the corn and agricultural produce trade towards Manchester, which increased from as far away as the Grantham area. Its existence did, however, cause many tolls to be lowered, for its line was competitive with that by way of the Trent & Mersey via Preston Brook or the Macclesfield Canal and Marple.

The canal age ended in this area when between 1839 and 1840 the Birmingham & Derby Junction, the Midland Counties and the North Midland Railways were all opened, seriously affecting the traffic on every navigation except the Grantham and the Trent below Nottingham, which had a few more years of respite.

Cromford Canal

The canal line ran from a junction with the Erewash at Langley Mill up the valley to what is now Ironville, where the Pinxton branch left it. The main line then swung west, passed through the

Butterley tunnel, 2,966 yd long* to Bullbridge where it crossed the
Amber on an aqueduct, and at Ambergate turned up the Derwent
valley to Cromford, crossing the river 1¼ miles from Cromford by
an aqueduct 30 ft high and with a single arch of 80 ft span. The
length of the main line was 14⅝ miles and of the branch 2⅜ miles,
with 14 locks on the main line and three other short tunnels. The
locks below the Butterley tunnel were built wide to take the
Erewash barges that served the collieries, but the tunnel itself and
the locks above it were narrow. Later these were shortened to
save water.

The authorized capital was £46,000. William Jessop was appointed engineer at £350 p.a. and expenses, he to give one-third of
his time to the works, with Benjamin Outram as full-time assistant,
and Thomas Dadford,† from the Trent & Mersey as one of the
two contractors. Early in 1791 the two engineers took over the
work by direct labour, Outram now receiving the high salary of
£400 p.a. At the beginning of 1792 the Amber aqueduct partially
failed, and Jessop, never very good on masonry aqueducts, offered
to pay £650, the cost of restoring it, and to give up his salary for
six months back and until the canal was finished. The first offer
was accepted, the second not.

By September 1791 the original share capital had been raised,
and further calls and loans were then authorized. In the end the
£100 shares were worth a fraction over £128; the total cost of the
canal was £78,880. It was opened throughout about August 1794,
though tolls had been taken below the tunnel from February 1792.
Once more, however, an aqueduct had cracked, this time the large
one over the Derwent. Jessop blames himself: 'the failure has
happened for want of a sufficient strength in the front walls and I
blame noone but myself for the consequence having often seen
much profusion of expence by an unnecessary consumption of
materials. . . . Painful as it is to me to lose the good opinion of my
Friends I would rather receive their censure for the faults of my
head than of my heart'.[1] The aqueduct had to be partly rebuilt.

The regulations made at the opening of the canal for the traffic
through Butterley showed clearly the limitations imposed by a
long narrow tunnel. Boats could enter the east end between 5 and

---

* So the Cromford Canal Minute Book of 29 May 1792 (while cutting) and Rees,
Cyclopaedia; Farey, *Derbyshire*, Vol III gives 2,978 yd, and the canal Minute Book
of 17 September 1799, 3,000 yd. It was later lengthened to its present extent of
3,063 yd when a railway was built above it.

† Probably senior.

6 a.m. and 1 and 2 p.m., and the west end between 9 and 10 a.m. and 5 and 6 p.m., and were not to take more than three hours in transit. In 1802, when traffic had increased, the tunnel was worked at night, an additional entry being allowed at the east end between 9 and 10 p.m., and at the west between 1 and 2 a.m.

In 1800 it was agreed that Peter Nightingale* should make a short branch, 2½ furlongs long, at his own cost from near the Derwent aqueduct to his wharves at Lea Wood, the company to contribute £100. It was probably finished in the early part of 1802, and served two leadworks, cotton mills, a hat factory, and quarries there. A branch proposed to Bakewell in 1802-3 came to nothing.

We shall best understand the usefulness of the canal if we compare some figures for the year ending mid-May 1803 with those for mid-May 1831 and mid-May 1841:

	Traffic 1802-3	1830-1	1840-1
	tons	*tons*	*tons*
Coal and coke	111,763½	218,007¾	210,798¾
Lime and limestone	29,727½	19,265	33,361¾
Gritstone	2,705	8,442	17,885
Calamine and slag	1,161½	1,739	463
Sand, timber and slate	2,089¼	3,534¼	3,729
Iron, ironstone and lead	3,605½	19,843½	19,731½
Sundries, corn, groceries	3,723½	18,385½	34,602¾
	154,775¾	289,217	320,571¾

Tonnage recorded at Bullbridge and Pinxton Junction indicates traffic originating above Langley Mill on the main line and passing upwards, or originating above Bullbridge or on the Pinxton branch and passing downwards; that at Langley Mill indicates all traffic entering the canal from the Erewash, and that originating on the main line below Pinxton Junction and passing downwards:

* The brother of the mother of William Edward Shore, who, having inherited his money, changed his name to Nightingale. His daughter was the famous Florence Nightingale. 'Peter Nightingale had been a dare-devil horseman, a rider in midnight steeplechases, a layer of wagers, given to hard drinking and low company.'[2] He died in 1803.

Traffic Distribution

		Pinxton Junction Bullbridge	Langley Mill
		tons	tons
Coal and coke	1802–3	27,990½	83,773
	1830–1	41,958¾	176,049
	1840–1	52,277¼	158,521½
Lime and limestone	1802–3	21,884	7,843½
	1830–1	17,618½	1,646¼
	1840–1	30,193½	3,168½
Other	1802–3	7,610¾	6,674
	1830–1	30,885½	21,058¾
	1840–1	38,363½	38,047¼

Tolls taken

1802–3	£5,780, or 9d per ton average*
1830–1	£9,664, or 8d per ton average*
1840–1	£12,086, or 9d per ton average*

Dividends

1802–3	£9 per share
1830–1	£18 per share
1840–1	£24 per share

* Variations in the length of haul mean that these figures only give a broad result.

Especially notable is the growth of coal exports—in the first period about three times the local trade, in the second about 4½ times. Most of the coal went down the Erewash and into the Leicester line (a heavy rise between 1809 and 1814 probably reflects the opening of a wider market by way of the Grand Union), some down the Nottingham Canal to the Grantham, or down the Trent to Newark, Gainsborough and Lincoln. The rise in stone traffic was probably the result of improved roads and of a demand for railway ballast—much Cromford Canal stone was used on the London & Birmingham Railway. The tonnages of iron, ironstone and lead cannot be separated, but much of the iron came from the Butterley works and of the ironstone from Somercotes on the Pinxton branch. The heavy rise in corn and groceries in the third period mainly reflects the trade to Manchester that followed the opening of the Cromford & High Peak Railway in July 1831 from the canal side above the Derwent aqueduct.

A large number of tramroads, from ¼ mile to 1½ miles long, were built to connect collieries, limestone quarries and ironstone workings to the canal. Three of special interest were the line down from the Crich limestone quarries to the canal at Ambergate, that from Fritchley to a wharf at Bullbridge, and the Mansfield & Pinxton line. This had been first projected as a canal in 1803;[3] then as a tramroad in 1809 and 1816. It was authorized in 1817 from Mansfield to the end of the Pinxton branch, and opened in April 1819. However, the canal company took little interest in it, and it does not seem that much interchange took place, most of the traffic being coal originating on the tramroad and carried upwards.[4]

The management was steady, with few changes on the committee except by death. It was shared by representatives of local families like the Gells with clergy, often prominent in canal management. In 1809 five out of the nine committee members were clergymen, in 1819 four, in 1829 three, and in 1839 two, perhaps a reflection of the growth of Evangelical and Tractarian ideas alike.

The company had favoured the construction of the Grand Union. When, therefore, in 1831 that company wrote asking the Cromford to reduce its coal tolls so that Derbyshire coal could compete with supplies from Staffordshire and Warwickshire, the Cromford company agreed to a 50 per cent drawback on all coal bound for the Grand Junction's line. No increase in tonnage resulted, and the concession seems to have been withdrawn in 1834, when the company decided that with few exceptions it would charge its full parliamentary tolls on all traffic. When, therefore, in late 1834 the Leicester, Loughborough and Erewash Canals asked for a tonnage reduction on coal 'with a view to the Derbyshire and Nottinghamshire Coal Masters competing with the Leicestershire Coal',[5] the answer was 'no', and again when the Grand Union wrote in 1841 asking for a reduction to ½d per ton per mile 'to compete with the charge of the Midland Counties Railway and London and Birmingham Railway Company for coal passing along their lines up to Watford Locks,* and into the London Market'.[6] However, later in the year they changed their minds; it was the first step in steady reductions that were to be made to meet railway competition. (*To continue the history of the Cromford Canal, turn to p. 186.*)

Nottingham Canal

Nottingham's coal, other than that carried by road, reached it by way of the Erewash Canal and the Trent. The passing of the

---

* On the Grand Union near Norton Junction.

Cromford's Act on 31 July 1789 made it likely that the collieries along its line, as well as those near the Erewash, would flourish at the expense of those near Nottingham, that the Erewash company might become a monopoly and behave accordingly, and that Nottingham would suffer by dependence upon a roundabout route for its coal supplies. Once it was clear that the danger was real, three Nottingham men, Thomas Oldknow,* John Morris† and Henry Green, encouraged the Common Hall to call a public meeting at the Guildhall on 26 October 1790 'to take into consideration the propriety of making a navigable Cut from the Cromford Canal to the Trent below the bridge to pass by the side of the Town'.[7] A plan was approved and a provisional committee elected, two of whom were connected with the Cromford company. It did not include the coalowners, though Lord Middleton supported the idea, and recommended a possible line.

William Jessop was asked to survey the canal, and also a branch from Lenton near Nottingham to the Trent at Beeston that would serve to bring Trent trade to Nottingham wharves and to by-pass the difficult Trent bridge. He looked at the country long enough to satisfy himself that Lord Middleton's line was impracticable because of deep cutting and tunnelling, and then fell ill with a poisoned face. He therefore suggested that James Green, a surveyor who worked for Lord Middleton at Wollaton, should do the work instead. The committee preferred to wait, but after Jessop had been ill for six months agreed in June 1791 to Green doing the work under Jessop's supervision, the latter saying hopefully: 'I am still confined but hope next week to be able to get out with my Head wrapped up.'[8]

This sign of activity brought an immediate letter from the threatened Erewash company to Nottingham Corporation asking for support in themselves making a cut from Beeston through Nottingham to the Trent, but the city snubbed them and supported its own child. In September 1791 Jessop submitted an estimate, which was accepted, and on 25 October a public meeting showed itself in favour of the proposed canal, the enthusiasm of those who were present having been increased by a promotion meeting held the previous day for the Grantham Canal, at which £40,000 had been subscribed in half an hour.[9] Public spiritedly, a

* Textile merchant in Nottingham, and partner at the Pleasley cotton mills near Mansfield. Uncle of Samuel Oldknow, later a principal supporter of the Peak Forest Canal.
† Stocking manufacturer.

dividend limitation of 10 per cent was suggested. Agreement was then reached with the Cromford company upon water supply, the Nottingham consenting to build reservoirs on the Cromford's line, but at its own expense.

It was the time of the canal mania. In November the clerk asked for instructions on how to allot shares among the many competitors for them. This produced rumblings from property owners, who promptly demanded a lower dividend limitation to 'destroy Speculations in Shares that have been sold at large premiums to the great prejudice of the principal Landowners & Coalowners who are liable to pay them out of their property'.[10] The committee agreed to coal tolls lower than had been proposed, and to an 8 per cent limitation; they also judiciously allotted £20,000 worth of shares to be subscribed for by the landowners. The Trent & Mersey and the Erewash opposed the bill because they were promoting a Trent Canal direct from the former across the Erewash to Nottingham and the Trent (see p. 64), and the Trent Navigation because they wanted to make the Beeston cut themselves. By dropping the Beeston cut from their bill, however, the Nottingham company got its Act[11] in May 1792, in Nottingham the news being received 'by the ringing of bells, and other demonstrations of joy'.[12]

The company's capital was £50,000 in £100 shares, and £25,000 more if necessary. Coal tolls were unusual; these were 4½d ton plus ½d per ton per mile, with a maximum of 1s; corn was 1d with a maximum of 1s, and lime and limestone ½d with a maximum of 6d. These were cheap rates for the time. The first meeting appointed William Jessop engineer at 3 gns a day and expenses, with James Green as his assistant at 300 gns p.a. The first sod was cut on 30 July, and work began. On 30 July 1793 the stretch from Trent Bridge to the town wharves was opened.[13] Thereafter troubles were many, and by September 1794 £140 had been called on each share. In October the committee minuted that 'Mr. Jessop shall be informed that the Committee and the Proprietors are much dissatisfyed with the erroneous construction of many works on the Canal and the very large expence incurred . . . the Committee had hoped that Mr. Jessop after undertaking the concern would have paid greater attention to it'.[14] There was reason for complaint, but by this time Jessop was the greatest canal engineer in the country, responsible also for the improvements on the Trent and for building simultaneously two of the biggest projects in the country, the Grand Junction and the Ellesmere. In March 1795 the calls reached

£150, and still the canal was unfinished, mainly due to the weather.
On 14 February the newspaper had said:

'On Sunday last, the FROST, which had been very severe for
near seven weeks, began to relax, and was succeeded by a rapid
THAW, which, in two or three days occasioned the GREAT-
EST FLOOD ever remembered . . . the beautiful canal cut,
which forms a collateral branch with the Leen,* has received
such immense fractures, as will make the repairs amount to a
considerable sum.'[15]

On 1 March 1796 Common Hall was told that a boat had passed
through the Beeston cut, and on 26 April the canal was considered
open, for on that date the company ceased to pay interest on the
calls. The canal had cost about £80,000 apart from funded interest, and so great had been the struggle to get it open, and
probably also the bickering that had followed, that most of the
committee of nine retired in the same year; by April 1798 no
member of the original 1793 committee remained.

At opening the canal was 14¾ miles long from Trent lock below
Trent bridge to Langley Mill where it joined the Cromford just
above that canal's junction with the Erewash. It had twenty broad
locks 85 ft by 14 ft 6 in., the last, at Langley, being a stop-lock.
After Trent lock, into which craft were pulled by a rope and
windlass, and two further locks at Castle and Leather Mill, the
latter above the junction with the Beeston Cut at Lenton, the canal
rose by two locks and then a flight of fourteen to the summit at
Wollaton, whence it ran level to Langley.

In Nottingham small branches were built at the same time as the
main line near the Castle (immediately west of Wilford Street
bridge) to some property of the Duke of Newcastle; there was also
one at Sneinton. This, called the Poplar arm, ran east from the
canal at the Bridge Street curve, crossed the Leen and then entered
it. It was extended in 1835–6 by a private canal built by Earl
Manvers,† who also agreed to widen part of the Poplar Arm.
From the Poplar Arm the Brewery branch curved back to the
north as far as Bridge Street again. There also seems to have been
an earlier connection between the canal near Trent bridge and the
basin there belonging to the Corporation. Above Wollaton locks
the Bilborough cut left the main line and ran level to a wharf in

* A small river that ran parallel to the canal line down from Nottingham to near
Trent Bridge. It is said formerly to have been navigable for small boats to a town
wharf at the end of Sussex Street.[16]
† By 1918[17] the canal had become Manvers Street.

Bilborough wood, whence tramroads ran to Bilborough and
Strelley collieries. This was a private canal built at the expense of
the landowners, but open to other users on payment of toll.[18] It
was probably open by June 1799. By 1813 most of it was disused
and parts filled in,[19] the rest being disused about 1874. The Greasley cut towards the Duke of Rutland's collieries at Greasley and
Fillingham, 1 furlong long, was probably built in 1800 and the 3
furlongs long Robinetts cut near Cossall by the end of 1796. These
cuts were served by tramroads, and others ran to canalside
wharves. The colliery owners spent much time in cajoling and
threatening the company to reduce rates or provide facilities,
every now and then threatening to take their lines to the Erewash
Canal, and occasionally doing so.

Relations with the Cromford company were good from the
start, and the two concerns shared toll-collecting staff at Langley.
With the Erewash, competition was keen, and in October 1797 a
special toll of 3d against the authorized 1s was introduced for coal
travelling from Langley to points west of Beeston. The result was
so financially painful that in November 1798 an agreement was
sensibly made with the Erewash to take full tolls on both lines,
and not to offer inducements to collieries and others to get trade
from each other. For the year ending 30 April 1801 the tonnage
carried was 136,102 tons, of which 101,222 was coal; 65,705 tons
went to the Trent or the Grantham Canal, less than 3,000 tons
through the Beeston cut. Toll revenue was £5,197. At the annual
meeting in May 1804, the loan debt having by now been paid off,
the company decided to start paying dividend at the rate of £12
per share (8 per cent on each £150 share), to which shareholders
were entitled from 26 April 1796, as funds would permit. This
meant that dividends were paid irregularly, two or three times a
year, and by the end of the canal's independent life were still in
arrears. The last full payment, made in May 1854, was that due in
October 1849.

In September 1797 Mr Redfern began to run a packet boat for
passengers twice weekly between Nottingham and Cromford,
charging 5s for the best cabin and 3s for the second. He also
started a similar boat to Leicester at 5s and 2s 6d. In 1798 Pearson,
perhaps Redfern's successor, was running a packet boat from
Nottingham to Leicester four times a week,[20] and at the end of
1800 Matthew Hopkinson of Crich established a 'Common Boat
for the Carriage of Goods on the Cromford and Nottingham
Canals',[21] presumably for parcels and small consignments.

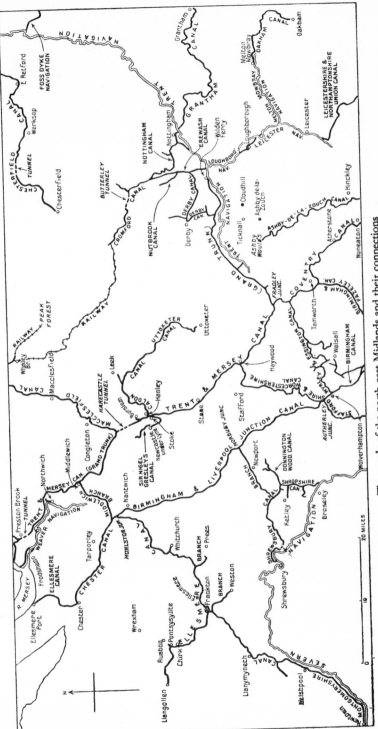

3. The canals of the north-east Midlands and their connections

On 28 September 1818

'a most distressing catastrophe . . . occurred at the Company's Wharf . . . by the explosion of Twenty one Barrels of Gunpowder which in its effect completely destroyed the Warehouse belonging to the Company near Wilford Street, Nottingham, and killed two men'.[22] 'This melancholy affair happened through a man named Musson, who was employed in one of the boats, observing a portion of gunpowder to have leaked from a cask, 21 of which he was just delivering, he said he would have a flash, and went to get a hot cinder from a boat which lay near, which, as soon as it was placed upon the train, caused the whole to explode, and by which he was thrown the distance of 126 yards in the most dreadful condition, the building and several vessels being also destroyed. . . . There are numberless instances in the town of furniture, and goods of great weight, having been thrown down with every appearance of an earthquake; the shock was so tremendous, as to be heard many miles distant from Nottingham.'[23]

The insurance company refused to pay on the grounds that the damage was exclusively the effect of explosion; the canal company then brought an action against the Nottingham Boat company, which they won. The Boat company had to pay £1,000 compensation and half the costs of the action. They could not, however, find the money, and in 1828 half the damages were remitted.

In May 1825 a general meeting had agreed that 'no Steam Packet or Vessel be permitted to pass . . . with the Engine at work'.[24] However, Messrs Hooton and Bradshaw seem to have run one, and were successfully prosecuted in January 1826. They protested that no injury had been caused, and in May the committee was given discretion to allow steam packets when they thought fit.

There was a hint of railway competition in 1830, when the company agreed to co-operate with the Loughborough and Leicester concerns in opposing a line from Cromford to Leicester. At this time, though, canal competition was their principal worry, the result of the opening of the Cromford & High Peak Railway, and so of rivalry between the canals serving it and the Trent & Mersey for the Manchester trade. For instance, in March 1832 German Wheatcroft asked that his flyboats should pass the locks at all hours 'to enable him to promote a new trade on the High Peak Railway from the Peak Forest Canal, and to compete with traders on other Canals, who are permitted to pass at all hours'.[25]

Early in 1837 protection clauses for the canal were included in the Midland Counties Railway Act. In August, however, the canal company had to apply for an injunction against the railway for interfering with the canal during the construction of its line. Negotiations settled the matter, and in March 1839, when the MCR proposed to make an interchange basin near their Nottingham station, the Nottingham company agreed.

In 1839 an Act[26] obtained by the West Croft Enclosure Commissioners enabled them to make a branch canal from near the Midland Counties station, which was opened in 1842. It formed a loop, leaving the main canal just below the station, and entering it again just east of Carrington Street, coal wharves being established on the curve where it turned north. This canal seems to have been disused by 1860, and in 1866 the Midland Railway obtained powers to acquire it and fill it in.[27]

On 4 May 1840 the Midland Counties Railway reached Leicester from Nottingham, and on 1 July the North Midland was opened from Derby to Leeds. Between the two dates we get the first toll reduction, in stone ex the Cromford Canal, on the Nottingham. An era was over. (*To continue the history of the Nottingham Canal, turn to p. 194.*)

Grantham Canal

On 27 August 1791, at a time when Jessop was just completing his survey and estimate for the Nottingham Canal, a canal was announced from Grantham to the Trent at Radcliffe below Nottingham.[28] It was promoted mainly by a group of Grantham men, who were spurred on by neighbouring proposals to build navigations to Sleaford and Melton Mowbray. As Jessop had carried out their own survey, they must have known that the Nottingham project was a likely starter, which would give them access to plentiful and cheap coal. In turn, a meeting at Grantham on 24 October was so enthusiastic that it encouraged the Nottingham promoters to go ahead.

Newark, which had been accustomed to supply Grantham and its district with its coal by road, and those who feared the River Witham would lose water, strongly opposed a bill of 1792 which was defeated. The subscribers met in August to decide upon a fresh attempt, the end being this time moved from Radcliffe to West Bridgford opposite Nottingham, and a branch, 3⅝ miles long, being added to Bingham. They were successful, and an

Act[29] was passed on 30 April 1793, a year after that for the Nottingham Canal. The capital was to be £75,000, with £30,000 more if necessary. Dividends were limited to 8 per cent, and in addition to normal mileage tolls, a charge of 2½d per ton was allowed for all traffic entering or leaving the Trent.

Such was the rejoicing that at a meeting in May a 'written extempore' was sung to the tune of 'The Roast Beef of old England', the last verses of which ran:

> Whilst politics trouble the heads of the great,
> We'll leave them alone to the wise ones of fate,
> For Boats, Locks, and Bridges our care does await,
>   To finish our new Navigation,
>   To finish the Grantham Canal.
>
> The Goddess of Peace shall her blessings unfold,
> Then open your treasures and pay down your gold,
> Our trade it will flourish—then freemen be bold
>   To finish your new Navigation,
>   To finish the Grantham Canal.[30]

Two engineers were appointed, James Green of Wollaton for the section from the Trent to the Leicestershire boundary about 1½ miles east of Hickling, and William King, the Duke of Rutland's agent, for the rest, including the reservoirs at Denton near Grantham and Knipton on the River Devon. William Jessop was employed from time to time to check progress. The initial board of nine included William King, an unusual arrangement as a paid servant, and also two members of the Trent Navigation board, Jonas Bettison and Robert Padley, Bettison being also on that of the Cromford Canal. The others were probably Grantham men, though many more of the shareholders came from Nottingham than from Grantham, and close links with the Nottingham company were to develop later. Construction began: on 1 February 1797 King reported that the eastern section was navigable, and this was probably opened in April, for a minute of the 18th records 'That Thos. Lockwood of Hickling be allowed the Amount of the Tonnage which he paid for a Boat Load of Coals (being the first) navigated upon the Canal to Grantham'.[31] The company now advertised coal and coke as being available at Grantham basin, and decided themselves to trade in them. The whole line was probably opened during the summer. The canal cost about £118,500, the extra money over the original authorization being raised by calling

£150 on each share and obtaining loans under an Act[32] of 1797
which also removed the 8 per cent dividend limitation to make
easier the raising of the additional money needed.

The canal was 33 miles long and rose 139 ft 9 in. to Grantham
by 18 broad locks (including Trent lock) admitting craft 75 ft by
14 ft. The main engineering features were the cutting at Harlaxton,
built at first only to take a single wide boat, but in which two
passing places were ordered to be made in 1801, and the leaky
section through gypsum beds in the parishes of Cropwell Bishop
and Cropwell Butler. Boats were worked into the Trent entrance
by a rope and capstan, for the use of which 1s 6d, then 3s, and then
in 1850 1s 6d again, was charged.

A maiden dividend of £3 per £150 share was paid for 1803.* In
the next two years substantial debts were repaid, the £3 being
repeated for 1806, after which dividends were paid regularly. In
1815 they reached £7 10s 0d or 5 per cent, then fell back before
reaching £8 in 1821, £10 in 1824 and a maximum of £13 in 1839,
1841 and 1842. Between 1801 and 1823 inclusive the receipts from
tolls did not exceed £9,000 in any year. Thereafter the amounts
collected slowly rose to a maximum of £13,079 in 1841. The
company also earned a few hundreds a year of other income,
mainly in wharfage, weighing and cranage charges at Grantham.

Traffic on the canal was mainly upwards, in coal, coke, lime,
building materials and groceries to the villages along the line, to
Grantham, and to places beyond to which goods were distributed
by land carriage. Downwards the canal carried corn, malt, beans,
wool and other agricultural products, Grantham and Harby acting
as collecting points for a wide area. In April 1798 a passage boat
was authorized from Cotgrave to Nottingham on Saturdays; I do
not know for how long it ran.

In 1827 the company, disturbed at what they considered to be
the inadequate stocks of coal carried by the merchants on Grantham wharf, returned to the coal trading business they had given
up in 1812. They were soon afterwards indicted at Lincoln Assizes
for conspiracy to enhance prices, and though the penalty was
nominal, they stopped trading after the merchants had agreed to
maintain a minimum stock of 2,660 tons. Though a concession in
the coal toll was made in 1838 after some years of pressure by the
merchants, it looks as if the company kept its tolls too high, and
thereby encouraged competition.

The natural link with the Nottingham Canal helped this con-

* Year ending 30 April in all cases.

servatism—in 1838 two of the Grantham's board were also members of that of the Nottingham—and probably also the advice of old William Ostler the clerk; he started in 1793, and was to remain till nis death in 1853. An illuminating memorial presented to the company in 1843 said that coal was being carried to Sleaford, Bridge End (Colsterworth) and places near, from Boston by the Witham and the South Forty Foot (the Black Sluice Drain), presumably being landed at Guthram Gowt, while groceries were coming in via Boston, the Witham and so up to Sleaford instead of via Gainsborough as formerly. It said also that owing to toll reductions made by the Oakham and Melton Mowbray Navigations, most of the corn grown between Colsterworth and Stamford was now sent away by those canals. Finally, it said that corn was being sent to Manchester by land carriage to Newark and then via Selby and connecting railways for 18s 6d a ton, against 21s 9d via the Grantham Canal and the Cromford & High Peak Railway, or 24s by canal all the way. In the reverse direction Yorkshire coal brought by sea to Gainsborough could reach Grantham by land from Newark more cheaply than coal carried on the Grantham Canal from the Nottingham area. The memorial finished by asking for a one-third reduction in tolls; the company must have been impressed, for they agreed, with the important exceptions of coal, coke and lime.

A little earlier, J. Rofe and his son had in 1833 proposed a 16 mile long canal to join Grantham and Sleaford,[33] so giving the Midlands an east coast outlet at Boston without the double transhipment that was necessary at Shardlow and Gainsborough were the route to Boston via the Fossdyke to be used, or were goods to be sent by way of Hull. But nothing came of it. (*To continue the history of the Grantham Canal, turn to p. 195.*)

Erewash Canal

The Cromford Canal was complementary to the Erewash by increasing the number of mines and works that it served, but the Nottingham Canal was competitive, and its construction threatened to remove much of the benefit the Cromford could bring.

The first move of the Erewash was to try itself to build the Beeston cut to ensure direct access to Nottingham and to the Trent and Grantham Canal trade. This having been blocked by the Nottingham company, they then allied themselves with the powerful Trent & Mersey during 1793 to promote the Trent Canal, to run direct from the end of the Trent & Mersey at Derwent Mouth across the Erewash on the level to Beeston, Nottingham and the Trent. Such a canal would much have improved the Erewash's access both to the Trent & Mersey and to Nottingham by cutting out the navigation of the Trent itself, but the river company succeeded in getting the bill withdrawn in exchange for an under-taking to introduce its own bill for the improvement of the river. Again defeated, the Erewash company then settled down to a rate war with the Nottingham which, combined with diversion of the traffic itself, reduced their takings from £10,784 in 1796* to £6,519 in 1797, £5,701 in 1798 and £5,110 in 1799, and brought the dividend from 30 to 20 per cent. In November 1798 the company made known their willingness to come to terms and, as we have seen, an agreement to eliminate rate-cutting and enticement of traffic was come to.

Except for the making of two new connections, the Nutbrook and Derby Canals, the Erewash's history was uneventful for some years to the opening of the Grand Union in 1814, which gave their coal a chance to compete farther south than before against that from Warwickshire and Staffordshire. Here are some figures:

Average of years ending 6 April	Receipts £	Dividend per cent
1791–3	6,730	24·2
1794–6	8,971	30
1797–9	5,777	20
1800–2	6,379	25
1803–5	6,891	23·3
1806–8	7,114	25·8
1809–11	7,922	33·3
1812–14	9,240	44·7
1815–17	10,134	51·3

The effort to export Derbyshire coal south of the Grand Union largely failed after the first burst of activity. The Erewash and other companies made considerable reductions, but the disadvan-tages of a line from the Cromford to the Grand Junction con-trolled by seven companies, all of which had to agree upon any change of toll, and each of which was intent upon throwing the burden on to the others, were as obvious then as they were to be later when railway competition was added. However, the canal maintained a comfortable and prosperous existence, an indication of which is the steadily increasing salary paid to the company's

* Year ended 6 April in all cases.

E

official at Trent Lock in charge of the wharf, toll-collecting, and transport of towing-horses across the Trent. It runs from 60 guineas and £10 gratuity in 1803 to £135 in 1824. Dividends rose to a maximum of 74 per cent for the year ended 1826, and then fell back.

In 1832 the Leicester & Swannington Railway was partially, and in 1834 completely, opened. It did what the Charnwood Forest branch of the Leicester Canal had failed to do; it brought Leicestershire coal into direct competition with that from Derbyshire. It seems likely that the opening of this line was the cause of the sharp reduction in the Erewash's revenue from £10,903 in 1831 to £9,398 in 1833 and £8,254 in 1834, with a reduction in dividend from 57 per cent for 1831 to 40 for 1834 and in the value of canal shares from £1,300 in 1832 to £500 in May 1834.

Trade then recovered well enough, but a much worse threat arose indirectly out of the Leicester & Swannington, when the Nottinghamshire and Derbyshire coalowners met at Eastwood and resolved to build a railway from Cromford and Pinxton to Leicester. Nothing followed immediately from their initiative, but in May 1833 the Midland Counties Railway first appears in the company's records, and the shareholders instruct the Committee to oppose 'any Railway that may be projected out of Derbyshire to supply the Leicestershire and distant Market with the Derbyshire and Nottinghamshire Coal'.[34] Before an extended line was authorized in 1836, the Erewash valley section was cut out, and promoted as a separate company, the Erewash Valley, in 1844. Before the Midland Counties reached Leicester in May 1840, reductions had been made in the canal's rates for long-distance traffic to the Grand Junction, mainly, it seems, because of competition on that line from coal from the Coventry area. Then early in 1840 the company received a letter from the Midland Counties asking the Cromford and themselves for reduced tolls on coal, stone, iron and other traffics along their canals 'to the merchandize station of the Midland Counties Railway Company at Long Eaton',[35] where a transhipment basin was built. In other words, the two canal companies were invited to share in the supply of the MCR's line southwards. A year later the Erewash agreed that coal should be carried on its water at the same cheap rate of 6d whether it was to continue onwards by rail or canal. Hereby it retained its tonnages, though not its revenue, which fell in 1841 to £8,412 from the £11,965 of the previous year, as did the dividend from 64 to 45 per cent. It was the end of the company's extreme prosperity, but for the next fifteen years it continued to enjoy the relative blessings of a dividend that never fell below 21 per cent, thanks partly to the age of the canal and so to its low original cost. (*To continue the history of the Erewash Canal, turn to p. 187.*)

Derby Canal

Though Brindley had about 1771 proposed a canal to join the Trent & Mersey to the Chesterfield via Derby, the true beginnings of the Derby Canal lie in a meeting held at the *Bell Inn* in that city on 14 September 1791,[36] which supported a canal from Derby to the Trent & Mersey at Swarkestone. The same issue of the local newspaper, however, also carried a notice for a canal from Derby to the Trent & Mersey at Shardlow, which was supported by the Erewash and Trent & Mersey companies as a branch from their proposed Trent Canal to Nottingham.

The second project waited upon the negotiations for the Trent Canal itself, while the first hung fire, probably because of the hostility of the Trent & Mersey. In August 1792 another meeting was held, at which additions to the original line were proposed, to the Smithy Houses at Denby, to Newhall and Swadlincote towards the proposed Ashby Canal, and to Cheadle through Sudbury and Uttoxeter. Benjamin Outram was commissioned to make the surveys.

Meanwhile the canal mania had gripped the country. On 9 August 'a number of people from Northampton, Harborough, and various parts of Leicestershire arrived in Derby with the supposed intention of buying shares in our intended Canal; but their chagrin and disappointment were inconceivable when they found . . . the meeting no other than a private one of the committee'.[37] Future notices of committee meetings had to state that no subscription would be entered into at them.

Outram reported, and a meeting on 8 September proposed a Trent–Swarkestone–Derby–Denby line, a branch to Sandiacre on the Erewash carried over the Derwent on an aqueduct, and the purchase of the Derwent Navigation. Soon afterwards shares were changing hands at £20 premium. The canal promoters now found themselves involved in the rivalries of other companies: the Trent & Mersey seeking to promote the Trent Canal and its Derby branch (the two together called the Derby & Nottingham Canal), to safeguard its tolls and by-pass the river, and the Erewash, which managed to make agreements both with the Derby for a junction and with the Trent & Mersey for a rival canal, but who eventually came down on the Derby's side.

Jessop re-surveyed Outram's proposals, and suggested a termination at Little Eaton instead of Denby, and a tramroad thence to the collieries; confirmed Outram's later idea of a level-crossing of the Derwent, and altered the position of the Swarkestone–Trent connection, which was mainly intended to link with a possible canal and tramroad to Breedon limeworks that Jessop had himself surveyed in 1787.

The bills for the Derby & Nottingham Canal and for the Derby reached Parliament. The former was strongly opposed by the Trent Navigation and first the Shardlow–Derby section, and then the Trent Canal, was dropped. That for the Derby went through, but during the next decades the company combined respect for the Trent & Mersey with firmness; for instance, in 1796 they decided not to support the competitive Commercial Canal project (see p. 117) if the Trent & Mersey would reduce tolls. In June of the following year a satisfactory toll agreement was reached.

The Act[38] was passed on 7 May 1793. Dividends were confined to 8 per cent; the Erewash were limited to 5d a ton on coal for the Derby Canal because of its anticipated benefits; the Trent & Mersey received a compensation toll of 1s on all goods passing to and from their canal to and from the Trent along the link between the two; the company—unusually—was bound to compensate the trustees of the Mansfield road for any loss of coal tolls;* had to carry 5,000 tons of coal a year toll-free for the poor of Derby; and agreed to buy the Derwent Navigation.

Benjamin Outram was appointed engineer. On 11 May 1795 'the Denby Line of the Derby Canal and Railway was opened for the conveyance of Coals &c',[39] and on 30 May the Sandiacre line. In February 1796 the weir across the Derwent and the iron aqueduct at the Holmes were reported complete, on 30 June the line to Swarkestone and the Trent was opened, and the canal was finished. The total cost was about £100,000, £150 having been called on each of the 600 shares and debts incurred.

The canal as built was 3 furlongs long from the Trent to Swarkestone, with four locks;[40] thence to Derby was 5 miles 2½ furlongs with two locks. It fell through two locks† to the river and crossed it on the level above a 300 ft long weir that also served

---

* The canal company guaranteed a revenue of £340 p.a., and for many years had to make up deficiencies.

† One a flood-lock.

local mills. Under this weir ran a water feeder to serve the Derby–
Trent section, and above it was a wooden towpath bridge. Beyond
the river crossing the canal rose by White Bear lock, beyond which
a short branch turned off to fall through Phoenix lock into the
river again, navigable for $1\frac{1}{2}$ miles upstream to Darley mills.
Beyond the junction the canal fell through four locks to Sandiacre,
$14\frac{1}{2}$ miles from the Trent & Mersey. Just beyond the Phoenix
branch the canal to Little Eaton, $3\frac{1}{8}$ miles long, turned off and rose
by four locks. The short Trent–Swarkestone length, burdened
with the Trent & Mersey's compensation toll of 1s as well as the
Derby's charges, was a failure from the start. By 1812 its maintenance exceeded its revenue, and traffic probably ended about
1817. It was dry and useless in 1837.

The tramroad, or Little Eaton gang-way as it was called locally,
ran from Little Eaton wharf for some 4 miles to Smithy Houses,
whence private lines extended it to Denby Old Colliery and other
mines and works. The tramroad was built of cast-iron plates of
28 lb to the yard, increased in December 1804 to 40 lb for new
plates. It was single-track, with passing places whose number
steadily increased till there were nine in 1825, and took 2-ton
waggons. It was the practice of the collieries to ship their coal in
boxes containing 33–$37\frac{1}{2}$ cwt. A box of coal was placed on each
waggon, carried to Little Eaton, and then transhipped by crane to
the barges. This was still the practice in 1831, when Bulmer & Co
were warned not to exceed the proper size of the boxes.

The canal soon had a passenger boat. Farey tells us that 'A
Market Boat, decked over, with seats, and a fire-place, for the
accommodation of passengers, starts from Swarkestone every
Friday morning, to carry market-people to Derby, at 6d each; and
which again leaves Derby at 4 o'clock for Swarkestone'.[41] It was
running in September 1816.

The lines of trade on the Derby Canal were complicated. Coal
came mainly down the Little Eaton railway to Derby itself, or into
the Swarkestone line. It also came into the canal from the Erewash.
Other trade, such as ironstone from the Nutbrook Canal and iron
from Stanton, entered the Sandiacre line and went past Derby to
Swarkestone for the Trent & Mersey. Other goods came up the
Trent to the Erewash and the Sandiacre line to Derby, or eastwards
from the Potteries or beyond to Swarkestone, Derby, and the
Sandiacre line to beyond Langley Mill. The company's toll structure, as approved in July 1798 after the adjustments necessary by
the opening of the Nottingham Canal, greatly encouraged the use

of the canal for through traffic, and not just to supply Derby itself.

The coal trade developed rapidly. In the year ended June 1798 28,571 tons were carried, 11,530 tons of which had come down the tramroad; by June 1803 this had grown to 50,374 tons, 27,771 tons having passed over the tramroad. Of this total, 39,110 tons was used from Derby wharf. Later figures are not available, but the tonnage must have grown steadily.

The shareholders were entitled to 5 per cent on their subscriptions, but payment had fallen behind. In 1802 the company agreed to treat unpaid interest up to June 1801 as an interesting-bearing debt. Spasmodic dividends were thereafter paid in 1803, 1806 and 1808, but the company was slower to become prosperous than its neighbours, and regular payments did not begin till 1811. In 1814 6 per cent was paid, which rose to 8 per cent in 1819, and then fluctuated about that figure, reaching 9½ in 1825, then falling back to about 7 per cent till 1836, thereafter rising rapidly to 12 in 1839, and then falling to 10½ in 1841 and 6 in 1843. Some of these payments were over the permitted maximum, and were presumably justified, as on the Nottingham, as contributions towards arrears properly due to the shareholders. Here are average dividend rates per cent:

Years	Per cent
1797–1801	1·5
1802–6	1·6
1807–11	1·2
1812–16	5·8
1817–21	7·4
1822–6	8·8
1827–31	6·5
1832–6	6·8
1837–42	10·6

The Derby Canal company had a curious road history. We have seen that under their Act they had to compensate the trustees of the Mansfield turnpike against a loss of coal tolls, a liability they got rid of in 1812 when the turnpike trustees' Act came up for renewal, and their liability ended. In 1802 the situation was reversed, when a turnpike bill for a road from Derby through Ripley to Alfreton was promoted. Into this the canal company got inserted a clause entitling them to the tolls on all coal, minerals and stone (other than for road maintenance) carried on the road, and on iron, lead, timber and goods made or got within 2,000 yd of the canal or tramroad. Such a protective clause was necessary, for the proposed road paralleled part of the tramroad and canal, and provided the colliery owners with an alternative means of carriage.

It was easier, however, to get such a clause passed than to extract the subsequent tolls from the turnpike trust, who naturally had no interest in collecting what it was bound to hand over. In 1810 the Derby company complained that they had received no tolls for two years, and a mandamus in 1811 did not improve matters. However, prosecutions against those who failed to pay, combined with threats to the toll-collectors and a commission to them on tolls collected, seem to have kept the trouble under control.

The tramroad from Smithy Houses worked busily. For instance, in April 1814, a time of scarcity, 27 boats and many carts and waggons were reported to be waiting for coal at Little Eaton.[42] In October 1820 the trade of the Denby potteries came on the line; in 1827-9 it was extended for 1,000 yd to Harrison, Pattinson & Davenport's collieries at Denby, in 1829 for 520 yd to a colliery at Kilburn and also to Salterwood pits near there. Altogether there were some 6 miles of tramroad.

In 1830 the canal committee, excited by the first railway mania, commissioned Stephenson (presumably George) to survey a new locomotive line from Smithy Houses to Derby that would eliminate road competition, and in 1832 considered a Little Eaton to Derby line for horse or locomotive working. Nothing happened, but the opening of the Cromford & High Peak Railway in 1831 at once increased competition for Belper traffic, and from 1834 there were toll reductions on the Little Eaton line. Then came the Midland Counties Railway, the building of which involved diverting the canal near Borrowash and building a new lock, the Birmingham & Derby Junction from Derby to Tamworth and Coleshill to the London & Birmingham at Hampton, and the North Midland from Derby to Leeds. By 1840 Derby was served by three main lines, and the canal company was faced with competition of a kind it had never felt before.

For the two months of February and March 1839 we have figures that give us some idea of canal traffic just before railway competition began. In these two months the Little Eaton line carried 13,332 tons, of which 7,057 were coal and 5,739½ were stone; the Sandiacre line 15,725 tons, of which 5,258½ tons were corn, 3,063½ tons were coal, and 1,670 stone; and the Swarkestone line 9,773 tons, of which 1,468 tons were corn, 898 tons stone, 878 tons cement, and 532 tons plaster. Coal came mainly from Salterwood and Marehay; Denby old colliery sent very little. It looks, therefore, as if the canal carried about 200,000 tons in this year. (*To continue the history of the Derby Canal, turn to p. 193.*)

Nutbrook Canal

Last of the linked canals in the area, the Nutbrook was first proposed in August 1791 as a branch to be built by the Erewash company,[43] to put trade on the Trent Canal, then being promoted, and their engineer, John Varley, surveyed it. No action followed, and in January 1793 that company received a letter telling them that 'Earl Stanhope's Tenants to his Iron Works are making a Railway and Canal from Dale Furnace to join the Erewash Canal . . . above the Heath Lock'.[44] The local colliery owners then promoted a canal downwards from Shipley to join that which had already been cut through Lord Stanhope's land, and the Act[45] was passed on 3 June 1793.

Jessop was paid for a preliminary survey, Outram was appointed engineer, and £300 was paid to Lord Stanhope for the cutting already done. The whole canal was probably open by the end of 1795, at a cost of some £22,800.[46] This had mostly been raised by calls of £156 7s 3d on each of the 130 shares, arrears of interest being then added to give them a nominal value of £175.[47] The canal was 4½ miles long from the head at Shipley wharf to the junction with the Erewash Canal at the White House at Stanton, and had 13 broad locks and three reservoirs. The old horse tramroad, probably still with wooden rails, that had been built steeply upwards from Newmanleys Mill to the collieries soon after the opening of the Erewash Canal was then closed, and removed in 1796.

Coal, ironstone and iron were either shipped directly on to the Nutbrook, or brought to it by horse tramroads. The first dividend, of 4 per cent, was paid for 1797, and ten years later this had risen to 5 per cent.[48] A peak of 7 per cent was reached in 1819. (*To continue the history of the Nutbrook Canal, turn to p. 192.*)

Woodeaves Canal

About 1802 this private canal, 1¼ miles long, parallel to the Woodeaves brook north of Ashbourne, was built as a long dam, and in order that small boats could carry limestone to the cotton mills ¾ mile east of Fenny Bentley.[49]

Chesterfield Canal

Farther to the east the Chesterfield Canal maintained a modest prosperity. The 1 per cent dividends of 1791 and 1792 had risen to 5 per cent by 1795 and a year later to 8. Between 1805 and 1810 they were 6 per cent; in 1826, they were 7 per cent, and shares were selling at £152 each; in 1836 the dividend was still 7 per cent.

As early as 1792 the proprietors of the River Dun had proposed what became the Sheffield Canal from that city to Rotherham to join their river, with a branch to the Chesterfield Canal near Eckington or Renishaw.[50] It was opposed by the landowners and dropped at the end of the year.[51]

In the early twenties the company had considered an extension to the coalfield near Barlow, and a communication thence to the limestone quarries near Calver and Stony Middleton to the west. The Sheffield Canal company were also looking westwards, and these ideas were caught up with older ones in a proposal put forward by Joseph Haslehurst, a colliery engineer at Chesterfield, in a prospectus of 24 June 1824 for the Grand Commercial (or Scarsdale & High Peak) Canal, 44 miles long, to run from the Peak Forest at Bugsworth by Hope and the Derwent valley to Grindleford and thence to the head of the Barlow brook, whence one line would run to the Sheffield Canal and another connect with the Chesterfield and continue to the Cromford at Buckland Hollow. The estimate was £574,130, the revenue being put at £62,250 p.a.[52] This scheme, 'not only uniting the Western with the Eastern ocean, but also causing an almost universal water communication between the existing Canals and Railroads of the united kingdom',[53] got support especially in Manchester and Sheffield, and Telford was employed to report on it. I have not traced whether he did, but interest concentrated upon a Peak Forest Canal to Sheffield connection, which developed into the Sheffield & Manchester Railway proposal with its inclined planes, and from that again into the Sheffield, Ashton-under-Lyne and Manchester Railway, opened in 1845.

In August 1852, however, a meeting was held in Sheffield to discuss a possible Sheffield & Chesterfield Junction Canal, at which it was reported that many thousands of pounds were subscribed[54]. As a result, Mr Burke surveyed a line 7¾ miles long from the head of the locks on the Sheffield Canal to the Chesterfield below Killamarsh forge. George Leather, asked his opinion, reported on 22 October[55] in favour of Burke's line, but with a

course about a mile longer at the Chesterfield Canal end to reduce
the earthworks needed. He referred to a possible trade from new
collieries on the line, to be carried to Sheffield and also down the
River Dun to compete with Silkstone coal from the Barnsley
Canal, and to other trade from Sheffield to Worksop, Retford and
beyond. He estimated the cost at £75,870, which was more than
the promoters had thought.

A newspaper report of October said that a plan had been
adopted which was 'so fair and honourable towards the subscribers, that there is not the slightest chance existing of the concern becoming, as had sometimes been the case, a matter of profit
to a few at the expense of the many'.[56] These ominous words
heralded the collapse of the scheme. Thereafter the Chesterfield
stayed content with its limits till railways appeared to threaten
them. (*To continue the history of the Chesterfield Canal, turn to p.* 196.)

Adelphi Canal

J. & E. Smith & Co, iron forgers and founders of Chesterfield,
built the Adelphi works between Calow and Duckmanton as a
munition plant manufacturing cannon balls for the East India
Company and the Army. As they were not on a main road, a ½ mile
private canal was made about 1799 from them to the lane leading
to Staveley and the Chesterfield Canal. Traffic in boats, carrying
about 1½ tons, was two-way: pig-iron from furnace to road, and
coal from pits near the road back to the furnaces. The canal was
also used as a reservoir for condensing water for the steam-engines
used at the works, which were closed about 1850. Some of the
buildings remain in farm use.[57]

Trent River

In the excitement of canal promotion at the beginning of the
1790s, the Trent Navigation had two main interests: to support a
by-pass to the dangerous passage of Trent Bridge at Nottingham,
but to prevent it being made by anyone else but themselves; and
to defeat the Trent Canal proposal of the Trent & Mersey and
Erewash companies for a canal parallel to the upper river.

They attained their first object by allowing the Nottingham
Canal company to prevent the Erewash making the Beeston cut,
and then themselves getting the same proposal removed from the
Nottingham's bill as the price of allowing it to pass. To defeat the

second was more difficult. It was done in the House in May 1793, when agreement was reached that the canal bill should be withdrawn on condition that a thorough survey should be made of the river as a preliminary to legislation by the Navigation company to obtain improvements.

This survey was made by William Jessop and Robert Whitworth. They reported on 8 July[58] that 65 out of the 71 miles of river between Cavendish bridge and Gainsborough had 3 ft of water or more, but that there were some 70 shallows in the rest, 42 of which had a minimum of 27 in. and 15 only 24 in., the worst one being opposite the entrance to the Soar. They recommended a cut and lock at Thrumpton* opposite Soar mouth, a cut and lock at Beeston to join the Nottingham Canal at Lenton, with a weir below the cut and a side-lock back into it, and a cut and lock below Nottingham at Holme. With other improvements, the estimate was £12,776 exclusive of the cost of the Act and the expenses of the Trent Canal promoters, which the river company had agreed to pay.

All was agreed, and the Act[59] was passed in 1794. It authorized a capital of £13,000 (which was in fact subscribed by the existing proprietors), doubled tolls which were still very moderate, and provided for a minimum depth of 30 in. at all seasons, so that 40-ton boats could pass. The Act also substituted a charge of 6d per loaded boat passing between the Erewash and the Loughborough for the old annual payments, and provided for the purchase of the Nottingham Corporation's capstan at Trent Bridge to encourage their approval of the by-pass. In the Beeston cut the Trent company took its own tolls, paying the Nottingham Canal 1s per boat for craft passing back to the city wharves.

At Sawley, which already had a lock, another with flood gates was built alongside; a lock was built at Cranfleet, with a weir just below the Soar entrance, so that craft could cross the river above it; another at Beeston into the cut to Lenton, and a side-lock back into the river below the weir, which was fitted with flood-gates; and at Holme a lock and a flood lock. These varied somewhat in size, the largest craft able to pass them all being 85 ft 9 in. by 14 ft 9 in., drawing 2 ft 6 in. Nature further improved the navigation when in 1792 a flood cut through the loop of river at No Man's Friend, and in 1797 through another at Burton Round, both between Torksey and Gainsborough.†

* Cranfleet.
† The towpath had not been built round either.

The company paid over £1,838 to the Trent Canal promoters, continued Jessop as engineer, and got down to work. The Beeston cut was finished early in 1796, the Cranfleet cut and lock during 1797, and the Holme cut and lock during 1800. The improvements were declared complete on 1 September 1801, by which time the company had already borrowed some thousands over the authorized £13,000, and was still to borrow £3,000 more. However, the limited 7 per cent dividend was henceforth paid on old and new shares alike.

By the turn of the century there was a large river trade, downwards in lead, copper, ironware, coal, Cheshire cheese, salt, beer and pottery, and upwards in Swedish iron (diminishing as home supplies increased), Norwegian timber, hemp, flax, malt, groceries and other London goods, and flints from Gravesend for the Potteries.[60] In 1799 there seem to have been about 140 barges on the river, usually about 70–72 ft long, 11–14 ft wide and carrying about 40 tons. They could be towed or sailed, in which case the horses were carried in a well-deck, and were extravagant in manpower. A by-law of 1802 required a boat carrying 18 tons or more to have a crew of three men and a boy. Decked boats seem only to have been introduced about 1860.

Shardlow was a transhipment point for the Trent & Mersey, along which flyboat and stage services ran westwards. Its population rose from 580 in 1801 to 1,306 in 1841, and then fell back to 842 in 1891. Nottingham, past whose wharves flowed all the Trent traffic, became an important inland port, and by 1817 had a steam packet service to Gainsborough. In 1830 such a packet carried passengers at 5s and 8s 6d, who were supplied with refreshment. The trade of Newark grew more slowly; below it, at Torksey, barges turned into the Fossdyke for Lincoln and beyond; Gainsborough, to which the Trent was tidal, was an interchange port for coastal shipping as well as a shipping place for the Rotherham iron industry. In 1815, 318 vessels entered the port; it was given customs facilities in 1841,* and it prospered till steam and motor craft were able to continue to Hull. Foretaste of change, a steamboat of 16 hp started running between Gainsborough and Hull in 1814; a steam tug worked regularly between the same places from 1818, and in 1830 a packet was running from Gainsborough to Goole, to connect with others for various places in Yorkshire.[61] Farther down the river there were the interchange ports of Stockwith, for the Chesterfield Canal, and Keadby, for that from the

* These were withdrawn in 1881.

Don and beyond. Below lay Trent Falls, the Humber and Hull, which by 1837 had become the third port in England.

Above Shardlow, however, the story was different. At some time before 1787 the Earl of Uxbridge and the Burton Boat Company had built a canal branch upwards from the river at Burton to a basin at Bond End, some 40 yd from the Trent & Mersey Canal at Shobnall. In August of that year they asked the canal company to extend their wide boat waterway onwards from Horninglow to Shobnall and build a barge connection through to the Bond End basin whence the Boat Company would widen to the Trent. The Burton company hopefully expected the Trent & Mersey to charge the same tolls for barges coming up the canal and into the new cut as they themselves took on the river, and to provide the water. The T & M refused, and the Boat Company then worked hard to link the upper Trent by tramroad or canal to some source of traffic. A line to the Breedon limeworks or to the mines near Swadlincote; a canal to join the Ashby or the Coventry; support for the Commercial Canal (see p. 117), which would have crossed it; all were tried, as well as sale to the Trent & Mersey and amalgamation with the Ashby. In desperation, they even cut the connection through the towpath at Shobnall without authority in 1791, 'which afterwards, on a little Consideration, they thought to fill up', as the Trent & Mersey put it after having compelled reinstatement.[62] The proposal to join the Coventry had, however, perturbed the T & M, and at an inter-company meeting in the Grand Junction's offices in December 1793, they agreed to build the Shobnall connection with one lock.* It was probably built in 1795.

In that year the Boat Company had 19 craft on the Staffordshire barge register, varying from 20 to 33 tons. But the upper Trent was often short of water in dry seasons, which meant that a nominal 33 tons became an actual 17 or 18,[63] and could not compete with the canal. Joseph Wilkes, a leading figure in the Boat Company, died in 1805, and the concern, which had partially changed hands the year before, closed down in the same year.[64] After that little, if any, through trade was carried on the river, though some local business probably lasted until the 90s. The Bond End branch had a Midland Railway transhipment siding in

---

* This was a stop-lock. The Bond End lock lower down the cut towards the Trent, with a fall of 3 ft 9 in., must have been put in at this time, and the level of canal thence to Shobnall raised to that of the Trent & Mersey, probably to save water.

1847, was reported disused in 1872, and had probably become so a year or two before that.[65]

On the main river all was going well: here are the tolls averaged over three-year periods:

Years	Average tolls
1805–7	£7,099
1808–10	£7,078
1811–13	£7,952
1814–16	£7,984
1817–19	£8,549
1820–2	£8,513
1823–5	£11,282

In 1823 the Newark Navigation Commissioners, who were far-seeing, suggested that the river should be improved for larger craft. They were snubbed by the Trent company: 'it will not be either for the Interest of the public or of this Company to make any alteration in or to deviate from the System of Improvement authorized'.[66] It was a bad moment to suggest reform, for takings had started to rise sharply in 1822, and by 1825 the company had a balance in hand that could not be used for the limited dividends. All tolls other than on coal and coke were therefore reduced by one-third from 1 January 1826, which brought the toll receipts down from £13,338 in 1825 to £8,280 in 1826. Under the old company they were never again to exceed £11,500. Once more, in 1831, the Newark Commissioners suggested improvement; once again they were repulsed. So passed a chance that would not recur, for on 4 June 1839 the Midland Counties Railway was opened between Nottingham and Derby, and on 4 August 1846 the (now Midland) branch from Nottingham to Lincoln. The first seriously affected the upper Trent traffic, and the second that into the Fossdyke. (*To continue the history of the Trent Navigation, turn to p. 198.*)

CHAPTER IV

The Leicester Line

THE story of the Leicester line is pleasantly complicated. Whereas the Loughborough, Leicester, Melton Mowbray and Oakham companies each had their own local reasons for existence, the Leicestershire & Northamptonshire Union was promoted to link Leicester and the Trent with the Grand Junction; it only got part way, and the connection had to be completed on a different line by a second linking canal, the Grand Union. As each of the six waterways tried to get the greatest advantage for itself out of the business of the line, these two were in the weakest position, the Union only having an internal trade to Market Harborough, and the Grand Union to Crick wharf.

Round the central story,[1] too, are many groups of interests. The Leicester Navigation was built in two portions, the River line to Loughborough to carry Derbyshire coal, and the Forest line from the Coleorton and Swannington collieries. Leicestershire coal failed to compete, however, the Forest line was both inconvenient and ill-fated, and Derbyshire had its own way till Leicestershire made a spectacular come-back with the Leicester & Swannington Railway, opened in 1832. The lime and limestone owners of Barrow Hill and Cloud Hill had the alternative of the Ashby Canal tramroads, but these were prevented from carrying much coal by a toll of 2s 6d a ton payable to the Leicester company. For a time in the 1780s and early 1790s, however, the Ashby Canal project had seemed to the Leicestershire coalowners a possible solution to their difficulties.

Again, the Leicester line, carrying Derbyshire and later Leicestershire coal, competed against the canals carrying Warwickshire and Staffordshire coal from the Coventry and Birmingham districts, and both against sea-coal imports to London and to such places as Northampton, to which they came up the Nene. In other traffic from north of Trent it competed against the route by way of Derwent Mouth, Fradley, Fazeley and Coventry to London. Finally, in and out of the story come and go the projects for extensions, such as that to Stamford and the Welland.

At the beginning of our period only the Loughborough Navigation had been built, whence Derbyshire coal was carried to Leicester by road to compete with the local product, also brought by land by way of Desford and Aylestone. As early as 1780, seemingly at the suggestion of the *Leicester and Nottingham Journal*, men began to consider its extension to Leicester and Melton Mowbray. The idea of a second line to the Charnwood Forest collieries also came up at this time. However, the impetus was not strong enough, and nothing happened for nearly five years. Meanwhile the first proposal was made for what later became the Ashby Canal from Ashby Woulds to the Coventry Canal, and a possible extension from the Woulds to the Trent. This in turn was dropped.

In 1785 the idea of extending the Loughborough Navigation upwards was revived, under the stimulus of the high charges for goods carried onwards by road. It was proposed to make the Soar navigable to Leicester, and also the Wreak to Melton Mowbray as a separate enterprise. These plans were supported by the Earl of Harborough of Stapleford Park, but strongly opposed by the Leicestershire coalowners, a number of riparian landowners and millers, and the Loughborough company, and also by the influential because fair-minded Lord Rawdon.* The promoters, with the support of Joseph Boultbee, a Leicester banker and tenant of a newly opened colliery near Thringstone, then proposed a canal branch from the Soar to that place. Lord Rawdon, however, whose interests lay in the Moira district, was not convinced, and opposition came also from other landowners. Rawdon then produced his own scheme for a canal from Moira to Leicester and on to Melton, but this was not accepted, and a tremendous argument began on a bill of 1786, on the edge of which hovered the promoters of other lines to Melton, to Oakham and to Stamford. The bill was lost, and again there was a lull until 1788, when the efforts of the *Leicester Journal*, Joseph Cradock of Gumley, and others, produced a bill in 1789 combining the lines to Leicester and to Melton Mowbray, which was once more defeated. Then, in 1790, Lord Rawdon was convinced. His conversion made easier a grouping of the landowners, colliery owners and town notabilities, the opposition of the Loughborough company being placated with a guaran-

* Later Earl of Moira and Marquess of Hastings.

(*above*) Erewash Canal lock at the junction with the Nutbrook Canal, which comes in from e left behind the lock-house. In the background are the Stanton works; (*below*) canal house t the junction of the Cromford Canal (to the left) with the Lea Wood branch (to the right)

VI. Chesterfield Canal: (*above*) Norwood bottom lock, at the beginning of the flight that lea
to the western end of Norwood tunnel. The far end building used to be a public hous
(*below*) the eastern end of Norwood tunnel

tee. In 1791 bills for the Leicester Navigation, with two lines from Loughborough to Leicester and from Loughborough to the Charnwood Forest collieries, and for the Melton Mowbray Navigation, were passed. The Leicester's two lines were intended 'to keep up the Competition between the Leicestershire and Derbyshire Coalowners and bring the Article of each fairly to market proportionate to its intrinsic Worth'.[2]

These led in turn to two other Acts of 1793, for the Oakham Canal to extend the Melton Mowbray to that town, and for the Leicestershire & Northamptonshire Union. The promotion of the Grand Junction in 1792 (see Chapter V) naturally led men to the idea of a broad canal to link it with Leicester by way of Northampton, so that Leicester would 'receive upon its quays the vessels from Thames and Trent . . . an inexhaustible source of commercial wealth'.[3] The Melton Navigation was probably opened throughout in 1797, and the Oakham in 1803, but the fortunes of the Union were very different. It reached Gumley Debdale in 1797, and there stopped, except for an extension to Market Harborough completed in 1809, Leicester getting its through connection to London by road services run by Pickfords and others from Brownsover wharf on the Oxford Canal or Hinckley on the Ashby. The line was eventually completed in 1814 by the Grand Union company, a protégé of the Grand Junction, along a different route and using narrow locks, so making it impossible for wide boats to work through the line to the Grand Junction, as later that company itself wanted them to do when it built the Foxton inclined plane. Within a few weeks of the opening, fly boats from Paddington wharf started running to Leicester, Loughborough and Derby, to parallel those already established between Derby and Leicester. On the other hand, the disadvantages of narrow locks became clear equally quickly, for in November 1814 Sale, the Grand Union's clerk, wrote to the Loughborough to propose a steam tug across the Trent 'to which should be attached a narrow Boat on each side or lengthways as occasion served which would prevent the necessity of unloading at Leicester and probably gain a day'.[4] It was not adopted.

The line was complete, and so it remained, though in 1810 there was a flurry of promotion for alternative lines to Stamford, an idea revived again later. For some years trade grew steadily, though Derbyshire coal on the whole competed unsuccessfully for the market south of the Grand Union with that from Warwickshire and Staffordshire, and from that brought along the Ashby Canal

F

from Moira. Stone was a good trade also, notably Mountsorrel and Quorndon granite.

Then, in 1830 the Leicester & Swannington Railway got its Act, and in August the Derbyshire coalowners agreed to reduce the price of coal if the canal companies would cut tolls. In the autumn came the threat also of a line from Pinxton to Leicester, and toll reductions were made in 1831 and 1832. The opening of the first section of the L & S in 1832 marked a major change. Coal from the Leicestershire collieries now competed seriously with that from Derbyshire at Leicester itself, so forcing the Leicester, Loughborough and Erewash companies to reduce their tolls on coal from across the Trent. This in turn brought the prices of their shares down heavily. Moreover, the attempts of the Leicester company to build their own railway to Swannington and so get their own access to the local coal was frustrated first by the dereliction of the old and inconvenient Forest line and second, by Lord Shaftesbury's blocking of a new Act in the interests of his pet reform, the abolition of rating privileges. On the other hand, the Union and Grand Union did not much mind whether they carried Leicestershire or Derbyshire coal south, so long as its price would enable it to compete with that from elsewhere. Therefore a split of interest occurred between the two groups of canal companies.

In the 1830s merchandise tolls on the line felt the pressure of the road carriers. In 1835, for instance, the Loughborough and Leicester companies reduced their tolls on sundries, 'finding a very considerable portion of the Traffic from Birmingham and the Neighbourhood to be coming by Waggon at very low Rates (lower than Canal Carriers can meet with present Tonnages)'.[5] In May 1840 the line faced a greater threat, when the Midland Counties Railway was opened from Derby and Nottingham to Leicester; by the end of the year, also, two railway lines were carrying Derbyshire coal south towards London in competition with all the canals. By June 1841 the Leicester company was carrying merchandise at ½d a mile, and by August was willing to reduce its tolls on coal for Paddington to 4d for its whole line, with building stone at the same rate. The good days were over.

Loughborough Navigation

Faced with three proposals for extensions upwards of their navigation to Leicester, a line to the Leicestershire collieries on

Charnwood Forest, an extension up the Soar to Leicester, and the making navigable of the River Wreak to Melton Mowbray, the Loughborough company opposed the first as likely to lessen its import trade in coal from north of the Trent. As for the other two, 'this Company will oppose in Parliament any Attempt to reduce or limit the Tonages in any respect which the Company have now a right and are authorized to take on all Coals, Goods etc. navigated on the Soar Navigation'.[6] However, they were brought to agree to the Leicester Canal bill of 1791 on condition that they were guaranteed £3,000 p.a.—the average gross receipts for the years 1787–90—five-sixths by the Leicester company and one-sixth by the Melton Mowbray. In return, they undertook not to charge more than 1s 6d or less than 10d for coal on their line. In 1794 they were compelled to raise all their tolls other than on coal and coke to the full Parliamentary rates in order to maintain their takings, but by 1798 they could reduce lime and limestone, and soon afterwards, such was their prosperity, they were free to adjust their tolls without concern for the guarantee.

Apart from coal, wool, and agricultural produce, an important trade developed in Mountsorrel granite going north, as the demand grew for paving. It went far afield; for instance, in 1834 the company gave a drawback on such stone passing Harecastle tunnel on the Trent & Mersey. As early as 1796 the company refused to reduce their tolls on the stone, but agreed that coal boats carrying it as back-carriage could do so at reduced rates. Later, a whole series of toll changes and drawbacks resulted from efforts to encourage its use.

The opening of the Leicester Navigation, the line to Melton Mowbray and on to Oakham, the extension beyond Leicester to Gumley and Market Harborough, and the completion of the through line to the Grand Junction, each brought an accession of trade to the Loughborough. With its key position, and having cost so little to construct, the market prices of the few shares in existence and the dividends upon them rose to fantastic heights which were maintained until the opening of the Leicester & Swannington Railway. The dividends (see table on the next page) are averaged over three-year periods.

Because they were so busy, the company jointly with the Leicester employed a full-time boat-gauger separate from the lock-keepers; oddly, too, they had always combined the posts of clerk and treasurer, and in 1804 put the current holder of both posts on to the committee also.

Years	per cent	Years	per cent
1779–81	3 1/3	1812–14	108 1/18
1782–4	1 1/2	1815–17	112 2/9
1785–7	13	1818–20	134 1/6
1788–90	20	1821–3	147 1/2
1791–3	27 1/2	1824–6	152 7/9
1794–6	30	1827–9	154 1/6
1797–9	40	1830–2	151 7/18
1800–2	63 1/3	1833–5	91 2/3
1803–5	80	1836–8	128 8/9
1806–8	82 1/2	1839–41	106 7/8
1809–11	94 1/6		

Little happened of special interest till 1819 when John Kiddey, then engineer, reported that 'the Line of the Navigation at or near the Devil's Elbow in the Parish of Long Whatton and by Kegworth bridge . . . is dangerous and very inconvenient to the Traders thereon and that the same might be improved by making fresh cuts at both places'.[7] It was agreed to carry out the improvements. There was difficulty with landowners, but in April 1826 it was reported that the 'new Cut Lock and Bridge made . . . near Kegworth Bridge (by) John Kiddey . . . has been completed in a very efficient and workmanlike manner'.[8] The other proposal seems to have been dropped.

The first hint of serious trouble appears in 1825: 'there are Railways proposed that will to all probability most materially affect the Interests of the Navigation'.[9] Though the company saved money by not petitioning against the Leicester & Swannington Railway's bill of 1830, they soon afterwards decided to oppose a projected line from Pinxton to Leicester. Tolls were reduced in 1831 and 1832. At the end of 1832 not only was the Leicester & Swannington open, but the Leicester Navigation were proposing to rebuild their Charnwood Forest line to carry still more Leicestershire coal in competition with that from Derbyshire coming up from the Loughborough. By December 1833 the company was in a frenzy. They were worried about the project that was to become the Midland Counties Railway, they were opposing the Leicester Navigation's projected line which included the proposed abolition of the £3,000 guarantee, they were considering building yet another line from the Soar near Zouch to the Leicestershire collieries themselves, and they thought 'someone should be employed to expose the falacy of the proposed advantages to the public of the above named railways'.[10] By May 1834 the value of

Loughborough shares had fallen from £2,300 each in 1832 to
£1,670.[11]

By August 1834 the Union Canal had negotiated joint drawbacks with the L & S R on Leicestershire coal to Market Harborough and beyond, and offered similar drawbacks on Derbyshire coal if the canal companies reduced their rates. The Loughborough agreed to bring theirs down to 7d. At this point they also
had to pay 'Mr. Richard Cort the Sum of £5 for his Pamphlets and
his exertions in shewing the falacy of Railways'.[12] They were not,
however, themselves convinced by his arguments, for by 1836
they were talking of either opposing the Midland Counties Railway bill, 'or making such arrangements with the Projectors thereof
as may appear advisable'.[13] No such arrangements were made, and
in 1840 that company's line was opened from Derby and Nottingham to Leicester. The Loughborough's palmy days were over.
(*To continue the history of the Loughborough Navigation, turn to p.* 188.)

Leicester Navigation

On 12 July 1790 a group of canal supporters met to consider
preliminary plans for lines to Leicester, Melton Mowbray and the
Charnwood Forest collieries, and decided to seek a bill, and to
commission William Jessop to make their survey. It had been
thought that a plan for the Ashby Canal should be part of the same
scheme, but Lord Rawdon, 'for the greater Assurance of the above
Plan succeeding', made that for the Ashby a separate project, to be
supported by the Leicester promoters, and so earned their thanks
for 'his peculiarly disinterested Conduct in making so great a
Sacrifice of his own Interests to the Publick Good'.[14]

Jessop and Staveley reported in the autumn, proposing a canal
and river line to Leicester, a canalization of the Wreak to Melton,
and a rail and water line to the Leicestershire collieries. The Melton
line was taken over by a separate company, their other proposals
were accepted, no difficulty was found in raising the £46,000
thought to be necessary, and an Act[15] was obtained on 13 May
1791. Jessop was appointed engineer at £300 p.a., Christopher
Staveley junior surveyor at £200, and it was decided to build the
River and Forest lines together, for the Act bound them not to
carry coal to Leicester until it could be brought from the Leicestershire collieries as well as from Derbyshire. At this point a certain
Morecroft proposed that lifts should be used on a canal from

Loughborough to Coleorton, cutting out the railways, but the idea was laid aside.

The Charnwood Forest line was planned as a tramroad from the basin of the Loughborough Navigation at that town for 2½ miles to Nanpantan, there to join a level canal 7½ miles long to a junction point, whence one arm would continue for ¼ mile to Thringstone bridge, and the other for 1 mile to Barrow Hill. From Thringstone there was to be a tramroad to Swannington, with a branch to two Coleorton collieries; from Barrow Hill basin a limeworks tramroad to Cloud Hill, with a branch to Barrow Hill. Altogether there were to be 8¾ miles of canal and 5¾ miles of tramroads. The rail and water line was built complete from Loughborough to Thringstone and Barrow Hill basins, together with the tramroads to Swannington and Coleorton. The track of the Cloud Hill and Barrow Hill branches was not prepared, nor were the rails laid, though the land was bought.

The line was formally opened on 24 October 1794, when 'a Boat Load of Coals of nearly Ten Tons . . . passed from Mr. Burslem's Collieries at Coleorton along the Waterlevels and Railways to Loughborough';[16] later, two ceremonial boatloads of coal arrived together at Leicester, one carrying this coal, and one a cargo from Derbyshire. It is often stated that these lines were built in 1789, and that they were the first edge-railways. As we have seen, they were constructed under the Act of 1791, and were probably completed about the end of 1793; they were certainly not the first edge-railways, for earlier lines are known, but they may have been the first to use fish-bellied rails. These were 3 ft long, one end terminating in a broad foot with a recess, in the centre of which is a hole for the spike, the other end having a smaller foot which lay in its neighbour's recess. They were spiked to pads of wood which in turn rested upon wooden sleepers. The rails were not, oddly enough, cast at Butterley as one would expect, but by Butler & Co and Smith & Co, both of Chesterfield. The line from Nanpantan to Loughborough had a fall of 170 ft, the first short section at 1 in 30, the rest at 1 in 70; those from Swannington and Coleorton to Thringstone were even steeper, with gradients up to 1 in 24 and 1 in 26.

It seems that, even before the Charnwood Forest line was opened, the Leicestershire colliery owners had decided that it would not help them. Perhaps this was because they felt unable to compete with Derbyshire coal, or perhaps they hoped to use the Ashby Canal instead. In December 1793 the committee learned

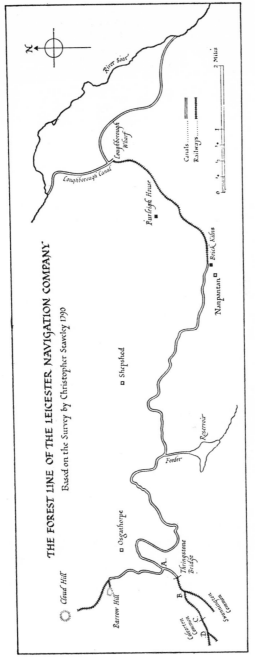

THE FOREST LINE OF THE LEICESTER NAVIGATION COMPANY

Based on the Survey by Christopher Stawley 1790

Canals ....
Railways ....

0   ¼   ½   ¾   1   2 Miles

River Soar

Loughborough Wharf

Loughborough Canal

Burleigh House

Brick Kilns

Nanpantan

Shepshed

Reservoir

Feeder

Osgathorpe

Cloud Hill

Barrow Hill

Thringstone Bridge

A.

B.

C.

D.

Coleorton Common

Swannington Common

N

4. The Forest Line of the Leicester Navigation

that neither Fenton & Raper nor Boultbee, two of the three coal-masters concerned, would be ready with their new mines by the probable date of opening, and in January 1794 that the former were making no effort to build waggons or boats. It seemed as if eyes were looking to the Ashby, and therefore the Leicester company obtained a compensation toll in the Ashby's Act. In May they wrote again to the coalmasters asking them to build boats and waggons; they then built a toll-house on the water level, appointed a toll-collector, and opened the line with their own boat on 24 October.

This opening was a demonstration one, to enable Derbyshire coal to be carried on the River line, for clearly the Charnwood water level was too short of water to be usable. Another demonstration boatload was navigated in April 1795, but Burslem, the only coalmaster interested, could not carry on without assistance, and the company agreed to help finance a stockpile of coal at Thringstone—they themselves also sold it at Leicester, presumably carrying it by road till they had enough water. Simultaneously work on a reservoir at Blackbrook was begun.

A few tolls now came in, but a full-time collector was not thought necessary for the time being. Then about June 1797 the reservoir was finished and filled, though it had to be emptied again to fit a new valve. On 10 October reduced tolls came into force on the line, 2d for the use of the tramroads to Thringstone basin, and 10d for the water level and tramroad to Loughborough, and we can probably claim the line as operational from this date. Prospects began to improve a little, for Sir George Beaumont, the most important owner, whose tenant Boultbee was, agreed to discuss building boats and waggons on the basis of the reduced tolls lasting for ten years, and of free passage for empties. The company agreed, and presumably Sir George started to build; in December 1798 he was advertising Coleorton coal for sale at 5½d cwt at Nanpantan, indicating perhaps that land carriage thence to Leicester was cheaper than rail and boat via Loughborough.

Then, in February 1799, 'owing to the Thaw and the Quantity of the Rain and Snow falling occasioning a violent Flood', the new reservoir burst, damaging farm land and a house; 'great injury was done to the Water Level . . . entirely destroying the Aqueduct near Chester's and doing great damage to the Embankment across the Valley'.[17] The cause was the flood, but its effects were aggravated by an insufficiently large discharging weir. Though, as we shall

see, the line was again restored, the flood was the end of its hopes
of activity.

The River line began in the Loughborough Navigation basin,
and ran for 15¾ miles to Leicester, partly as an artificial canal, and
partly as a river navigation, there being 9 broad locks and a flood
lock at Loughborough. Near Cossington, 7 miles from Loughborough, the Melton Mowbray Navigation turned off eastwards
along the course of the Wreak. The making of the River line went
on uneventfully, though the plans were somewhat modified when
the Act for the Union Canal was passed in April 1793, and through
barge traffic from the Grand Junction seemed likely. It was opened
on 21 February 1794, when two craft arrived at Leicester from
Gainsborough with merchandise and left again with wool,[18]
though coal could not be carried till the Charnwood line was
opened on 24 October. On 31 October the newspaper reported
that both Leicestershire and Derbyshire waterborne coal was on
sale at Leicester. There was much building on ground near the
wharves, but the takings of the turnpike trust controlling the
Loughborough–Leicester road fell.[19] By 6 July 1795, when the
works were complete except for Blackbrook reservoir, the amount
spent was £73,621. The total cost was probably about £80,000,
between £40,000 and £50,000 being attributable to the Forest
line.

Christopher Staveley was now appointed engineer to the completed concern. The main line proved steadily prosperous, still
more so after the Grand Union was opened in 1814, the principal
traffics being coal, wool, Mountsorrel and Quorndon granite,
Crich lime from the Cromford, plaster-rock, iron, lead, pottery,
and merchandise from the Trent.

Expenditure above the estimate required the Act[20] of 1797,
which gave the company power to raise additional money, and to
levy tolls of 1s 8d for coal on the River line (against 1s 2d) and 10d
to the Melton junction (against 7d) until their dividends reached
5 per cent. These were imposed from 15 May 1797, and taken off
on 1 January 1810. The final financial position, reached in July
1804, was that 540 shares had had £140 called upon them. Five,
whose holders had refused calls over £110, received proportionately lower dividends. The first dividend of £3 10s 0d per share
was paid for 1797, and £7 10s 0d in 1798, an earnest of the
potential earning capacity of the River line.

Here are the toll and dividend figures:

Years	Average tolls	Average Dividends per £140 share		
	£	£	s	d
1794–6	3,312*	—		
1797–9	5,154*	3	13	4
1800–2	6,377*	6	16	8
1803–5	6,782*	7	0	0
1806–8	6,815*	8	0	0
1809–11	7,545*	7	10	0
1812–14	8,053	10	3	4
1815–17	8,733	11	6	8
1818–20	9,928	13	3	4
1821–3	10,907	13	13	4
1824–6	12,569	16	6	8
1827–9	12,017	16	13	4
1830–2	11,788	15	10	0
1833–5	8,882	10	3	4
1836–8	10,273	14	6	8
1839–41	8,434	12	6	8

* Including up to £200 of wharfage.

Then came the burst reservoir of February 1799, and Jessop's estimate of £6,193 for repairs and compensation. James Barnes of the Grand Junction took over work on the reservoir, and by about the end of 1801 it was open again, with a trunk over the break in the embankment. No one was willing to use it, so Telford was called in to see whether the Nanpantan–Loughborough rail link could be replaced by a canal. I do not know what he proposed, but the colliery owners were unenthusiastic, and then once again the reservoir failed and the embankment was found to be dangerous. The company gave up; their agent on the line was moved, and in 1808 they sought legal advice upon whether they could abandon it, especially as the Forest was about to be enclosed, and they would have to pay for the land they had taken. They were told that they could not, and paid £1,900 for their land. Though untrue, the unfortunate history of the Forest line lent colour to the story later put about that the Derbyshire colliery owners had influenced the canal company to build a line that would not be able to compete economically with them. That Jessop's son William was later a leading Derbyshire colliery owner certainly added to the story's interest.

Like most river navigations, the company had endless trouble with the millers over water shortage and consequent claims for compensation. There were ten mills on the line, including one at Leicester and two at Loughborough, to whom annual payments had to be made for leakages and the passage of boats. In 1824 they thought it worth while to buy Barrow mill for £4,000.

The Leicester line of canal had become an important outlet for the Derbyshire coalowners, and it was therefore with concern that they wrote in November 1827 to the canal company to draw their attention to a projected railway from Whitwick (near Swanning-ton) to Leicester, and to ask for a meeting with the navigation companies. The line became the Leicester & Swannington author-ized in 1830.[21] It was supported, not only as a means of developing the Leicestershire collieries, but of breaking down the high prices of the Derbyshire coalmasters and the high tolls of the waterway companies. It achieved all its objects. The canal company did not oppose the bill but preferred to concentrate mainly on seeing that no one tried to make them reopen the Forest line to prevent a new monopoly by the railway company.

This indeed happened, for Lord Stamford formally required the company to put the line in order for lime and goods to Breedon. W. A. Provis was called in, and eventually the committee agreed to a plan for making the Forest line a horse railway throughout, with the possibility of conversion to a locomotive line later, at a cost of £44,585. However, the draft bill failed to pass the share-holders by 73 votes to 70.

Tolls were cut heavily, not only in anticipation of the opening of the L & S, but because of the abolition of the duty on seaborne coal in 1831, which brought down canal rates elsewhere at this most inconvenient moment. Then in 1832 the L & S opened, and once again tolls were cut; unlike the Erewash and the Lough-borough, however, the Leicester did not oppose the proposed Pinxton to Leicester railway, the Derbyshire coalowners' answer to the L & S. At this trying time Edward Staveley, who had succeeded his father as engineer and superintendent in 1827, called at his solicitor's to say that he owed the company £1,400 and then bolted, leaving his records inaccessible. They got back the records, but there was no trace of Staveley or the cash.

At the beginning of 1833 the canal committee, who now wanted a Leicestershire colliery line of their own, were again considering a route to the mines, not necessarily along the Forest line. Rastrick and Thomas Hill were called into consultation before a horse line roughly along the Forest line, proposed by Provis and estimated at £31,849, was chosen. A bill was introduced in 1834. The L & S, Coleorton Railway (a private line owned by Sir George Beaumont), Loughborough and Union companies all petitioned against it, but its withdrawal was mainly due to Lord Shaftesbury, who would not let it proceed unless the company gavé up its 1791 exemption from poor rates. The Leicester shareholders now decided to sell the land of the Forest line, but even here they were pursued by the ill-luck of the Charnwood venture. After starting to sell, they took Counsel's opinion, and found they would need an Act to do so. When a bill was introduced, once more they came up against Lord Shaftesbury, and had to withdraw it. At last they agreed with a landowner who wanted some of the land that he would introduce a private bill; thus, curiously, the Forest line was abandoned in 1848, and over the following years the land was sold.

Competition from the L & S, the recurrent threat of a railway from Derbyshire, and competition between the Leicester canal line and those from Warwickshire and Staffordshire, combined to cause a drop in toll receipts on the Leicester Navigation from £12,027 in 1831, the year before the L & S was opened, to £7,683 in 1835, though the tonnage carried probably increased. A newspaper of August 1834 said that the canal was carrying 160,000 tons of coal a year. Tolls then started to climb back as lower charges took effect, but having reached £10,603 in 1837 and £10,535 in 1838, they fell back again after the Midland Counties Railway was opened from Derby and Nottingham to Leicester on 4 May 1840, and soon afterwards through to Rugby to join the London & Birmingham. The Leicester company had tried to get restrictions on coal carrying inserted in the MCR bill, but unsuccessfully, and was now faced with a railway to Derbyshire, and two to London competing with each other and so keeping rates low. By 1842 the toll revenue was down to £6,166. (*To continue the history of the Leicester Navigation, turn to p.* 188.)

Melton Mowbray Navigation

In 1777 the inhabitants of Melton had petitioned in favour of the Erewash Canal,[22] and by 1780 the success of this and the Loughborough Navigation caused proposals to be made for continuing the waterways to Leicester and making the Wreak navigable. Nothing then resulted, but in 1785 the Wreak proposal was revived as a separate though related scheme supported by Lord

Harborough whose estate was in the Wreak valley, and connected also with the possibility of an Oakham Canal, and £6,000 was subscribed on the day the books opened.

A bill was prepared and introduced in 1786, but was dropped after the defeat of that for the Leicester Navigation itself, and though a meeting was called at Stamford to consider a possible through line to that town via Melton, there was an interval of inaction. In early 1789 another bill was introduced for navigations to both Leicester and Melton, but was defeated, upon which the *Leicester Journal* remarked that Melton was 'paying 18d a hundred-weight for coals which a water convenience would reduce to about 9d.'.[23] Once more in 1790 the Leicester project was revived, with the Melton supporters also deciding to try again, using a survey made by Christopher Staveley junior under William Jessop's guidance in 1790. At a meeting at Melton in July 'Mr Craddock spoke as to the general utility of the plan and the hand-some manner in which the Melton interests were united with those of Leicester . . . the plan seemed to be generally approved'.[24] In August it was decided to apply for a bill.

The Act[25] was passed in 1791. It authorized the making navi-gable of the rivers Wreak and Eye from a junction with the Leicester Navigation at Turnwater meadow to Melton Mowbray, and the raising of £25,000 in £100 shares, with £5,000 more if necessary. The clerk was Charles Latham, a solicitor of Melton, and the shareholders included the Dukes of Rutland and New-castle, Earl Ferrers and the Earl of Harborough, and Lords Middleton and Melbourne. The *Leicester Journal* of 10 January 1794 announced that in a few days the Leicester Navigation would be open from Loughborough upwards as far as the junction, whence the Wreak would be navigable to Rearsby, and probably in November of the same year to Melton.[26] However, in April 1795 another paper reported that the company had agreed to raise a further £2,500 'for making and compleating the Navigation, so as to admit the passage of boats',[27] and through navigation prob-ably did not begin until 1797.[28] Its length was 14¾ miles, there being 12 broad locks each 91 ft by 15 ft to overcome a rise of 71 ft 2 in.

In 1800 a second Act,[29] having explained that the full £30,000 had been spent and also £7,000 of receipts, and that there was a debt of £4,000, authorized a further £10,000. In 1804 the shares seem to have been rated at £120 each, advances beyond that being repaid with interest; at the same time a dividend of £2 8s 0d was declared;[30] soon afterwards repayments of excess calls must have brought them back to £100, for in 1809 their price was reported as £131, and the dividend as £7 10s 0d.[31]

The navigation seems to have become prosperous, for in 1832, when the canals on the Leicester line were considering toll reductions, coal into the Wreak was excluded. In 1833 a newspaper reported that the shares were standing at £200, and the dividend at 10 per cent.[32] In 1838 the waterway carried 40,001 tons, and still paid 10 per cent.

The navigation felt competition for the Melton trade from land carriage from the wharves at Hickling and Harby on the Grantham Canal, and each line tried to attract traffic from the other. In 1824, for instance, tolls on grain on the Oakham Canal, or originating on the Melton line, were reduced by half.[33] Again, goods for Melton originating at Nottingham, or brought up the Trent, in 1831 only paid 1s 7½d in tolls if carried on the Grantham, against 7s 3d on the Leicester line. In that year the Loughborough, Leicester and Melton companies agreed to cut these tolls to 4s 3d, 1s 6d of the reduction being contributed by the Melton company, and the carriers to reduce their freight charges by 2s. I am not sure whether these reductions were carried out, but in 1841 the three companies did agree toll reductions on grain and timber, and in 1842 the Oakham Canal suggested lowered tolls on coal and coke on the line to the Erewash. These obviously took effect, for in May 1845 a meeting of the Grantham Canal shareholders was told that owing to toll reductions by the Oakham and Melton companies, much corn grown between Colsterworth and Stamford had been attracted away from Grantham to that line, which was supplying coal in return.[34] (*To continue the history of the Melton Mowbray Navigation, turn to p.* 190.)

Oakham Canal

The first mention of a navigation to Oakham[35] occurs in 1785, when a group of those interested in a line to Melton and onwards commissioned William Jessop to make a survey.[36] The work was actually done by Robert Whitworth, who mapped a line well to the west of Stapleford to Leesthorpe, and thence by Ashwell to Oakham. This line was shorter than that later adopted, and would have had thirteen locks against nineteen. In December this activity also caused meetings to be held in Stamford to consider extending the line thither from Oakham.[37]

The Act of 1791 for the Leicester and the Melton Mowbray Navigations naturally raised new hopes, and a meeting at Oakham in April 1792, supported by the Earls of Harborough and Winchilsea, ordered new plans to be made.[38] Notice of a bill was given in September, and in November £51,000 was subscribed at a meeting which again had in mind a possible extension to Stamford. On 7 May 1793 the Act[39] was passed, to authorize a capital of £56,000, and £20,000 more if necessary.

Construction began at a time of increasing scarcity of money, and in March 1794 it was reported that many subscribers wanted to limit expenditure to a fixed amount each year, or stop work till peace came. William Jessop had done the general survey and Christopher Staveley junior the detailed work, the latter becoming engineer till late in 1797 when, perhaps because he was so busy elsewhere, Col. Frewen Turner, a leading committeeman, obtained the services of William Dunn from Sheffield. Dunn was not a canal engineer, but a grinder-cutter who later took to coal mining, but he completed the works.

Construction cost more than had been expected, and money was difficult to raise. A second Act[40] of 1800 authorized £30,000 more, of which £15,000 might be raised by further calls upon the existing shareholders. In the end, calls of £130 were made upon the 545 shares issued, a little money was borrowed, and the company was left £1,000 in Lord Harborough's will; the final cost was probably about £65,000–£70,000. The line was opened to Saxby in November 1800 and was reported finished in June 1802, but water, always scarce on this canal, was still needed, and boats probably did not reach Oakham till about January 1803.[41] The waterway was 15¼ miles long; it rose 126 ft from its junction with the Melton Mowbray Navigation by 19 broad locks to reach the summit at Oakham. The principal wharves were at Saxby, Stapleford, Market Overton, Cottesmore and Oakham.

The canal served its neighbourhood, bringing coal and other necessaries, and carrying away agricultural produce, but it was financially unsuccessful. The only figures we have for receipts are those of £1,838 for 1807, £1,824 for 1808 and £2,013 for 1809, though a newspaper report of 1815 said that the 'trade and finances of the Oakham Canal Company seem annually to be improving' after many years of struggle with great difficulties,[42] and we know that the company did better in its later years. Dividends were paid of £2 per £130 share in 1814 and £3 in 1815; apart from these, regular payments are not known to have begun till that of £2 for

THE

COMPANY OF PROPRIETORS

OF THE

Oakham Canal.

—————◗|◖|◗|◖|◗|———◗|◖|◗|◖|◗|—————

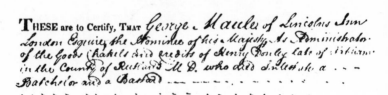

THESE are to Certify, T**HAT** *George Maule of Lincolns Inn London Esquire the Nominee of his Majesty As Administrator of the Goods Chattels and credits of Henry Donley late of Ashwell in the County of Rutland M.D. who died Intestate a Batchelor and a Bastard*

is on the Day of the Date hereof, a Proprietor of O**NE** S**HARE** of *One Hundred and Thirty* P**OUNDS** in the O**AKHAM** N**AVIGATION**, being Number *177* , in the S**HARES** of the said Navigation, subject to the Rules, Regulations, and Orders of the said C**OMPANY**, and T**HAT** he, his Executors, Administrators, and Assigns are entitled to the Profits, and Advantages of such S**HARE**.

Given under the Common SEAL of the said Company the *Twenty second* Day of *May* , in the Year of our Lord, One Thousand Eight Hundred and *twenty.*

Clerk to the said Company of Proprietors.

————◗◖◗◖◗————
John Snodin, Printer, Oakham.

5. Oakham Canal share certificate

II. The Charnwood Forest line of the Leicester Navigation: (*above*) the Junction house near Osgathorpe; (*below*) Thompson's bridge, the only one now remaining

VIII. (*above*) The opening of a short diversion, Ashby-de-la-Zouch Canal, in 1919; (*below*) the granite company's wharf at Mountsorrel on the Leicester Navigation, about 1870. Note the wide boat with centre cabin

1827. In 1831 and 1836 £2 10s 0d was paid, and a peak of £5 in 1840.

In 1809 the Stamford project was revived again, but this time as alternative lines, one from the Union Canal at Harborough, the other from Oakham. One scheme supported by J. Jepson Oddy (whose book, *A Sketch for the Improvement of the Political, Commercial, and Local Interests of Britain*, 1810, should be consulted,) and surveyed by Hamilton Fulton under Telford's supervision, ran from Oakham to Stamford, with extensions from the Welland near Market Deeping in one direction to join the South Forty Foot (the Black Sluice drain) leading to Boston, and in the other to the Nene at Peterborough; the second, surveyed by Benjamin Bevan and supported particularly by the Grand Junction, ran from Market Harborough to Stamford with a similar extension to the South Forty Foot. Bills for each were introduced in 1811, but both were defeated by large majorities. Similar ideas were discussed in 1815 and 1828.

Otherwise the concern had little history till the coming of the railway threat, though its influence may be seen in the growth of Oakham's population from 1,630 in 1801 to 2,726 in 1841, Melton Mowbray's having increased from 1,730 to 3,740 in the same period. It did not, however, have a local monopoly, for the Grantham company competed with it in its later period for the trade of the country in the triangle between Stamford, Grantham and Oakham. Competition was greatest in the early 1840s. The Rutland company seems to have come off best, but at the cost of toll reductions. (*To continue the history of the Oakham Canal, turn to p. 190.*)

Leicestershire & Northamptonshire Union Canal

Early in February 1792 the *Leicester Journal* carried an advertisement calling a meeting at Market Harborough to consider a bill to 'extend the Navigation from Leicester to Market Harborough'.[43] The moving spirits were Lord Rawdon, Earl Ferrers and other country gentlemen, and a group of Leicester businessmen. The meeting approved the project and asked Christopher Staveley to make a survey. After a rule had been made that no one person could subscribe more than £500, a total of £29,600 out of the £30,000 thought necessary was raised on the spot.

This proposal lead to another, that an extension be built to Northampton, and early in June a meeting was held there which

G

approved the project and appointed a committee.[44] On 27 June
another meeting at Harborough received Staveley's report and
also considered a letter from Jessop which seems to have com-
mented on the proposed extension, for the meeting thought it
practicable. They resolved to go ahead and get the surveyor to lay
down a final line. Another meeting on 6 August, held in a field
because of the crowd,[45] decided that £80,000 would be needed, of
which £31,300 had already been subscribed. Landowners were to
be given the chance of subscribing for eight shares per mile of
canal passing through their land, and the rest were to be offered
to the original subscribers. The canal mania was in full spate, and
£170,000 was offered at the meeting. This new subscription was
to be considered as separate from that for the Leicester–Harborough line, a second committee being appointed to work with
that for the original project. Jessop was appointed engineer, with
Varley to do the survey. About this time there was a suggestion
that the line should be continued to Hertford on the Lee, with a
connection to the Ouse at Bedford,[46] but the meeting had clearly
seen the purpose of the extension as to join the Grand Junction
which had been launched at a meeting at Stony Stratford in July,
and so 'to connect Thames and Trent',[47] by a canal with broad
locks that would be better than the narrow-lock route by Coventry
and the Trent & Mersey that had just been opened, and, moreover,
one that would promote Leicestershire trade.

After considering a possible junction with the Grand Junction
near Blisworth, Varley finally recommended a line to join that
canal at Gayton, with a branch to Northampton and the River
Nene if the cost were reasonable, the latter being seen as a means
of importing Norwegian and Baltic goods. It was now decided to
seek a bill, the two projects to be considered as one in every
respect except the subscription. Staveley and Varley did the final
plans, which Jessop was given authority to alter, and, though
some wanted to wait till the Grand Junction had actually got its
own Act, the majority decided to rely upon their good relations
with the promoters, and to go ahead. Other concerns sent their
good wishes, the Grand Junction decided on a Northampton
branch, a committee at Uppingham wanted a clause authorizing a
future junction with a branch from that place, Kettering wanted
a junction, and M.P.'s promised support. In all this whirl the
Act[48] was passed on 30 April 1793, on the same day as that for the
Grand Junction.

It authorized a capital of £200,000, with £100,000 more if

necessary, to make navigable the River Soar from the West bridge in Leicester to Aylestone bridge, and to build a canal thence by Saddington, Foxton and a great curve by Theddingworth, East Farndon and Great Oxendon to Kelmarsh, Maidwell and the northern Nene valley down to Northampton. There it crossed the northern Nene and then the Nene itself on the level, to join the Grand Junction's proposed branch. There was also to be a spur from near Foxton to Market Harborough. The length of the main line was to be 43¾ miles, and of the branch 3¾ miles. Apart from the very winding course round Market Harborough, the main features were to be the tunnels at Saddington, Foxton, Kelmarsh and Great Oxendon, estimated at 880, 1056, 990 and 286 yd long respectively.

Work started at the Leicester end with John Varley and Christopher Staveley as engineers, though Staveley soon dropped out. A winter excitement was a march of 300 canal workmen into Leicester after a wage dispute that could have led to trouble, and in February someone put an advertisement into the paper saying that work would shortly be suspended, as to squeeze £100,000 out of the inhabitants of Leicester in the economic situation caused by the war would be ruinous.[49] The canal company's solicitor immediately denied this, but further versions of the story were put about, and had again to be denied at the general assembly on 5 May.

On 25 October 1794 'The Leicester Navigation being reported to be opened on Monday next (it had in fact already been opened on the 24th) & the Engineer having informed the Committee that the Union Canal is navigable as far as Blaby, Ordered that Mr. Varley the Engineer do contract for a Boat load of good coal to be conveyed as far as it will pass on the Union line on Monday to be sold for the benefit of the company'.[50] By about March 1795 the canal was open to Kilby bridge, and in that month the company decided itself to trade in coal there and at Blaby. It seems that in this year the company was already contemplating abandoning the Northampton line and ending at Market Harborough, for a plan to do so was deposited.

In April 1795 there was more excitement with the navvies at Kibworth. A mob of them overpowered a group of Fencibles, and town volunteers and yeomanry had to be sent from Leicester. By July several tunnelling contracts were let, but with scarcity of money, quarrels with landowners and labour troubles, the company was losing heart. In October they resolved that no work was

to be done beyond Gumley without a special order. There was
more trouble in July 1796 when William Fletcher, the assistant
engineer, discovered that Saddington tunnel was out of straight.
Varley then offered to pay the cost if it were so, and entered into
a £2,000 bond. Oldham was called in, and said it was; James
Barnes confirmed this, but did not consider the trouble very
serious. Three lengths of 11, 6 and 5½ yd had to be taken down on
one side only and widened 6 to 8 in. to make sure that broad
barges of Thames type, as broad at the bottom as at the top, as
used on the lower section of the Grand Junction, would be able
to pass. He gave some advice upon how to proceed, and added:
'I experienced some obstacles from the differences which exist
between the Company's Servants, were they to exert themselves as
much to serve the Concern, as they do to injure each other, it
might be more to the Company's advantage'.[51]

While tunnelling was going on, the company had evidently
decided to carry on as far as Gumley Debdale, a mile short of the
present junction with the Market Harborough branch. The tunnel,
880 yd long, was finished in February 1797, and in March the
company wrote to the highway surveyors of Gumley and Smeeton
Westerby to tell them that the Gumley–Market Harborough road
was likely to be much used, and that they were willing to contribute to its improvement. This was done by the company finding
the gravel and the parishes the men, the company also undertaking
to maintain the Foxton road for ten years, the parishes contributing £20 p.a. On 7 April the line was opened to Gumley Debdale
wharf, and the company resolved 'that the Tonage taken for the
first Boat that passed through the Tunnell to Gumley Debdale
belonging to James Gibson be returned to him'.[52] It was a heroic
gesture, for they owed money. Seventeen miles of canal had been
built, with 25 locks and a reservoir at Saddington, and there the
work remained.

In 1799 the company borrowed James Barnes from the Grand
Junction to look for a way of joining that canal at Braunston. In
1802 he again surveyed for a connection, this time deciding on a
line from Gumley by Welford, Crick and Watford to Norton, with
16 locks and two tunnels, and a branch to Market Harborough, at
an estimate of £146,960 for the main line—very much that which
was built. Telford was then called in, agreed on the same starting
and finishing points, but proposed a longer course with less
lockage more to the east, using part of the old Parliamentary line
via Market Harborough, the upper Welland valley, Maidwell,

Cottesbrooke, Hollowell, Ravensthorpe and Holdenby, with a branch to Rushton near Kettering. His estimate for the main line was £228,207. Telford thought his line would pick up local traffic and have better water supplies, though his revenue estimate of £46,787 10s od seems unusually hopeful.[53]

One would have thought that the opening of the Grand Junction throughout on 25 March 1805 and of the tramroad branch to Northampton on 7 October of the same year would have caused the company to take action towards a junction. But in fact the general assembly of 1804 only discussed plans for taking the canal forward along Telford's line through Foxton to Market Harborough, an Act[54] being obtained in 1805.

Even now there were fears, for in November the company minuted that if only the Derbyshire and Notts coalowners would reduce prices, and the canals in between would lower tolls, 'such Diminution wou'd enable the Traders upon the Union Canal to keep up the Competition with other Canals, and very much conduce to the Enlargement and spreading the Sale of Coal at . . . Gumley Debdale Wharf without which it is probable that all Idea of the Extension of this Canal must be abandoned'.[55] However, Barnes had finally surveyed the line to Market Harborough, Thomas Newbold was appointed to build it, and at a cost of some £40,500 the extension of 6¾ miles, with the necessary basin and buildings, was opened on 13 October 1809. Upwards of 10,000 people were there, and afterwards a sumptuous entertainment was given at the *Angel* in Harborough to about 180 gentlemen interested in the concern. The main line and extension together had cost about £205,000.

In May 1807 the committee was asked again to investigate how best to join the Grand Junction; they corresponded with that company and with the Trent & Mersey, and concluded in November 1808 that neither company would be prepared to invest, though individual shareholders might, and that therefore 'the Present time is not a proper one to set on Foot a Subscription for the purpose of bringing about such Junction'.[56] It is probable, indeed, that the committee's approach had stimulated the Grand Junction to decide that such a junction had better be made under its own control. About the end of 1808 a group of largely Grand Junction interests employed Barnes and Telford once more to survey for a new connection. The Union were probably relieved; anyway, in May 1808 the committee recommended that 'it should be resolved by this Assembly that the Union Canal should finally

terminate at Harborough'.[57] The shareholders agreed, and William
Gresley of the committee was despatched to tell the Grand Junction and promise support for the new venture, which was initiated
as the Grand Union Canal at a meeting in London on 11 June. He
seems, however, to have gone further than his brief, because on
25 July the Grand Union wrote 'expressing the surprise and regret
of this Committee at finding the Subscriptions from that Company
fall so very short of the representations which Mr. Gresley had
been authorised by that Company to make'.[58] To which the Union
replied that 'this Company never did promise to subscribe £50,000
towards the completion of the Grand Union Canal'.[59] In fact,
Union shareholders had taken up about £20,000 worth of shares,
though no Union committeeman was also on that of the Grand
Union.

By 1810 the company was feeling more cheerful. The Harborough extension, which also allowed Kettering to be supplied
by road, had brought increased trade, and receipts had shot up
from £1,957 in 1808 to £4,833 in 1810 and were to go to £7,573
in 1811. The Grand Union promised increased trade, and a bill
was in prospect for a canal from Stamford to the Harborough
branch, which would open another through line to London via
Spalding and Boston. 'With such a Trade in Possession', they
said, 'and such prospects . . . it is not perhaps very bold . . . to
predict the Realization, at no very distant period, of all those
hopes and expectations now so long deferred but so confidently
entertained by the original Proprietors.'[60] They happily presented
a gilt cup to Joseph Cradock, who is credited with having first
promoted the canal. Here is the financial record of its earlier days:

Years	Average receipts £	Average dividend £100 shares
1807–8 (2 years)	1,928	—
1809–11	5,106	—
1812–14	7,412	2
1815–17	9,002	3½
1818–20	9,925	3½
1821–3	9,359	3½
1824–6	10,584	4
1827–9	10,076	4
1830–2	8,907	3½
1833–5	9,714	3½
1836–8	14,458	6
1839–41	12,776	5

By 1812 the company could pay its first dividend on the 1,892 shares that were eligible.

The Grand Union was opened in 1814, and immediately brought an increase of trade, which might have been greater had not the canal companies concerned failed to carry the Leicester Navigation with them upon what the through tolls for Derbyshire coal ought to be.

In 1823 the shareholders resolved that it would be very useful to make the Welland navigable from the Union Canal to Stamford, and took some soundings. Again in 1830, when a railway between Stamford and Oakham was talked of, the project was considered, but came to nothing.

Then came the company's great chance, an alliance with the Leicester & Swannington Railway, opened in July 1832, to promote and carry Leicestershire coal coming off the railway rather than Derbyshire coal off the Leicester Navigation. The railway's first chairman, Clement Winstanley, and two other members of its first committee, James Goddard and Thomas Leach, were also members of the canal committee at the time. In November 1831 they had minuted that 'the contemplated reduction of Coals of at least 3s per Ton on the completion of the Leicester & Swannington Railway will ensure the delivery of it at Harborough at so low a price as to render any reduction on the Union Canal unnecessary'.[61] In May 1832 they co-operated by leasing nearly 4,000 sq yd of canal land at Augustin Friars to the railway company (it was sold to them in 1835), so making unnecessary the basin that the Leicester Navigation wanted them to make. They also built a short railway extension into the canal wharf there at a cost of £190.

This new source of cheap coal was probably the cause of the large increase in revenue and near doubling of the dividend that has been recorded. This prosperity led to another revival of the Stamford plan in 1837, with the support of the L & S R, but though Stamford corporation was favourable and the Union offered to raise a fair proportion of the capital, nothing happened.

The year 1837 saw receipts at their peak of £15,227 and a dividend of 7 per cent. Thereafter there was a slow decline. Railways were about. In 1839 the company joined others in giving drawbacks on all coal, Leicestershire and Derbyshire alike, in the hope of increasing revenue to compensate for 'a Reduction in the Revenue of their Merchandize which sooner or later will ensue from a Competition with Railways'.[62] By May 1841 railway competition for merchandise was described as 'strenuous'.[63] (*To continue the history of the Union Canal, turn to p. 191.*)

Grand Union Canal

James Barnes and Thomas Telford having made their preliminary surveys in 1808, a meeting on 11 June in London, with William Praed, banker and chairman of the Grand Junction, in the chair, resolved that a canal would be useful 'by bringing the Trade of the River Trent to the Metropolis from the Counties of York, Lincoln, Nottingham, Derby and Leicester . . . and also . . . promote the agricultural Interests of . . . Leicester, Northampton, Buckingham and other Counties'.[64] R. C. Sale, clerk of the Grand Junction and J. E. Carter of the Leicester Navigation were appointed joint clerks, and subscription books for £220,000 were opened.

It was now decided to build the canal with narrow locks, though the Grand Junction and the line from Gumley to the coalfields were broad, because the former company had realized that barges meant one-way traffic through Blisworth tunnel, and were no longer prepared to allow them. Also, carriers who had been asked their opinion forecast that most of the trade would be carried in narrow boats even if it were made bigger. Yet the tunnels and bridges were built broad, presumably with the possibility of later barge traffic in mind.

Benjamin Bevan, a Leighton Buzzard man who had worked on the Grand Junction and elsewhere, was now brought in as engineer, and must have had a trying time before the final line was settled. A proposal to make it from near Blaby on the Union to Cosford on the Oxford Canal had first to be got out of the way; then he had the delicate task of throwing overboard Telford's proposed line in favour of one based on James Barnes's original ideas, which was seven miles shorter and much cheaper.

Then followed further proposals to join the Oxford Canal at Hillmorton and to carry the canal to the Kilsby side of Crick into the Ashby St. Ledgers valley. Bevan himself favoured a line from Crick to Braunston without a tunnel, but, while rejecting the actual tunnel line put forward by John Woodhouse, another Grand Junction engineer, with the support of a Leicester group, he acquiesced in a Crick tunnel, and his final line to Norton on the Grand Junction was agreed in May 1809. On an estimate of

£205,000 and with a strengthened board, the promoters decided to go ahead, and by June the subscription list was over-filled.

The Grand Junction was of course a strong supporter of the bill, with the double object of opening a communication with the Trent and the canals that communicated with it, and also of supporting a canal project across the Peak by connecting the Cromford Canal with the Peak Forest Canal,[65] a line that would considerably shorten the route to Manchester compared with that by the Trent & Mersey and the Bridgewater.* However, both those concerns promptly opposed the Grand Union bill, and were only placated when the Grand Junction withdrew its support for the Peak project. Northampton and the Western Division of the Nene Commissioners were promised a canal branch to Northampton instead of a tramroad by the Grand Junction company, against a guarantee of revenue equal to 5 per cent on the cost of the tramroad and canal from the Grand Union and the Union, the Oxford Canal were indemnified against any loss to them that might result from the new canal, and the Grand Union and Union agreed between themselves not to charge more for the 54 miles from Leicester to Gayton than would have been charged on the 49 miles of the original Leicestershire & Northamptonshire line. These things settled, the Act[66] was passed on 24 May 1810, authorizing a capital of £245,000 in £100 and £50 shares, and £50,000 more if necessary. Benjamin Bevan was made engineer at the high salary of £500 p.a. and £200 p.a. expenses.

The locks on the canal were to be grouped into two flights at Foxton and Watford at opposite ends of the line; they were built as staircases, at Foxton two of five locks each with a passing place in the middle, at Watford one of four and three single locks, with large side ponds. Construction began at the Foxton end, and by June 1812 the canal line above it to the cutting before Husband's Bosworth tunnel was open; on 1 October Foxton locks were finished, and coal boats could get to Welford. By now Bevan had found that unfavourable strata, including quicksands, lay in the line of his proposed tunnel at Crick, and a new tunnel line 1,528 yd long to run east of Crick village was authorized at an excess cost of £7,000. By the end of May 1813 Husband's Bosworth tunnel, 1,166 yd long, had been finished, and 10 miles of the main line were open, as well as a mile of the navigable feeder towards Welford.

Tolls were reduced from the Parliamentary rates to get trade started, but meanwhile more money was needed. Including over

* It must be remembered that the Macclesfield Canal had not yet been built.

a hundred forfeitures, 238½ shares were still available for issue, and it was decided that shareholders could subscribe for these at £75, together with as many new shares as they liked. Alternatively, they could subscribe for loan notes, convertible into shares at par up to Lady Day 1816, and otherwise repayable 1816–19. In the event, £44,500 was raised from such issues and £5,000 was borrowed from the Treasurers, and this was enough to open the canal. To avoid a deep cutting and short tunnel, the company had to pay Mrs Bennett of Watford £2,000 and £125 per acre for the land they needed. This lady also asked to have a pleasure boat on the summit level, and to appoint the lock-keeper at Watford, 'that she might ensure civility towards herself and Tenants and also proper attention to the Boatmen to prevent them doing any Injury to her property'.[67] The company agreed to the lock-keeper, provided he were qualified, and to the boat.

The Welford arm, used mainly for the carriage of coal with lime burnt at Welford wharf as back carriage, was not completed till at least November 1814, but the rest of the canal was opened on 9 August. A boat

'amply supplied with refreshments was brought to, and moored alongside, into which the company went and partook of abundance of good things—this was a necessary precaution, as the boats had shortly to pass the long and dark tunnel . . . strong symptoms of fear were at first evinced by some of the ladies—which were at last surmounted by the gallantry and polite attention of the gentlemen—a close package, great hilarity and good humour during the interval of darkness, brought them again into the face of day'.

Arrived at Market Harborough, the party settled down to turtle soup, turbot and venison, a specially written ode was delivered, and all was gaiety and good humour.[68]

When the canal was opened, 23¼ miles long plus the 1⅜ miles of the Welford branch, it seems that about £292,000 had been spent, with another £13,500 to come in the following year. From the beginning it suffered from one great disadvantage. It lay in a line of canal controlled by an extraordinarily large number of different companies: Derbyshire coal to London probably had to pass the Cromford, Erewash, Loughborough, Leicester, Union, Grand Union and Grand Junction Canals, and perhaps the Regent's also. The Grand Union was the weakest link, for as its motto *Juncta Jovebunt*, implied, it depended almost entirely upon its through trade, whereas each of the others had substantial local business.

Therefore when bargaining was to be done the Grand Union usually came off worst. Soon after it was opened the charge for 20-ton boatloads of coal was 1s 9d per ton, just over 1d per ton per mile, against an authorized toll of 3d. Bar iron, pig iron and heavy castings, still paying 5d per ton per mile on the Monmouthshire Canal, were being carried on the Grand Union for 3s 2d for 23¼ miles.* With this poor bargaining position the company also possessed the summit level of the canal line between the Trent and Leighton Buzzard, and therefore had the privilege of maintaining reservoirs at Naseby, Sulby and Welford, and of supplying water to both the Union and the Grand Junction. Finally, because of the number of companies involved, it was extraordinarily difficult to get anything done on the Leicester line, and the Grand Union, in many ways the liveliest company, was always struggling with complicated inter-company correspondence.

Financially, they were unsuccessful. In 1818 they had been able to sell their forfeited shares for £95 each, but by 1825 their prospects had so weakened that shares were at £25. By November 1826, when the company had paid off a good deal of debt, though something under £15,000 remained, a maiden dividend of 1 per cent was paid. Not till 1836 was the loan debt extinguished, or till 1840 did the dividend rise to 25s. An interesting index to the probable view of the canal's prospects taken by the Grand Junction is given us by the Grand Union shareholdings of R. C. Sale, the clerk of both companies. He started in 1810 with 15 shares, and this hardly varied for ten years. Then he began buying, and held 32 shares in 1825 and 50 in 1830. Then, presumably foreseeing greater competition and lower tolls from the London & Birmingham Railway, then building, he reduced his holding to 16 in 1835. At that point the Grand Junction must have decided to seek financial control, for in 1840 Sale's shareholding had risen to 118, the Praed banking house (W. T. Praed, B. J. M. Praed and Vere Fane) held 433½ shares, and Samuel Mills, a committeeman of the Grand Junction, had increased his holding from 48 to 122. These figures were much the same in 1845.

In 1838 the London & Birmingham's line was opened throughout, and bitter competition lay ahead. (*To continue the history of the Grand Union Canal, turn to p. 192.*)

* These rates constantly altered, usually downwards.

CHAPTER V

The Great Grand Junction

+++++++++++++++++++++++++++++++◆+++++++++++++++++++++++++++++++

A DIRECT canal line from Aynho or Braunston on the Oxford Canal to London was first planned at the end of 1791.[1] Probably the hope of a good trade and profit came mainly from the immediate increase of traffic that had followed the completion of the Coventry Canal between Atherstone and Fazeley. Goods from Birmingham and the Staffs & Worcs via the Birmingham & Fazeley, and from Manchester, Liverpool, the Potteries or Burton via the Trent & Mersey, could now reach the Oxford Canal, to add to its existing trade in coal and produce. All traffic between London and these centres had, however, to be transhipped between narrow boats and barges at Oxford, and to use the unsatisfactory Thames navigation.[2] A good canal from Braunston to Brentford would shorten this line by sixty miles, and give the London trade an efficient modern waterway.

The plan was known to the Oxford Canal committee in early January 1792, and thenceforward was publicly and busily pressed. Its importance was so great that plans for many other canals were made in 1792 and 1793 on the assumption that the Grand Junction, as it was called, would be built, even though it was not in fact authorized till 30 April 1793; these plans in turn strengthened the case for the Grand Junction itself. We have seen that the Union was promoted in February 1792 to join it, a project that promised the Grand Junction's supporters a feeder route to Leicester, the Trent and the Derbyshire coalfields. Again, the canals that were to form the Warwick line to Birmingham and that to Stratford were planned with the Grand Junction idea in mind, and again increased the latter's hope of success by suggesting a far shorter route to Birmingham, with access also to the Dudley, Stourbridge and upper Severn trade.

In the prevailing excitement one company stood to lose, the Oxford, for much of the trade hoped for would not travel the whole length of their line, but for less than half; indeed, some of it for only a few miles were the Warwick ideas to bear fruit. As soon as they heard of the Grand Junction's plan they decided to promote an alternative which would use as much of their own canal as possible. This was the London & Western, or Hampton Gay, Canal, surveyed by Samuel Simcock and Samuel Weston, and intended to run from Hampton Gay six miles above Oxford, at first to Marylebone, later to Isleworth on the Thames by way of Thame, Wendover, Amersham and Uxbridge, some 60 miles, with a branch to Aylesbury. During 1792 two additional plans took this canal into account; one for a line from the end of the Stratford-upon-Avon Canal at Stratford to Cropredy,[3] another from the Westcountry by means of projected canals from Exeter via Bristol to Lechlade (where it would be joined by Severn traffic from the Thames & Severn), and Oxford.[4] Hampton Gay shares became a brisk speculative counter. In September 1792 five on which two guineas each had probably been paid up were sold for 60 guineas,[5] and in November three for 48 guineas.[6]

The scheme was well supported financially, but the Grand Junction had the greater power. The latter refused a suggestion of a junction at Uxbridge and a common line thence to the Thames, and eventually, having failed to lease the northern part of the Oxford so that it could be widened, persuaded that company into acquiescence with a guarantee of £10,000 p.a. of income from the Grand Junction. No more was heard of the London & Western.

The original survey for the Grand Junction was made by James Barnes, who had formerly worked on the Oxford. In the autumn William Jessop re-surveyed it, but found little to alter in a line which, he said, was only fifteen miles longer than the road. However, a meeting in October decided not to adopt Barnes's route from Watford via Harrow to Brentford, but to follow that of the London & Western by way of Uxbridge.[7] Jessop pointed out that the main engineering problems lay in the high ground at Braunston, Blisworth, Tring and Langley Bury near Watford, and in the provision of water to the summits at Braunston and Tring; at the former he saw no difficulty, but at Tring pumping might be necessary. He was right.

The canal was planned and built to take barges carrying up to 70 tons, 'such as will navigate with safety on the Thames, on the Trent if the communication should take place with the Navigation to Leicester, and on the Mersey if the present Canals should hereafter be widened, which is not improbable';[8] the locks would also take two narrow boats. It was authorized on 30 April 1793[9] with a capital of £600,000, to be over 90 miles long from Braunston to Brentford, with branches to Daventry, Northampton (to meet the Union), Stony Stratford and Watford.*

The successful leader of the promoters was William Praed, after whom Praed Street in Paddington is named. He had been born in 1749, and when aged thirty had been a partner in the Cornish Bank at Truro. He then turned to London banking, becoming a partner in Cocks, Biddulph, Eliot & Praed before founding Praed & Co of Fleet Street in 1803. In promoting the Grand Junction he had the considerable help of the Marquess of Buckingham, whose arms were to form part of the company's seal, and the support on the board also of the Duke of Grafton, Earls of Clarendon and Essex, Earl Spencer, and the Hon. Edward Bouverie, as well as of an influential group of commoners. Later the company preferred members of Parliament to peers; in 1812, for instance, five sat on the board. This political influence was a source of grievance to weaker bodies: E. L. Loveden, M.P., a Thames Commissioner, wrote in 1811: 'confiding in the supposed omnipotence of the Grand Junction Company, projectors think they can carry on their plans without any regard to public or private property, or rendering any satisfaction for the loss it may sustain. That Company is certainly very powerful, much more so, perhaps, than Parliament should have suffered'.[10] Praed became chairman and William Jessop was appointed to take charge of construction, with James Barnes as resident engineer. All three were still active in the company's affairs in 1805, when the canal was opened throughout.† Let us first follow the construction side, and then return to consider the company's relations with others while building was going on.

Work on the main line began quickly at each end, and by December 3,000 men were at work. In the north the cutting of Braunston and Blisworth tunnels began. At Braunston quicksands caused difficulty, and a contractor made a mistake in the direction, so that the tunnel now has a slight 'S' bend in it. On 21 June 1796 Braunston was open, and the canal finished to Weedon;[11] not long afterwards it extended to the wharf at Blisworth. Blisworth tunnel had also been begun, but by January 1796 had failed, seemingly

* Branches to Buckingham (an extension of that to Stony Stratford), Aylesbury and Wendover were authorized in 1794.
† Jessop was not regularly employed after September 1797, but was frequently consulted.

due to excessive water finding its way into the workings, the use of an unsatisfactory form of arch, and bad materials. Jessop was discouraged and suggested flights of locks, 29 in all, but Barnes, supported by Whitworth and Rennie, who were called in to advise, proposed a new tunnel on a slightly different line.* The company agreed, but had too many worries, financial and otherwise, to start till the autumn of 1802. Meanwhile in 1797 they built a toll-road over the hill, seemingly with access to Stony Stratford, which was replaced by November 1800 by a double-track horse tramroad constructed by Benjamin Outram, which ran from Blisworth wharf to what is now the foot of Stoke Bruerne locks.[12] The new tunnel caused fewer difficulties, thanks to undertunnel headings built first to drain water; it was opened on 25 March 1805, and with it the whole canal was complete.

At the southern end building began at Brentford, whence the canal used the course of the River Brent as far as Greenford, where it ran westwards to the Colne and followed it to Watford. It reached Uxbridge on 3 November 1794.[13] Beyond, a change had been made in the line. Instead of building a ½-mile tunnel at Langley, special payments† were made to Lords Essex and Clarendon for permission to pass through Cassiobury and Grove parks, on condition that these stretches were made as ornamental as possible. By the end of 1797 the line had been built as far as Hemel Hempstead. Meanwhile in 1796 a London wharf and warehouse were opened at Whitefriars above Blackfriars bridge as a depot for canal trade, but were soon afterwards let to Pickfords, and were sold about 1810, presumably because more trade centred at Paddington.

Tring was reached in 1799, when the Wendover navigable feeder was opened, and Fenny Stratford‡ on 28 May 1800.[14] In September the line was open to the bottom of Stoke Bruerne locks, and trade was possible over the whole canal using the tramroad thence to Blisworth. The Ouse near Wolverton was originally crossed on the level, four locks leading down to it on the southern side, and five up from it on the northern.[15] In 1799 Barnes proposed that, because of danger from Ouse floods, they

* The original tunnel was to have been longer than the present one; its southern exit was about 130 yd to the east, and its northern a little to the west, of the present tunnel.

† £15,000 to the Earl of Essex for the land and permission to pass through Cassiobury Park, and £5,000 without the land to Lord Clarendon for Grove Park. Lord Essex, but not Lord Clarendon, was then on the Board.

‡ Bletchley.

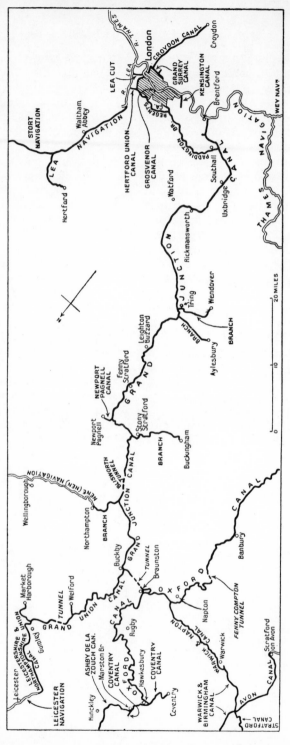

6. The Grand Junction Canal and its connections

be replaced by an embankment and aqueduct, which Jessop designed as a three-arched masonry structure. When these were finished the Ouse locks were no longer used, but the contractor's work had been faulty; the embankment partially collapsed in January 1806, and was closed for some time and then reopened, and then on 20 February 1808 the aqueduct itself collapsed, fortunately leaving one arch standing to allow the river water to pass. A temporary wooden trunk was installed and opened on 14 June, and an iron trunk from Ketley ironworks on 21 January 1811.*

Early in its existence, the company had decided that a canal route into London to supplement that by way of Brentford and the Thames was desirable. The curious may see ancestors of the Paddington branch in Sir Edward Forde's scheme of 1641 to bring water from the Colne to London in a 'navigable river',[16] or in two canals proposed about 1766 from the Colne, one at Uxbridge and one near West Drayton, to Marylebone.[17] This time a branch from the Grand Junction at Bulls Bridge was authorized in April 1795;[18] it was to run level for 13½ miles to Paddington, where a basin was laid out and built after much bargaining with the Bishop of London's men of business. It was opened on 10 July 1801 with two committee boats, the City shallop† and seven pleasure boats, the Buckinghamshire band, several cannon, volleys of musketry, 20,000 spectators, and a good dinner and party for the celebrants at the *Yorkshire Stingo*.

At Paddington basin warehouses were soon built and wharves laid out to form a busy terminus. Farther out, as early as 1803 the company were advertising 'There is a good Brick Earth along the . . . line of canal for several miles',[19] and soon many brickfields sprang up along the line, especially near West Drayton and Hayes, some served by private branch canals. Farther in, the building of the Paddington arm encouraged ideas of extension through London to the Thames that in 1812 became the Regent's Canal.

As for the other branches, that to Daventry was never constructed, and in 1803 a reservoir was built over part of the line. A short arm ⅜ mile long was built into the new military depot at Weedon, which had been opened in April 1804. That to Northampton was delayed while the company waited to see whether the Union Canal would be completed; it was not, but Northampton agitated, and the reluctant company agreed to a double-track tram-

---

* It is known that the Ouse locks were reopened during the troubles, first with the embankment, and then with the aqueduct. Their remains are still visible.
† The City of London controlled the Thames up to Staines.

H

road, opened on 7 October 1805 at a cost of £12,000, most of the materials having come from the now-disused tramroad over Blisworth tunnel. However, the town was dissatisfied with the substitute, and the bill for the Grand Union gave their leaders a chance. As a result, the canal branch, 5 miles long and falling through 17 locks from Gayton junction, was opened on 1 May 1815.[20] South of Blisworth tunnel the Stony Stratford branch had been built for 1¼ miles from Cosgrove, and then extended another 9¼ miles to Buckingham with two locks, and opened on 1 May 1801.

There were a number of proposals to link the Grand Junction with Bedford and the Ouse Navigation. The first was probably in November 1811, when a meeting at Bedford with Samuel Whitbread in the chair, supported by William Praed and Charles Harvey of the Grand Junction company, decided to seek a bill for a canal that might be extended beyond Bedford to join the London & Cambridge Canal, authorized in 1812 but never built. A survey was made and prospectus issued, but not enough money was subscribed, and the project failed.[21] Then the independent Newport Pagnell Canal (see p. 126) was built from the Grand Junction near Wolverton and opened early in 1817. It offered another possible route towards the Ouse, and Lord St John commissioned a new survey. In January 1817 this proposed a navigation for 20-ton boats to join the Newport Pagnell Canal at that town to the Ouse, which would be made navigable past William Praed's property at Tyringham to Sharnbrook, whence a canal would be made to St Neots on the Ouse, with a possible branch to Kimbolton. No action followed.[22]

In 1812 the Newport Pagnell company was considering an extension; in 1824 there was a plan to link the Grand Junction both to the Ouse at Bedford and the Ivel Navigation at Shefford;[23] in 1838 the old idea of linking the Newport Pagnell Canal to an upper Ouse navigation was revived, and in 1844 the original idea of a canal to Bedford. The answer turned out to be the Bedford Railway from Bletchley to Bedford roughly along the canal line originally proposed, from which a branch was built to a wharf on the Ouse at Bedford.[24] Finally, in 1892, a plan was deposited for a canal from Soulbury on the Grand Junction to Kempston on the Ouse, which was to be made navigable thence to Bedford[25]—so long did the idea linger.

Farther south again was the Aylesbury branch. The Grand Junction company interested itself in two main schemes for canal links to the westwards, intended to by-pass the difficult navigation of the Thames, and join it directly to the Kennet & Avon or the Wilts & Berks. One was the Western Union from Cowley on the Grand Junction to Maidenhead or Marlow and so to the Kennet & Avon, a bill for which the shareholders approved in 1802. However, landowners and Thames Commissioners opposed, and the application was postponed till 'the present hostility to the Measure will shortly yield to that perfect satisfaction of Mind, which must result from mature reflection and a full conviction of its public utility'.[26] The second became the Aylesbury branch.

Though authorized in 1793, no action was taken till 1800, when a tramroad was proposed, and the tramplates actually bought.* No work was done, and in 1803 the Grand Junction was approached by the Wilts & Berks (then building) and agreed that the engineers of the two companies should survey from Aylesbury or Thame to Abingdon, opposite the Wilts & Berks's proposed entrance. There was no result, and the company steadfastly refused to make the Aylesbury branch, which promised to lose more water than it would gain trade, in spite of threats from the inhabitants and a notice for a canal to link Aylesbury to the Oxford Canal.

In 1809 the Wilts & Berks, its own line now almost open, again approached the Grand Junction. This time, threatened by the Marquess of Buckingham that he would oppose the Grand Union bill unless the Aylesbury branch were built, the shareholders agreed to subscribe £100,000 towards the estimated cost of what was now called the Western Junction Canal from Marsworth near Tring on the Grand Junction (near Bulbourne, where the Aylesbury branch leaves the main line) through Aylesbury to Abingdon, the Wilts & Berks shareholders agreeing also to subscribe £100,000, the balance being left for the landowners. A bill was introduced in 1811, but failed, mainly owing to Kennet & Avon opposition in the interests of their own trade and a revived Western Union scheme.[27] Now, however, the Grand Junction agreed to build the Aylesbury branch if those who had subscribed to the Western Junction would lend their money. Preparations began towards the end of the year, but the branch, 6⅜ miles long with 16 locks falling towards Aylesbury, was not reported complete till May 1815.[28] There was interest in the Western Junction scheme till 1819, after which no more is heard of it.

From Tring summit a branch, partly also a navigable feeder, ran

* They were later used by the contractor on the Wolverton embankment.

to Wendover, 6¾ miles long and level. Lower down the valley the Watford branch was never built, nor the canal or tramroad later proposed to St Albans. Finally, at Rickmansworth a side lock gave access to wharves along ¼ mile of river.

Apart from the branches, the length of the Grand Junction Canal was 93½ miles with 101 locks; including them, it totalled 136¾ miles with 137 locks.* By the end of 1811, when only the Northampton and Aylesbury branches remained to be built, about £1,646,000 had been spent.

While the main line was building, the company were concerned with many hopes and interests. One was the encouragement of a shorter line to Birmingham by way of Warwick, fulfilled in 1800 when the Warwick & Birmingham and Warwick & Napton lines (see Chapter VIII) were opened to Napton on the Oxford Canal five miles from Braunston. Thereafter the canal lines to Birmingham via Warwick and via Fazeley competed with each other for the trade to the Grand Junction.

Another preoccupation was the improvement of the canal route to Burton, the Potteries, Liverpool and Manchester. The company had built a broad canal suitable for Trent barges in the hope of the successful construction of the Union Canal, and in faith that the Oxford, Coventry and Trent & Mersey concerns could be persuaded to widen theirs. We have seen that they tried to lease the northern part of the Oxford in order to widen it, and failed. As soon as their Act was passed, the Grand Junction called a meeting at Meriden of the Trent & Mersey, Oxford, Coventry, Staffs & Worcs, Birmingham† and Trent (Burton) Navigations, all of which were narrow except the Trent & Mersey east of Burton and west of Middlewich, and the Trent (Burton) Navigation. Unfortunately the Oxford, perhaps sulking from its defeat over the London & Western, and the Staffs & Worcs did not attend the meeting, which resolved 'that if a general communication by a wide canal can be effected at reasonable expence, it will be very advantageous to the commerce of this Country';[29] it does not sound very enthusiastic. However, the companies agreed to study the costs and the advantages, and to meet again. The Grand Junction then approached the Oxford, and even got Barnes to survey the northern section to show how it could be shortened and widened. In the autumn the Oxford company actually agreed to rebuild, and during 1794 there was a fever of meetings and pres-

* Excluding those of the Ouse crossing.
† Because of the section from Fazeley to Whittington Brook.

sures, as the Grand Junction, the Ashby (another broad canal just authorized as a branch from the Coventry) and the Trent (Burton) Navigation tried to get the line from Braunston to Fradley and thence to Burton widened. It died away, but was revived in 1796 when the Grand Junction threatened to oppose a Trent & Mersey bill for the Leek branch and the badly needed Rudyard reservoir unless a clause were inserted requiring the latter company to widen after a certain time. They agreed to do so from Fradley to Harecastle within two years of the Coventry and Oxford widening from Braunston to Fradley. To this the Oxford had already agreed, and it seems that the Coventry did also. Unfortunately for the Grand Junction, in this year 1796 an entirely new broad canal, the Commercial, was promoted to run from the Chester Canal at Nantwich (whence there was wide boat communication with the Dee or the Mersey at Ellesmere Port) through a tunnel a few miles south-west of Harecastle to join Sir Nigel Gresley's Canal or its projected extension the Newcastle-under-Lyme Junction, then to cross the Trent & Mersey at Burslem and later the Caldon branch, and pass by the Dilhorne and Cheadle coalfield to Uttoxeter and down the Dove valley to join the wide portion of the Trent & Mersey at Burton. Then it would cross the Trent below Burton and join the broad Ashby Canal, so providing a broad waterway that would only require about 3½ miles of the Coventry Canal from Marston junction to Hawkesbury, and the northern section of the Oxford to Braunston, to be improved, to provide a barge waterway linking London with the Trent, the Mersey and the Dee.

The new project was strongly supported by Sir Nigel Gresley, the Burton Navigation, the Ashby promoters, and some who did not like the Trent & Mersey's monopoly position. The Grand Junction refused to support it, however, relying on its arrangement with the Trent & Mersey. The scheme was defeated in 1797, and released the Trent & Mersey from any feeling that they must take action. Combined with the increasing financial stringency, it was enough to cause widening plans to be shelved. Once more, in 1804, the Grand Junction tried to call a meeting, but unsuccessfully. Not long afterwards the convenience of narrow boats being able to pass in Braunston and Blisworth tunnels was thought to outweigh the advantage of using wide boats which could not in any case move beyond Braunston, and on 25 July 1805 their passage through either tunnel was prohibited.[30] Writing in Rees's *Cyclopaedia* in this year, John Farey tells us that, in addtion to narrow boats, 'barges with square heads and sterns, and flat

bottoms, that carry 60 tons' were in use. This prohibition led the
Grand Union, which was largely built with the money of Grand
Junction shareholders, to construct narrow locks, so cutting off
the Leicester line from barges, and though further efforts at agreement were made in this year, in 1814 and in 1824, the year of
railway scares, nothing happened till a final effort to pass wide
boats through the Leicester line at the end of the century.

Before we take the history of the Grand Junction forward from
its opening date, we must notice its water supply undertaking.
The building of the long lockless pound to Paddington gave the
company a huge supply of water which could be augmented from
their reservoir at Ruislip (now the lido) and from water brought
down from the Wendover feeder. As early as June 1796 the company was considering the provision of water in Paddington and
Marylebone, and in 1798 obtained power to supply it. Nothing
was done immediately, though in 1799 there were abortive negotiations for amalgamation with the Chelsea Waterworks Co. In
1801 these were renewed, as also discussions with the New River
Co, and in 1808 others with the West Middlesex Co. These all
proving unsuccessful, an agreement was made with outside interests in 1810 for the formation of a separate company, which was
authorized in 1811[31] with a capital of £150,000. This drew its
water from the canal till public criticism of its quality became so
loud that in 1820 a supply from the Thames at Chelsea (see p. 131)
was substituted. The Grand Junction Water Works Company
survived till the Metropolitan Water Board was formed in 1902.[32]
The curious can still see an occasional G JWW hydrant plate in the
pavements of Paddington.

The trade of the Grand Junction before railway competition
was great and varied. The biggest single item was coal, but here
the company faced the total prohibition inserted in their original
Act in the interests of the City of London against bringing coal
nearer to London than the entrance to Langley Bury tunnel, later
altered to Lady Capel's wharf at the north-east end of Grove Park
near Watford. Inland coal was landed here to pay the City's duty
before being distributed. The canal Act of 1805, however, allowed
50,000 tons a year to pass to Paddington on payment of a duty
equal to the Thames duty on sea-coal and later the limitation was
removed. In 1831 the duty was consolidated at 1s 1d a ton; it was
reduced to 4d in 1889 and abolished in 1890.

In 1810, a total of 109,844 tons of inland coal was carried on the
canal, with 22,209 tons of sea-coal also which had been brought

into the canal at Brentford. Twenty years later these figures had
increased to 149,004 and 39,804 tons.

Coal was a smaller proportion of the total trade than on most
canals, for there was so much else to be carried. Iron, for instance,
taken towards London for manufacturing, or in the finished form
of castings and iron pipes for factories and waterworks. This trade
from Shropshire and Staffordshire amounted in 1810 to 24,264
tons; it came down the Severn and through the Thames & Severn
to Oxford, and thence encouraged by Grand Junction drawbacks
to Braunston and the main line; or more often via the Stourbridge
and Dudley lines and the Stratford Canal to Lapworth and the
Warwick line; or, keeping Grand Junction rates low, by the Trent
& Mersey and Trent River to Gainsborough for shipment by
coastal craft. In 1830 the figure was steady at 26,890 tons, and
then, encouraged by cheaper tolls, grew rapidly to 55,694 tons in
1840.[33]

The steady growth of London created an important trade in
house-building materials, of which bricks, timber and lime carried
to London between them accounted for 72,797 tons in 1810. For
the rest, agricultural produce of all kinds moved towards London
from the Birmingham, Leicester and Oxford lines, a flourishing
hay, straw, vegetable and cattle market being maintained round
Paddington basin. Salt came from Cheshire; glass from Stourbridge; pottery from Staffordshire and light goods from Manchester and Birmingham sometimes ballasted with pig-iron; nails
from Derby; stone from Mountsorrel and Quorndon on the
Leicester line and from Derbyshire; paving stones from Yorkshire; and much else. Outwards from London were carried its
groceries and other goods, whether manufactured or imported, on
their way to supply the Midlands, and also its ashes, breeze and
manure. In 1810 the 343,560 tons of London trade was centred as
follows:

		tons	tons
Towards London:	to Paddington	113,220	
	to the Thames	78,476	
	total		191,696
From London:	from Paddington	67,728	
	from the Thames	84,136	
	total		151,864

Not many canals possessed so nicely balanced a trade.

The carriage of passengers was never of much importance. In
July 1801 the company began to run a service from Paddington to

Uxbridge with one and later with three boats, the *Royal George*, *Marquis of Buckingham* and *William Praed*. The turnout must have been smart, for it was ordered that

> 'the Steersman of the Passage Boat be provided with a Blue Waterman's Jacket with Yellow Stand-up-Cape and a double Row of Yellow Buttons and that the Postillions be also provided with Blue Jackets with Yellow Stand-up-Capes with plain yellow Buttons and to have yellow Badges on the left Arm with the letters GJC thereon'.[34]

But the passage boats were a trouble to manage, and the company hoped to make more by leasing the rights. A series of lessees tried to make them pay after the company's charges had been met, but failed, for regular services do not seem to have been run after about 1810. A private service from Paddington to Buckingham was also maintained for a time after the branch's opening, but 'the number of passengers and parcels were found inadequate to support the expence'.[35]

Excursions from Paddington took the place of regular services; they are described in the *Illustrated London News* of 1849[36] as among the holidays available to the poor. Today craft like *Jason* still provide a link with the gay boats of 1801.

The development of the canal trade went steadily on, so much so that it often outran water supply. In 1814, for instance, the Loughborough company complained that owing to short water on the Grand Junction, boats had taken fourteen days instead of four. By 1828 receipts had reached £181,932 from tolls, £150,800 being distributed as a 13 per cent dividend.*

In 1808 one of the company's engineers saw at Bridgnorth 'a Steam Engine invented by Mr Trevithick on a very simple construction',[37] and one of 4 hp was ordered for pumping out water during repairs. In 1811 there was a pleasant exchange between Lords Clarendon and Essex over Sunday work. The former wrote to protest against the navigation of boats on Sunday. The company replied that they would prohibit movement during the hours of church services, only to receive a strong protest from Lord Essex against boaters stopping work, and 'ill consequences which must inevitably ensue from a number of lawless, ignorant and untractable Men being collected together . . . without employment to keep them from Acts of depredation, drunkenness and riot'.[38] Tactfully the committee took no further action, but diverted their

---

* Receipts and dividends from 1806 to 1843 will be found set out in full on pp. 175-7 of Charles Hadfield, *British Canals*, 2nd ed., 1959.

THE PADDINGTON CANAL, 1840.

7. Excursion boats on the Grand Junction Canal, 1840

benevolence and perhaps the Earl's attention by contributing 100 guineas to the relief of the sufferers in Portugal.[39]

As 1814 was a year of boom—'the unprecedented demand for Boats of every description for the conveyance of general Merchandize'[40]—so the post-war 1816 was one of slump, when drawbacks on tolls were introduced to support 'the different branches of Manufacture in the Interior of the Country'.[41] In this year Pickfords, the great canal carriers, owed the company £16,000, and were asked to liquidate it by instalments. However, tolls which in 1816 had fallen to £127,130 had by 1818 recovered to a more normal £169,922.

In 1818 a new line for the canal was authorized between Frog-more End, near Apsley, and Nash Mills, which would take the canal along the course of the rivers Bulbourne and Gade. This was the result of a dispute with John Dickinson, who had in 1808 bought a water-powered paper mill beside the canal at Apsley and in 1811 another at Nash Mills, and who complained of loss of water power. Six years later these mills had gone over to steam, but in 1826 he bought the water-powered Home Park Mills below Nash, and those at Croxley in 1830. From those days till recently Dickinson's provided the canal with traffic.[42]

Then in 1824 a cloud appeared and grew, for in January Rennie had been ordered to survey for a proposed London–Birmingham railway. A meeting of canal companies was held in Birmingham in November, where it was proposed to investigate the 'Expediency and feasability' of 'Rail Roads with Locomotive Engines',[43] and meanwhile to examine the possibility of improving the London–Birmingham–Liverpool canal route, removing any hindrances to traders, and claiming the protection of Parliament for canal pro-prietors. After the meeting there was something like panic, and in March 1825 the chairman of the Select Committee was authorized to use part of the reserve fund to buy the company's shares 'to counteract to a certain extent the extreme and sudden variation in the price of Shares'.[44] Share prices fell from £350 in 1824 with an 11 per cent dividend to £225 in 1831 when 13 per cent was paid.

For a time the London & Birmingham railway project was in abeyance because of the financial crisis of the time, and the Grand Junction did their best to prevent its successful revival. In 1828 they rationalized their complicated system of tolls and drawbacks and reduced them in 1830 and 1831 in concert with other canals on the Manchester route. At the same time they investigated the possibility of 'expediting Boats through the Tunnels by the power of Steam'[45] and of haulage by locomotives on the banks. They also encouraged opposition to the railway; they were not, how-ever, prepared to oppose the bill single-handed, and co-operative opposition was not supported by other canal companies. It passed in May 1833.

While the railway was being built there grew larger and then burst the bubble of a modernized canal line from Birmingham to London, part of a great project for an up-to-date waterway from Liverpool to London, with the earlier stages of which Telford was associated. The first section was the Birmingham & Liverpool Junction Canal, authorized in 1826 and opened in March 1835, a new waterway from Autherley on the Staffs & Worcs near the foot of the Wolverhampton locks to Nantwich to join the old Chester Canal, whence traffic could pass via Chester to Ellesmere Port and the Mersey or via the Middlewich branch to the Trent & Mersey and so to Preston Brook and Manchester. The engineer was Telford, who was also employed on the earlier stages of the major reconstruction of the Birmingham Canal Navigations' main line between Deepfields junction and Birmingham that took place between 1825 and 1838, the two together providing as good a line from Birmingham to Manchester and Liverpool as could be built within the limits imposed by narrow locks. The cost of the Birmingham & Liverpool Junction had been some £800,000, and of the Birmingham improvements about £500,000.

The moving spirit of both had been the energetic Birmingham solicitor Thomas Eyre Lee, who with Telford's support, had in mind at the same time an extension of this improved modern line right through to London. It first appears in *Aris's Birmingham Gazette* for 12 November 1827 as the London & Birmingham Junction with Telford as engineer from the Stratford-upon-Avon Canal ten miles from Birmingham (whence there was a level pound via King's Norton, the Worcester & Birmingham and Worcester Bar to the Birmingham main line) to the Grand Junction at Braunston (after passing under the Oxford), with a branch to the Coventry Canal. By avoiding the Avon valley the projected line had only 20 locks, instead of 77 via the Warwick canals or 54 via Fazeley, while the branch would shorten the line to the north by ten miles.

The Trent & Mersey and Warwick canals naturally opposed the plan, and the Oxford company, whose northern section would have been seriously affected by the loss of most of the trade from the Birmingham area via Fazeley, after minuting one week later that 'such a Canal would be highly injurious to the interests of the Company',[46] wasted no time in argument, but proceeded at once with surveys for straightening and improving the northern section of their line, and got their own authorizing Act in 1829.

This action becoming known, a new line was drawn for the proposed canal in 1828, to run from a point three miles farther down the Stratford Canal across the Warwick & Birmingham and past the southern side of Coventry to the northern end of the Oxford Canal at Ansty. In 1830 this was altered again to end farther down the Oxford Canal at Brinklow. A bill was introduced in February 1830, but ran into serious trouble, for it was found that all the subscribers had had their names entered without their consent, that many were 'needy and indigent persons', and some were of 'doubtful character'. Though Eyre Lee seems to have been more careless in failing to check the subscribers' list than culpable in compiling it, he was called to the Bar of the House in May and reprimanded, and the bill was thrown out.[47] The proceedings cannot have done either Eyre Lee or Telford much good.

Telford dropped out after the débâcle, and later Cubitt (Telford's assistant on the Birmingham & Liverpool Junction and consultant on the straightening of the Oxford) produced in 1832 a survey for the Central Union Canal, this time from the Worcester & Birmingham near Worcester Bar to the Warwick & Birmingham near Bordesley and from the Warwick & Birmingham near Solihull south of Coventry to the Oxford Canal at Ansty. This seems to have been Cubitt's own idea, perhaps in consultation with Eyre Lee, but not to have been discussed with any canal company.

At the end of 1833, however, a group of promoters, one at any rate of whom had been connected with the old Junction scheme, and who seem to have been backed by Lord Dudley and other Staffordshire coal and iron masters who disliked the rates agreement between the Coventry and Warwick canals, planned the London & Birmingham Canal. It was surveyed by James Green the west-country canal engineer who had rebuilt the Exeter Canal and in 1828 had surveyed a proposed ship canal at Cardiff for Lord Bute, a company was formed in March 1836, and a prospectus issued. This proposed a line from the Stratford Canal direct to the Regent's, 113 miles long against 149¼, with a level pound of 71⅝ miles, 9¾ miles of tunnelling, and an aqueduct over the Avon valley that was at one point to be 208 ft high. Locks were reduced from 172 to 48, three of which, at St Albans, would take the canal down to Highgate, whence goods for London could be delivered, though there would be a flight of 22 locks to join the Regent's Canal.

'The proposed navigation will possess all the improvements of the best modern canals. Where tunnelling is necessary, two tunnels with a towing path under each will be made; the sides of the canal will be walled; and the greatest of all modern improvements, the double towing path, will be carried throughout the whole line . . . the promoters of this undertaking have no hesitation in submitting their plan to the public, in face of the numerous Railways now in course of formation, every day, in their judgment, furnishing further and satisfactory proof, that although Railway conveyance may be preferred for passengers and light goods, that require dispatch and will bear high rates of transit, the great bulk of the trade of the country will still be carried on through the medium of cheap navigable communications. . . . By the proposed route, goods will be delivered in London in thirty-two hours, instead of seventy, by the existing route.'

The capital was three million pounds, and a saving in freight costs of £1 a ton was estimated.

The public did not take such an optimistic view, while the opposition of the Grand Junction Canal and of the London & Birmingham Railway could be assumed. Therefore we find in 1836 compromise proposals to join the Grand Junction at Stoke Bruerne, Braunston or Weedon instead of continuing an independent line, and in 1837 one to join the Buckingham branch. The last heard of it is a meeting in Cubitt's office in March 1838. As the earlier Junction proposal had pushed the Oxford company into improving its northern section, so the later plan, together with the threat of railway competition, had stimulating effects upon the Grand Junction. In 1835, a year in which the canal carried 192,859 tons of through trade to London, and 631,815 tons of local traffic, the doubling of the flight of seven locks at Stoke Bruerne was authorized to ease congestion there. The chronic water shortage whereby boats travelling singly had to wait until they could find a partner with whom to pass the locks, or pay extra, ended towards the end of 1838, when a new reservoir and pump were put into service at Tring summit and all restrictions lifted. Again, on 2 January 1837 a notice appeared in the newspaper that 'in consequence of an Agreement between the Grand Junction Canal Company, and the directors of the projected improved line of the Canal between Birmingham and the northern part of the Grand Junction Canal . . . the tonnage rates of Goods, &c. carried along the Grand Junction Canal have been materially simplified and reduced; and that Boats may pass at all hours through the Locks, and without extra charge, unless when single'.[48] The reductions were in fact considerable—a quarter off merchandise tolls, and coal through to London at a farthing per ton mile.

On 12 November 1838 the London & Birmingham Railway was opened throughout to Euston for goods traffic; the Grand Junction did not sell itself, did not slide into apathy, but fought back. Though it was on the losing side, it could still be thought of as 'the great Grand Junction'. (*To continue the history of the Grand Junction Canal, turn to p. 217.*)
(*To continue the history of the Grand Junction Canal, turn to p. 217.*)

Newport Pagnell Canal

The idea of making a branch to Newport Pagnell was as old as the Grand Junction itself; such a cut was suggested to the company in 1793, perhaps by the citizens, and James Barnes was instructed to make a survey. It was after they had seen his report that the canal committee decided not to make it themselves.

The idea was revived at a meeting at the *Swan Inn*, Newport Pagnell on 2 January 1813 'to consider the Propriety and local Utility of making a branch canal from the Grand Junction Canal at Great Linford, to the Town of Newport Pagnell, under the Powers and Provisions of the Grand Junction Canal Acts, or of applying to Parliament for leave to bring in a Bill for making a Railway upon or near to the present Road from Newport Pagnell to Great Linford'.[49]

The Grand Junction refused to make the branch, the railway idea was discarded, and another meeting on 20 August resolved to seek an Act, the promoting committee being told to keep a possible extension to Olney and the Ouse at Bedford in mind.

Benjamin Bevan, then working for the Grand Junction, made the survey, the Act[50] was passed in June 1814, construction probably began early in 1815, and the line seems to have been opened early in 1817.[51] The waterway was built to the same dimensions as the Northampton branch of the Grand Junction, 1¼ miles long, falling 50¾ ft by seven locks to the town, and having been made ornamental where it passed through the grounds of the Rev W. Uthwatt. The cost seems to have been £14,200.

Its main purpose was to carry coal, mainly from Shipley (a wharf at Newport was called Old Shipley Wharf) on the Nutbrook Canal and Moira on the Ashby to Newport Pagnell for sale there, and for transfer by land carriage to Bedford and its district. About 7,500 tons a year was carried, with another 2,500 tons of lime, manure, bricks, timber, grain and other cargoes. This steady trade was nurtured on high tolls, that for coal varying from 9d to 1s for 1¼ miles, and being maintained at 9d when the Grand Junction were taking less than 1d per mile. However, the revenue produced an average dividend throughout the company's life of £2 14s 0d per cent, the highest figure being 6 per cent for 1845, when the tonnage reached its maximum of 14,887. (*To continue the history of the Newport Pagnell Canal, turn to p. 228.*)

CHAPTER VI

The Canals of London

LONDON lies in the angle between the tidal Thames and the ancient navigation of the River Lee. After the Great Fire the lower part of the Fleet River was canalized, but for a true canal the city had to wait till 1799, when the Isle of Dogs Canal was authorized, and 1801, which saw the Acts for the Grand Surrey and the Croydon, which have been described in my *The Canals of Southern England*. Then came in 1812 the Regent's, to link the Grand Junction at Paddington to the Thames, and in 1824 its branch the Hertford Union or Sir George Duckett's Canal, to provide a waterway to the Lee. In that year also London's score was completed with the beginnings of the Kensington and the Grosvenor Canals. Of these, far the most important was the Regent's.

Regent's Canal

The first proposal for a canal eastwards from Marylebone was that of Robert Whitworth in 1773. He had been asked by the City authorities to plan a canal from Waltham Abbey to Moorfields and also from Moorfields to Marylebone, and in his report the latter emerges as a line from what would now be near the top of Baker Street (where he envisaged it joining on a level the canal proposed earlier from Uxbridge), then following much the same curve as the later Regent's to Islington but passing under the Pentonville Road and over the New River near Sadler's Wells to lock down nearly 50 ft to the Waltham Abbey line.[1]

The completion of the Paddington branch of the Grand Junction in 1801 produced schemes for joining it to the Thames below London bridge. In 1802 a horse tramroad was proposed to London docks, to join another possible line from Portsmouth.[2] In the same year the Grand Junction committee itself thought of building an extension on this route, but, soon finding itself too occupied,

promised support to 'the Gentlemen who are desirous to promote
that Undertaking',[3] then called the London Canal. In July a line
was surveyed from Paddington basin to the New River Head and
on to Commercial Road and London docks,[4] nearly seven miles.
The subscription of £400,000 was quickly filled, and the chairman
of the temporary committee, Sir Christopher Baynes, asked the
Grand Junction about water supplies. The latter refused to part
with any—as we have seen, the company was interested in public
supply as well as in navigation—and on this point and on opposition by landlords to interference with their building projects the
scheme was reported postponed in June 1803.

It was not until 1810 that the proposed London Canal was again
mentioned to the Grand Junction, this time by Thomas Homer,
who attended a committee meeting in November with a vague
project for a line to join the Limehouse Cut, which ran from the
River Lea to the Thames. Homer, a Coventry man, had been from
1789 to 1793 joint clerk of the Coventry Canal and from 1794 to
1807 on its committee. He was an original shareholder to the tune
of 60 £100 shares in the Grand Junction, had been Comptroller
from 1793 to 1802, and then for a period part-time Inspector
General and Superintendent of Trade, Packet Boats and Navigation. In 1802 he took wharves at Paddington and went in for
carrying and operating packet boats, but got into financial difficulties in 1808 and had to sell his wharves to pay his debts to the
Grand Junction. Having clearly not been discouraged by the
meeting, Homer then got in touch with John Nash. At this time
the lease of the Crown estate of Marylebone Park to the Duke of
Portland was coming to an end, and in 1810 the Commissioners
of Woods and Forests asked for plans for its development from
the two pairs of official architects to the Department, Thomas
Leverton and Thomas Chawner on the one hand, John Nash and
his assistant James Morgan (who had worked for Nash in his
private practice for ten years) on the other. These were submitted
in July, and Nash's was chosen. Homer then saw Nash, who
agreed enthusiastically to the canal passing through the Park,
joined the promotion committee, helped to raise money, subscribed heavily himself, and got the consent of the Prince Regent
to allow the undertaking to be called after him.[5] Finally, the promoters met the Grand Junction company, and reached agreement
upon water supplies.

After a somewhat rough passage the Act[6] was passed on 13 July
1812 for a canal to connect the Grand Junction near Paddington

(*above*) Eye Kettleby lock, looking west, on the Melton Mowbray Navigation; (*below*) Market Overton wharf on the Oakham Canal

X. (*above*) Foxton inclined plane; (*below*) the southern end of Saddington tunnel on the o̶
Union Canal

basin to the Thames at Limehouse near the Limehouse Cut. When built, it was 8⅝ miles long, with two tunnels, Islington (960 yd) and Maida Hill (272 yd). The canal was intended to have a double use: to be a means of exchanging goods between the Thames wharves and docks and the Grand Junction line to the Midlands, and to supply the local needs of the parts of London through which it ran, mainly with coal carried upwards from the river. As it turned out, the local trade proved the more important.

The first directors' list was impressive: the Earl of Yarmouth, Lord Robert Seymour, Lord Dundas, Sir Thomas Baring, Bt, Sir Thomas Bernard, Bt, Sir Bateson Harvey, Bt, John Nash, Harvey Combe the brewer, and Lt-Col John Drinkwater, deputy-chairman for over twenty years. The first meeting gave special thanks to Earl Stanhope, John Nash and Sir Thomas Bernard for their help in promoting the undertaking, and to the Earl of Bridgewater, who had been chairman of the House of Lords Committee on the bill. James Morgan, who was to remain with the company till 1835, was appointed engineer, and Homer superintendent.

Almost immediately the company was in difficulties. The supply of water was likely to be troublesome, for the canal fell towards Limehouse. The main authorized source was from the Thames (when above half-tide), with only limited amounts from the Grand Junction, which was protected by a stop lock. The first meeting had authorized pairs of locks side by side, which were economical of water because some of the supply from an emptying lock could be used to help fill its neighbour, but soon afterwards Colonel Congreve, later Sir William Congreve, of rocket fame,[7] put forward a scheme for lifts on a hydro-pneumatic principle. Canal lifts which would raise and lower boats vertically in tanks, so saving lockage water, were favourite objects of patents by inventors and experiment by engineers. Two varieties of counterbalance lift had so far been tried, one between 1800 and 1802 at Mells on the Dorset & Somerset Canal[8] which had been tested but never used in practical operation because the canal on which it stood had never been opened, the other at Tardebigge on the Worcester & Birmingham Canal, which had worked satisfactorily enough but was not considered sturdy enough for daily operation. Of a third, Weldon's effort on the Somersetshire Coal Canal in 1797,[9] the less said the better. Congreve's lift[10] had two caissons which were connected by chains passing over overhead wheels. The two pit chambers were interconnected at the bottom, and the vertical movement of the caissons was brought about by hand operation

I

assisted by the movement from one chamber to another of compressed air trapped beneath the water.

The directors were properly cautious. However, after an engineers' report they agreed to Maudslay & Co building one at Camden Town. On 7 June 1815 Congreve reported that there were some leaks where screws had been used instead of rivets, but every other part had been proved, 'and the sufficiency of the powers of the moving Apparatus ascertained, by lifting the Caissons without the Assistance of the Air underneath them'.[11] However, Earl Stanhope, a canal experimenter in Cornwall,[12] was a conservative in London, and suggested single locks instead. A year later Congreve's lift still would not work properly, and after having spent £12,000 the proprietors went back to the beginning and ordered twelve ordinary locks in pairs.

Meanwhile construction had begun from the Paddington end and upon the Islington tunnel, though at the end of 1814 only £254,100 had been subscribed out of the authorized £400,000. Homer reduced the company's balances still further when in April 1815 he absconded with £1,359; he was caught and sentenced to transportation. So hard up did they become that the first section of canal from Paddington to Camden Town, together with the branch to Cumberland Basin (authorized under an Act[13] of 1813) where an agricultural produce market rivalling that of Paddington was established, was only opened on 12 August 1816, the Prince Regent's birthday, after a whip-round of £100 from each member of the Committee.

It had become clear that much more than £400,000 would be needed, and an Act of 1816 authorized an increase to £600,000. Authority was one thing, to raise the money was another. At this crisis, in a whirl of discussion about redeemable annuities, tontines, annuities on lives with survivorship and new shares, the Earl of Macclesfield became chairman in place of Charles Munro, and Lt-Col Drinkwater Deputy. The Earl remained chairman till 1842, and between them they led the company out of its difficulties.

The first thing was to be businesslike. A new system of administration was put in, with sub-committees of the General Committee for purchases, works and accounts. The next was to raise money. A £300,000 tontine was tried, but only £500 came in from the public. Then a fortunate meeting took place between Munro and the Committee of the Society for relieving the Manufacturing Poor, which was concerned with post-war unemployment. The

Committee suggested a government loan which would enable the canal to be built and also the poor to be employed. From this interview, and the subsequent negotiations with the Government, probably sprang the Poor Employment Act of 1817, which set up the Exchequer Bill Loan Commissioners, empowered to make loans for public works that would reduce unemployment.[14] The scene was changed. Telford surveyed the canal on behalf of the Commissioners, who agreed to lend £200,000 if £100,000 was raised in shares together with whatever further money was needed to complete the undertaking. The £100,000 was quickly found under these conditions, and work re-started in December 1817. In 1819 power was given to build the great City Road basin, that was to add so greatly to the company's prosperity; the same Act[15] laid down the powers given in 1812 to make a Shoreditch cut to Aske Terrace. At the end of 1819 another £105,000 had to be raised, but prospects were good, and on 1 August 1820 the canal was opened throughout 'under circumstances of a particularly flattering nature, since on the very day of the Ceremony, Boats joined the procession with freights from Manchester, delivering their cargoes at the New Basin,* and returning towards the interior of the Kingdom in the course of the same day'.[16] This City Road basin below Islington tunnel, more centrally situated than that at Paddington, now began to form a distributing point for London trade, and an exodus from Paddington began, Pickfords being one of the firms that moved. At Limehouse a ship basin of about 4 acres had been built instead of that for barges originally planned, with an entrance lock some 125 ft by 31 ft, and in the middle of August the first collier discharged at this ancestor of the present Regent's Canal Dock. To finish the outstanding works another £50,000 was lent by the Commissioners, who also agreed to postpone capital repayments for five years.

In 1819 the company's water supply problems were lessened when they agreed to build their authorized supply from the Thames at Chelsea,[17] and then to transfer it to the Grand Junction Water Works company in exchange for water from the Grand Junction's canal. When they started to execute this arrangement the Regent's company had a severe shock, for they were asked £33,000 by Lord Grosvenor's agent for half an acre of Chelsea, 'swampy land unfit at present for any other purpose than Gardens'.[18] After arbitration they got it for £2,850, which they still considered excessive, and put in two Boulton & Watt beam en-

* City Road basin.

gines and pumps. Later, a broad agreement with the Grand Junction enabled the Regent's to share supplies from Ruislip and Aldenham reservoirs. Then in 1833 the company took over the Grand Junction's powers to build an additional reservoir at the Welsh Harp, and this was opened in June 1835. Aldenham was given up in 1861. The Chelsea supply was later condemned as tainted, and a new intake at Kew Bridge for the Grand Junction Water Works company was authorized in 1835. The Chelsea engines were transferred there, and one still remains.

Trading began. It was soon clear that much more traffic in such articles as coal (soon to be carried to London gasworks), timber, road materials, and bricks, lime, sand and other building materials, would pass upwards to places along the canal than would move downwards from the Grand Junction to points lower than City Road basin, though tolls were kept low to attract business and enable traders on the canal to compete for longer hauls with those using the Thames to Brentford.

The tonnage carried rapidly increased. Here are some figures:

Y.e. 1 April	Tons	Receipts £
1822–3	279,008	NK
1823–4	379,550	18,492 (10 months)
1824–5	454,256	25,684
1825–6	498,706	26,484
1826–7	456,554	24,389
1827–8	482,105	24,863
1828–9	488,721	23,614
1829–30	467,900	22,696
1830–1	533,115	24,481
1831–2	573,690	24,372
1832–3	570,362	23,900
1833–4	604,254	26,877
1834–5	624,827	28,930

This growing trade attracted building development along the line of the canal. At the end of 1823, for instance, it was reported that trade had increased 'on the lower Line, to the Eastward, where the increase of building contiguous to the Canal, is to an extent that excites general astonishment'.[19] This section also presented problems of hooliganism that required the employment of special police.[20] Basin accommodation improved; in addition to those at City Road and the end of the Cumberland arm, to which the Haymarket was statutorily removed in 1830 from the position 'long held in St. James's Parish',[21] the privately owned Horsfall basin and that at St Pancras became available in 1825, and the privately owned Wenlock basin adjoining that at City Road was opened in 1826. Another improvement was the 'introduction of a newly constructed Towing Boat,* worked by a Steam Engine of small power, for accelerating the passage of Barges thro' the Islington Tunnel . . . four Barges, containing nearly 200 Tons, have been carried thro' the Tunnel . . . in 30 Minutes!'[22] In 1830 the canal acquired a direct connection with the River Lea when the Hertford Union Canal (see p. 134) was opened.

In 1835 it was reported that three-quarters of the canal's trade came from the Thames and one-quarter from the interior; one-fifth of all the coal imported into London entered the canal, mostly for local use, though some passed upwards as far as Bulls Bridge, or exceptionally to Aylesbury.

The cost of the canal had been about £710,000, a figure much nearer the estimate of £506,697 made in 1812 by Peter Potter, a surveyor who appeared for E. B. Portman, who opposed the original bill, than the £299,729 of James Morgan. In 1827 it became possible to clear up the capital structure. The company owed the Commissioners £235,000 plus some arrears of interest, but were told they could settle for a quick payment of £220,885. New £100 shares were issued at £25, quickly subscribed, and by the middle of 1828 the 'Company was finally relieved from foreign controul and its affairs disencumbered of all pecuniary embarrassments'.[23] A first dividend of 12s 6d per £100 share was paid for the year ending 31 March 1830. Some shareholders had to wait a long time for a small return, and hopes of anything better were frustrated by the need for new capital expenditure and then by railway competition. The dividend for 1839, ten years later, was only 8s, and for 1845 21s.

Railways were to be important to the Regent's—indeed, it was to become a railway company; they first entered its life in 1824, when some shareholders asked 'what course the Committee propose to take, with regard to the various Plans lately recommended to the Public, for establishing Rail Roads in different parts of the Kingdom, some of which are proposed to be formed in connection with the new Coal Docks projected on the River Thames, below Limehouse'.[24] The committee decided to watch developments, but there were none till 1830, when notices were given for

* It hauled itself along a chain laid on the bottom of the canal. The same system remained till the 1930s.

the London & Birmingham. The company opposed the bill in
1832, but subsequently had talks with the railway promoters, for
when the railway Act was passed in 1833, the canal shareholders
were told that 'should the benefits held out by the Rail Road
Company prove to be such as the Canal Company have been told
they may expect, no backwardness will be shown on the part of
the Regent's Canal Committee to cultivate a connection, that may
promise to be mutually advantageous'.[25]

It was then thought that the railway would end near the canal
at Camden Town, but soon afterwards it was decided to cross it
to Euston. The opening in 1838 caused immediate pressure for
toll reductions, from the Grand Junction and from such carriers
as Shipton & Co, who said that 'unless the Regent's Canal Company's Tonnage Rates on Manufactured goods, be speedily reduced, they should remove their establishment from the City Road
Basin. . . . The Committee being informed that other important
Carriers had intimated their intention to remove their trade from
the Canal to the Railway, unless immediate alteration be made to
the Tonnage rates',[26] the sundries toll from Paddington to City
Road was reduced from 2s 6d to 1s 6d, and other changes made.
In this same month of January 1839 Pickfords were reported to
have diverted part of their trade; however, Joseph Baxendale, one
of the firm's partners, was also a considerable shareholder in the
canal, and he offered that Pickfords would build a dock near
Camden Town station which would be a transhipment point from
rail to water for goods bound for the Thames. By August Shipton's were using the transhipment facilities to carry goods from
Birmingham to their wharf at City Road basin by railway and
canal.[27] At the end of 1840 a through rate of 1s a ton was set.
Probably Pickfords did not build the dock, and transhipment took
place without it, for in 1845 the canal company agreed to sell the
L & BR land near Hampstead Road 'to make a Dock, which will
connect the Canal with their Goods Station'.[28] This was completed in 1848, and suggested that the company might do well
enough out of railways. (*To continue the history of the Regent's Canal,
turn to p. 230.*)

Hertford Union Canal*

Sir George Jackson, sole owner of the River Stort navigation,
former Second Secretary to the Admiralty, M.P. for Weymouth

* It was also called the Lea Union or Sir George Duckett's Canal.

and Melcombe Regis and later for Colchester, had changed his name to Duckett in 1797 because of a bequest. He died in 1822. His son, also Sir George, sought and obtained in 1824 an Act[29] authorizing him to build a canal 1¼ miles long with three locks from Old Ford on the Regent's Canal to the Lee Navigation; he was presumably moved to do so because of his interest in the Stort and so in the Lee, though he was also a committeeman of the Grand Union. His object was to divert the Lee trade, which passed to or from the Thames wharves or docks by way of Bow Creek or the Limehouse Cut (opened in 1770), into the canal and so to the Regent's Canal dock, as well as making a useful connection with the Grand Junction line.

He was authorized to raise £50,000, of which £20,000 was lent by the Exchequer Bill Loan Commissioners. Engineered by Francis Giles, the Hertford Union was opened in the second half of 1830, a time of low tolls and stagnation of trade, but it did not attract business, and in 1835 Duckett sadly wrote to the Regent's company to say that his attempt to divert trade from the Lee navigation 'had not answered the expectation'.[30] The trouble was that the combined tolls asked by Duckett and the Regent's company for goods to the Thames was unattractive to Lee traffic. In 1836 and 1837 Duckett offered to allow goods to pass toll-free if the Regent's would pay him 2d a ton, but the latter would not budge, probably thinking the trade not worth having. However, in July 1840 they did agree to reduce their own tolls from Old Ford to the Thames from 7d to 4d for all goods except manure, already on a low rate, and in December threw in a reduction to 6d a ton on goods from the Hertford Union to Paddington or any intermediate point also. For the moment prospects looked brighter.

Let us now briefly consider four separate London canals, the Fleet, Isle of Dogs, Grosvenor and Kensington. (*To continue the history of the Hertford Union Canal, turn to p. 237.*)

Fleet Canal

The Fleet River from the Thames to Holborn was navigable in the twelfth century; in the Middle Ages and later its wharves were busy with trade, and its water smelly with the sewage and rubbish it received.

After the Great Fire, Wren and Hooke deepened and widened the lower 700 yd of the Fleet River to form an impressive canal

50 ft wide, lined with wharves and crossed by bridges. It ended at
Holborn bridge, also designed by Wren. The canal, finished about
1674, cost £50,000, Wren having had great difficulty in preventing
it silting up.

Though much used, revenue from its wharves were small, and
the space it occupied was valuable. It was partially arched over in
1733, the canal itself becoming a long arcaded covered market and
the wharves roads; the rest was covered in 1766. The market was
replaced in 1829 by Farringdon Street.[31]

Isle of Dogs Canal

The River Thames flows in a three-mile loop from Blackwall to
Limehouse round the Isle of Dogs. This stretch was difficult to
navigate with sailing ships because of the number of craft moored
in the river, there being in the eighteenth century no enclosed
docks other than the Greenland, now part of the Surrey Commercial Docks system. A canal across the top of the loop was
therefore an obvious idea. It was discussed in 1771, for a newspaper of that year wrote that they were informed that the making
of a cut from Blackwall to Limehouse would produce enough
gravel for a century of highway upkeep, and that its cost would
be only one-tenth of what it would have been fifty years earlier
because Mr Morris's plough, using sixteen horses four abreast,
could be used to dig it. The canal would serve a number of new
shipbuilding docks and enable supplies to get quicker to market;
'tis imagined this will be the most beneficial Undertaking of any
during his present Majesty's Reign'.[32]

When the wars with the French broke out in 1793, a number of
suggestions were considered for improving access to the port of
London. One of them was for a canal across the Isle of Dogs and
for the building there of the West India Docks. After a good deal
of Parliamentary discussion the plan was authorized by the West
India Docks Act, 1799.[33] The canal, 900 yd long, 6 ft deep, and
142 ft wide at top,[34] with flood locks at each end, was to be built
by the City of London, the Consolidated Fund advancing the
necessary money for construction and for three years' maintenance, while a tonnage duty was to be levied on all shipping
entering the Port.

The work took a long time, during which the City returned
several times to Parliament for increases in the sum of £72,000
originally advanced for the canal and for various port improve-

ments. In July 1805 the canal was

'nearly finished, and was to have been opened with great pomp on the 12th August; when, about twelve o'clock, being near high tide, while a number of people were at work at the extremity next the river, they were suddenly alarmed by a hissing noise, and the appearance of water entering from below. Scarcely had they time to make a precipitate retreat, when the outward dam burst with astonishing violence; and what a

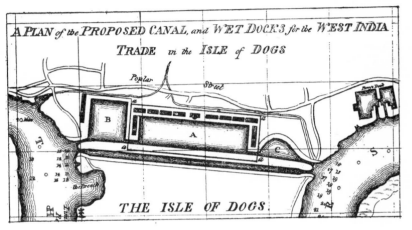

8. The Isle of Dogs Canal

minute before was dry land, was instantly covered with twelve feet of water:* the second dam, about fifty yards further on, composed of logs of wood twelve inches thick, besides a strong diagonal log by way of bar, was in like manner forced by the current, and this amazing strong bar snapped in two, as if it had been a piece of lath. The canal was immediately filled, as far as the second flood-gate next to Limehouse, which being shut, happily resisted the force of the current. Considerable injury has been done. . . .'[35]

The canal was eventually opened on 9 December 1805.

By 1807 £327,000 had been advanced from the Consolidated Fund and £5,000 lent by the City to make the canal and carry out other improvements—the two accounts are not separable. The cost of the canal alone is given as £168,000 in a Parliamentary

---

* This does not necessarily indicate that the canal had been built deeper than originally intended, though this was probably so.

report of 1829 on the sale bill,[36] and as £133,850 in *A New Steam Boat Companion*, published about 1840. For three years no tolls were charged on the canal in order to encourage craft to use it. Once they were levied, however, the waterway on the whole failed even to earn its repair and maintenance charges of about £2,600 p.a., much less wages and overhead expenses, much less again interest charges on the sums advanced.

Indeed, almost from the start, the canal earned more as a place to moor ships that were laid up than it did in transit tolls. Here are the three-year averages for each from 1812, when the figures become available:

Years	Transit Tolls £	Laying up Dues £	Total £
1812–14	711	1,570	2,281
1815–17	824	1,063	1,887
1818–20	812	978	1,790
1821–3	718	1,343	2,061
1824–6	581	916	1,497
1827–9	376	866	1,242

There are, perhaps, three reasons for the canal's failure. First, in ordinary conditions it was not much more difficult to take a small sailing craft on the tide round the loop of river than to take her through the canal and pay toll for it. Second, the former river congestion had eased by the building of a number of docks. Lastly, and perhaps most potent in the later years, the coming of the steam vessel and even more of the steam tug made craft independent of wind. In 1808 there were no steam vessels on the river; by 1823 there were 945.

The city realized as early as 1809 that the canal was not going to pay, and got Treasury permission to negotiate its sale, but pressure by ship owners prevented action for many years. In time their views and circumstances changed, and finally on 20 March 1829 the canal was sold to the West India Dock Company for £120,000 and, after an Act had been passed, conveyed to them on 13 August, it being agreed between the City and the Treasury that the tonnage duty levied on shipping generally in the Port should now be used only to repay the debt, of which that for building the canal was a considerable part, and no longer to pay interest. The Isle of Dogs Canal now became the South West India Dock.[37]

This canal, like the Caledonian in Scotland and the Royal Military in Kent, was built with Government money; many others, like the Regent's earlier in this chapter, were of course partly financed by Government loans through the Exchequer Bill Loan Commissioners.

Grosvenor Canal

This short canal left the north bank of the Thames between Chelsea Bridge and the bridge carrying the railway into Victoria station, and ran for ¾ mile to the south-east of Upper and Lower Belgrave Places, and underneath Ebury and Eccleston bridges, to a basin under what is now Victoria station.

It began life as a tidal creek. When the Chelsea waterworks were authorized by an Act of 1722,[38] their supply of water was to be taken by the waterworks company from the Thames by 'One or more Cutt or Cutts' which led the water into the marshes at high tide. As it ebbed it was to work a tide-mill which would pump it to the reservoirs in Hyde and St James's Parks.[39] The tidal creek and the land between the river and what is now Victoria station were leased from Sir Richard Grosvenor in 1724,[40] the creek was enlarged, and was used with the tide-mill till the latter ceased to work in 1775, steam engines being afterwards used for pumping.

In 1809 the company was authorized[41] to take water directly from the Thames, and the cut presumably then went out of use till the lease expired in 1823, when it reverted to its owner, the Earl of Grosvenor. In 1824 he turned the cut into a navigable canal, by building a basin at the upper end and a tide lock near the river, and began to use the waterway for commercial traffic, probably mainly the import of coal to the developing neighbourhood. The waterworks company were still allowed to use it, the basin being also a reservoir, until the Metropolis Water Act of 1852 forbade domestic water being taken from the Thames below Teddington lock.[42] (*To continue the history of the Grosvenor Canal, turn to p. 238.*)

Kensington Canal

The Kensington Canal was promoted because 'the Town and Parish of Saint Mary Abbot's Kensington . . . and the Neighbourhood thereof, are very populous'. A stream ran downwards from Kensal Green and it was proposed to make navigable the lower 1¾ miles of this, from the Hammersmith Road by Olympia to Chelsea Creek on the Thames. This stream had several names, but in the Act it is called Counter's Creek.

Among the promoters were Lord Kensington, Sir John Scott Lillie, Harvey Combe the brewer and William Ward, the last two being directors of the Regent's Canal. As built, the canal seems to have had a lock only at the entrance to the basin, 400 ft by 200 ft, at Warwick Road, the rest being tidal. The estimate was £7,969.

The authorizing Act[43] was passed in 1824. It was then decided to build the canal wider than had originally been intended, and to give the banks a greater slope, presumably because of the expected tidal action. A second Act, permitting additional capital, was therefore passed in 1826, the canal being opened on 12 August 1828.

'This ceremony, which had been reserved for the anniversary of his majesty's birth, was performed by lord Kensington, and a number of friends of the undertaking, embarking in a barge at Battersea-bridge, and proceeding up the canal, accompanied by a number a craft loaded with timber, coals, sand, etc., the first fruits of the speculation. The canal . . . is one hundred feet broad, and capable of affording passage for craft of one hundred tons burden . . . (it) has been completed at the expense of about 40,000£, and its income from wharfs, tonnage, etc., is calculated at about 2,500£ per annum.'[44]

Perhaps it was soon afterwards that an extension to join the Grand Junction was contemplated.[45]

In February 1836, when the traffic on the canal was described as 'very limited',[46] the proprietors made a provisional agreement with the promoters of the Birmingham, Bristol & Thames Junction Railway (later the West London Railway) for the sale of the canal to that company for £10,000 in cash, £26,000 of railway shares, and £1,587 7s 6d in payment of debts. In June the railway company was incorporated to build a line from the basin of the Kensington Canal to the Great Western Railway near Wormwood Scrubs, and on to the London & Birmingham at what was later Willesden Junction. There was, however, some delay in the purchase, and it was not until August 1839 that the railway company told its shareholders that terms had finally been settled with the canal company 'by which settlement a considerable increase in the respectable Proprietory has been obtained'. This may mean that the canal company agreed to take more in shares and less in cash. Possession of the canal was given up to the railway company on 24 July 1839. (*To continue the history of the Kensington Canal, turn to p. 238.*)

CHAPTER VII

The Line from Fazeley
to Oxford

++++++++++++++++++++++++++++++++++++◆++++++++++++++++++++++++++++++++++++

THE old and winding line of the Coventry and Oxford Canals was in 1790 the only Midlands route for goods making their way to London from Birmingham, Liverpool, Manchester, the Potteries and the upper Trent. Such a monopoly was too vulnerable to last. Yet, thanks to shrewd management, the line's position at the end of the canal age was far better than we might have expected.

The first ten years of the period, from 1790 to 1800, saw the opening of a new canal line from Birmingham to London by way of the Warwick canals to Napton and the Grand Junction from Braunston, using only five miles of the old route. The Oxford company, however, secure in a guarantee of revenue from the Grand Junction and substantial compensation tolls from the War-wick & Napton, did not too greatly regret the failure of their own rival to the Grand Junction, the London & Western. The Coventry suffered a sharp drop in receipts for a few years after the Warwick line opened, but additional trade between Liverpool, Manchester, the Potteries and London more than compensated; later a sharp bout of price cutting against the Warwick line was ended by a rates agreement.

The Coventry, but much more the Oxford, benefited from the opening of the Ashby-de-la-Zouch Canal in 1804, for much Moira coal passed the whole length to Oxford.

The route was affected to some extent by the opening of the Leicester line in 1814, for Derbyshire and Nottinghamshire coal now entered the Grand Junction in competition with that from the Warwickshire collieries along the Coventry Canal and from Staffordshire via either the Coventry or the Warwick line. But an expanding market prevented anyone from being seriously hurt, while consumers benefited from the competition.

A renewed threat to the line came in 1827 with the promotion of the London & Birmingham Junction Canal from Birmingham by way of Coventry to Braunston. The Oxford company saw at once that they had better wait no longer to straighten their winding northern section; it was completed in 1834.

Coventry Canal

On 13 July 1790 the last section of the Coventry's line to Fazeley had been opened, and the London market was free to the trade of the north. Before the excitement had died down, the company became involved with other canal schemes, for the mania was starting. They were sufficiently allied with the Trent & Mersey to oppose a canal project from the upper Trent (Burton) Navigation to its own detached portion at Fradley, and also one from the upper Trent via Ashby-de-la-Zouch to their waterway, both of which would have hit at potential traffic off the Trent & Mersey, but later they accepted a modified Ashby scheme after suitable compensation payments had been arranged. They were lyrically in favour of the Grand Junction: 'the same will be productive of more public benefit than any Thing of the Kind that has yet been done in this Kingdom'.[1] It offered the Coventry a far better line to London, and soon involved them in discussions with other companies on Grand Junction initiative upon the possible widening and straightening of their own line, for which, however, they never showed enthusiasm.

An interesting feature of contemporary canal promotion methods was the arrival on the committee of the Coventry in 1792, before the Grand Junction Act of 1793 had been passed, of Kenelm Digby, a large subscriber to and committeeman of that canal from its commencement, followed by Thomas Homer in 1794, William Praed himself in 1795 and John Farr in 1796. Between them they held 179 original £100 shares in the Grand Junction, and must have had considerable influence within the Coventry committee.

Another canal scheme to affect the Coventry was the Wyrley & Essington, authorized in 1792, which offered a new source of Staffordshire coal. By the beginning of 1796 the latter's delegates were examining the proposed junction with the detached portion at Huddlesford, and the canal was opened about May 1797.

By the end of 1800 the Grand Junction was usable, thanks to the

recently built horse tramroad over Blisworth Hill. Between its
promotion and opening, its prospective benefit to the Coventry
had been partially offset by the construction of the Warwick
canals, which together provided a shorter route from Birmingham
than that by Fazeley. These were opened in 1800, and their temporary effect is shown in the reduction of the Coventry's dividend
from 25 per cent for 1800 to 17 per cent for 1801, 15 per cent for
1802 and 14 per cent for 1803. The effect was sharp enough to
cause delegates from the company to visit the two Warwick concerns in October 1802 to seek an agreement on tolls that would
prevent mutual price-cutting. The Warwick companies had the
shorter route—though more heavily locked—but they were hampered by their heavy compensation payments to the Oxford. At
first they sought too much, and by the time the bargaining had
ended in agreement in 1810, the Coventry's dividends were higher
than they had ever been, at 32 per cent, and their power greater.
The essence of the agreement then made was that both canal lines
would raise their tolls on coal by 1s a ton, and each would then
guarantee the other within stated limits against any deficiency in
their receipts.

Prosperity had now set in, so much so that in 1808 a reserve
fund was set up to ensure that the dividend would not fall below
28 per cent. Dividends were as follows, averaged over five-year
periods.

Years	Percentage	Years	Percentage
1774–8	2	1809–13	35 4/5
1779–83	2 1/2	1814–18	43 1/5
1784–8	2 7/10	1819–23	41 1/5*
1789–93	8	1824–8	50*
1794–8	14 4/5	1829–33	42 3/5
1799–1803	19	1834–8	46 3/5
1804–8	23 3/5	1839–43	27 3/5

* Including bonuses.

In September 1817 it was decided to pay off the loan debt of
£40,000, and repayment was completed by March 1823, after
which the company began to compound for the rents it paid. By
this time the shares had become so valuable that an Act was sought
to enable fractional parts of shares, not less than one-tenth, to be
bought and sold. Like so many other canal bills of the time, this
one ran against the reforming zeal of Lord Shaftesbury, chairman
of House of Lords committees on canal bills, who insisted as the
price of acquiescence that petitioning companies should separate

the offices of Clerk and Treasurer, and should give up any old exemptions from paying rates they might possess. The former stipulation alone was extracted from the Coventry Company, and their Act passed in 1819. They got their own back on Lord Shaftesbury when their Treasurer resigned his Clerkship and his son was appointed instead. In 1825 two £100 shares were sold for £1,220 and £1,230.

At this time the town of Nuneaton was often enlivened by the troops who stopped there while on their way to London, Liverpool or Weedon by canal. In 1822, for instance, a local inhabitant noted in April a party of foot soldiers from Ireland, and part of the 31st Regiment of Foot from Chatham to Liverpool; in July, 300 men of the 1st Regiment of Guards from Paddington to Liverpool and in August some of the 3rd Grenadier Guards from Liverpool to London. In August 1824 a single convoy of 28 boats went through with troops from Ireland.[2]

In January 1829 the company considered the London & Birmingham Junction Canal, then proposed to run from the Stratford to the Oxford near Ansty. They decided strongly to oppose it in the light of improvements which, they said, had been carried out on the Trent & Mersey and their own waterway at a cost of £50,000. Their own canal, they thought, was 'complete for all purposes of Navigation, and fully adequate to the Conveyance of any extended Trade this great Manufacturing Country may require'.[3]

A week later they heard of the proposed bill of the Oxford's to shorten that company's line in association with the new project, and decided to oppose it, presumably as a holding operation pending consideration of a proposal of their own for a new junction between their own canal near Bedworth and the Oxford Canal near Ansty by a line 4 miles long through Bulkington, which was submitted to the Oxford Company in November, and for which notices were issued and plans deposited. At the same time they proposed to improve the other end of their canal by building a 1¾ mile cut from Streethay near Lichfield on the detached portion to Wood End on the Trent & Mersey to eliminate the loop through Fradley. Both these improvements were included in a bill of 1830, but they were unlucky, and therefore the Coventry company failed to follow the Oxford in shortening its line. The first cut had to be withdrawn 'in consequence of the threatened opposition of Mr. Secretary Peel* . . . communicated to them by

* Robert Peel, Home Secretary, soon to be Sir Robert. An industrialist of Tamworth.

I. Grand Junction Canal: (*above*) an ice-boat, crew, and 14 horses at Bridge 77, Linford. On e right is the former entrance to the Newport Pagnell Canal; (*below*) near the southern end f Braunston tunnel; the craft have been towed through by the steam-tug blowing off on the right. The other craft is T. W. Millner's steam inspection launch *Gadfly*

XII. Grand Junction Canal: (*above*) the steamer *Sultan* in the Buckby flight; (*below*) the experimental barge *Progress*, 12 ft 6 in beam, built by the Grand Union Canal company

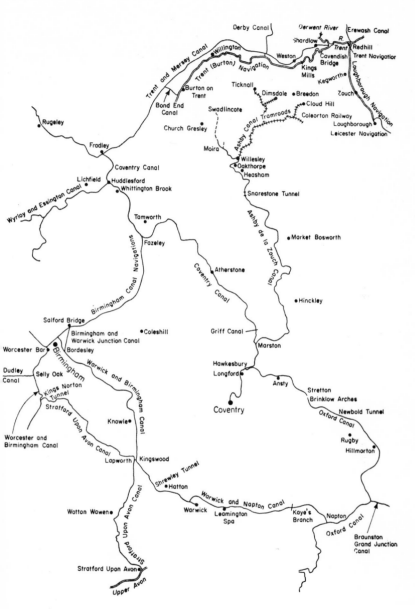

9. The Coventry and Warwick Canals and their connections

him in person', and the second because of 'the threatened opposi-
tion of Lord Anson . . . communicated to them by Mr. Wyatt his
Lordship's Agent'.[4] Lord Anson was sufficiently influential to
ensure nothing was done at the north end, though talks with the
Oxford company for an improved junction went on till 1836.
Landowners were often a trial to energetic canal proprietors.

The company decided that the threats to their section of the
through route represented by the new canal project and by
rumours of a London & Birmingham Railway made it necessary
to encourage the through trade, and in May 1830 a drawback of
20 per cent of the Parliamentary tolls was given on goods from
London to Preston Brook (junction between the Trent & Mersey
and the Bridgewater Canal), beer and porter from London to
Staffordshire, and crates of pottery from Staffordshire to London,
if other canal companies would also act. Soon afterwards they
supported cheap rates for Staffordshire coal to points beyond
Leighton Buzzard, and later for all coal passing Braunston. There
seems also to have been a heavy reduction in iron tolls, which had
the effect not only of reducing railway prospects, but of diverting
trade from the Warwick line of canal. In assessing these toll reductions, we must remember that the Coventry, being a pre-war
canal, had a low maximum Parliamentary toll of 1½d.

In 1833 another rates agreement was made with the Warwick
canals, with the object of raising the Coventry's revenue and
eliminating rate-cutting. The Birmingham company protested that
'the great object of the compact between the companies was to
raise the rates on the Coventry Canal, and by such means force the
Trade from the Fazeley route into the Warwick route'.[5] They
considered it had caused a fall of 75,000 tons in the yearly export
of Staffordshire coal to the Midlands. Later the agreement was
dissolved after public criticism, and competition re-established,
but by then Leicestershire and Derbyshire coal had, so the Birmingham company considered, got a foothold.[6] (*To continue the
history of the Coventry Canal, turn to p. 208.*)

Ashby-de-la-Zouch Canal

We can look for the origin of the Ashby Canal partly to efforts
by the upper Trent (Burton) Navigation to link themselves to an
independent source of coal supply, and so improve their competitive position against the Trent & Mersey, partly to action

taken by those who wanted to develop the coalfields round Ashby Woulds.

The first suggestion for a canal from Burton to the Coventry Canal at Marston reached the latter company in December 1781; they decided to oppose it, presumably because they hoped soon to complete their own line to the Trent & Mersey at Fradley—it was just before the Coleshill meeting (see p. 23). A few days later, however, they were aware of a bill for a canal 31⅜ miles long from Ashby Woulds to their waterway at Griff, and this they decided not to oppose in the light of the clauses it contained to safeguard the Coventry and Oxford companies. The line by way of Market Bosworth and Hinckley had been estimated by Robert Whitworth at £46,396, but this was thought to be an under-estimate. For this reason, doubts upon its profitability, the reported hostility of many landowners, and the probability of cheaper Staffordshire coal if the Birmingham & Fazeley were to be made, the project was dropped at the end of 1782, after some talk of extending it to the Burton Navigation.

A possible link with the Trent was revived in 1787, when William Jessop reported in September on making a communication between the Earl of Stamford's limeworks at Breedon and the river. He suggested a mile of double-track horse tramroad (or a stone road) and then 1½ miles of canal with three locks to the Trent, and a short length of canal from the far bank, with two locks, to join the Trent & Mersey Canal. Again nothing happened.

On 12 July 1790, the night before the completion of the Coventry's own canal to Fazeley that would link it with the Birmingham and the Trent & Mersey, a county meeting was held at Leicester to revive the idea of a canal from Ashby Woulds. Though the meeting was unanimously in favour, enough opposition showed itself afterwards to prevent a bill being brought forward. A plan followed for a canal from the collieries at Newhall and Swadlincote on Ashby Woulds to the Trent at Burton. A notice was published in September 1791,[7] and the project was actively discussed between September 1792 and April 1793.[8] But action waited for the canal mania.

A meeting at Ashby on 30 August 1792 declared itself in favour of 'a Canal from the Limeworks at Ticknall to Ashby Woulds and from thence to unite with the Coventry Canal at or near Griff'. Among the canal's supporters were the Earl of Stamford (owner of Cloud Hill and Breedon limeworks), Earl Ferrers (owner of the Staunton Harold limeworks), Francis Burdett of Foremark in

Derbyshire, Edward Dawson of Long Whatton, Thomas Pares the Leicester attorney, and Thomas Paget, father of the banker. Lord Rawdon (later Earl of Moira, then Marquess of Hastings and Viceroy of India), also supported the project, but told the committee that he would take no active part unless the Hon Penn Assheton Curzon of Gopsall House, a landowner and one of the members for the county, also agreed. Curzon himself announced that he would have no objection if the line were altered so as not to interfere with his plan for extending his park. When the committee pointed out that a variation would be expensive, he merely replied that 'the Expence to the undertaking was no consideration to him'.[9] Before long he had also discovered a possible danger to the spring that supplied his estate with water, and a conviction that it was impractical to make the canal to the limeworks anyway.

In mid-October Robert Whitworth put in a plan, revised from that of 1781. The main line was to run level from Griff to Ashby Woulds; then rise 139 ft by locks, with a reservoir 51 ft below the summit, to which water would be pumped by steam engine; then five miles of level canal, and 84 ft of lockage down; then level branches to Ticknall, Cloud Hill (via Coleorton collieries) and Staunton Harold if necessary. His estimate was £63,402 for the Griff–Ashby Woulds section, and £82,143 for the rest. Having asked Jessop to check the line, the committee decided to proceed, with a capital of £150,000 and very low tolls: only 1d a ton per mile for coal and ¼d for limestone. Since there were interests to be appeased, and because canal shares appreciated quickly at the time of the mania, 150 shares were reserved for landowners, 150 for holders of turnpike securities, and 150 'to be distributed or disposed of by the Committee as occasion may require during the Progress of the Bill in Parliament',[10] while the rest were to be offered widely. By the end of November, £110,000 had been subscribed. Though the company minuted that 'strict attention shall be paid to the responsibility of the proposed subscribers'[11] and that no share should be transferred till 15 per cent in calls had been paid upon it, there was clearly much speculation. Of the 55 names from Ashby itself, 13 were described as spinsters and six as widows, of the remainder there were two parsons and four doctors; a comber, four hosiers and a cordwainer; a butcher, a skinner, a victualler and two grocers; a joiner, a perukemaker and a cabinetmaker, and even a serving man and a postilion.

The company had to do some hard bargaining with the Coventry company over a junction at Griff, for the latter preferred coal to pass along its own canal for a longer distance than traffic from the Ashby promised. At first they decided to oppose the bill; then they turned down a proposal for compensation tolls as inadequate; then they suggested an alternative and shorter line from Ashby Woulds to Polesworth, which would earn the Coventry more, together with a branch from Griff to Hinckley, and said they would build these canals themselves if the Ashby company did not want to. Finally, they offered to take 8d a ton in compensation for a junction at Griff, and a guarantee against any loss of tonnage of Staffordshire and Warwickshire coal by the opening of the Ashby. At this point the Ashby promoters stood up for themselves, and offered 3d a ton with a guarantee, or 5d without. The Coventry promptly took the 5d.

After both Jessop and Whitworth had reported that Curzon's spring would be unaffected, the company offered to pledge their whole capital upon its survival intact. In spite of this, the bill was lost on technicalities of Standing Orders that read as if Curzon's hand had been behind them. It was therefore essential to satisfy Curzon if progress were to be made; his price was a penalty of £50,000 if any water were abstracted from his spring, and this preposterous figure was indeed embodied in the later Act. Curzon appeased, Lord Moira (as Lord Rawdon now was) spoke in favour of the bill at a meeting at Leicester in September and thenceforward supported the enterprise. Another opponent, the Leicester Canal, was quietened by a promise not to build a branch to Swannington to compete with the Forest line, and minimum tolls for carrying coal from the Leicestershire collieries were embodied in the Act.

It will be remembered that during 1793 the Grand Junction company was doing its best to get the whole canal line to Liverpool and Manchester, including the Oxford and Coventry canals, straightened and widened to the barge standard to which they proposed to build their own waterway. The Ashby therefore could itself form part of a barge canal route from London that might one day extend to the Trent; indeed, a clause was inserted in the Derby Canal Act of the same year compelling that company to make a canal from the Trent at Weston Cliff to the Trent & Mersey, whenever an Ashby/Trent link should have been adopted, to facilitate the sale of lime in Derbyshire. In November the company pressed the Coventry to widen to barge standard, and in July 1794 decided to build their own canal 'for the Navigation of River Boats'.[12]

In March 1794 revised tolls were agreed, still low at 1¼d for coal, lime and slate, ¾d for limestone and bricks, and 2d for most other traffic. In May, the Act[13] was passed, authorizing a canal about 50 miles long with a capital of £150,000, Jessop and Whitworth having together estimated it at £138,238, of which only £27,317 was attributable to the section from Ashby Woulds to the Coventry Canal, the point of junction now being Marston and not Griff. The deposited plan shows the main canal as 30⅜ miles long to Ashby Woulds; running thence via Ashby, a 700-yd tunnel and 11 locks to a junction. The left hand branch went for 1¼ miles to a further junction, when one line, ⅞ mile long, led to Staunton Harold and the other, 3⅜ miles long, to Ticknall. The right hand branch from the first junction ran for 5⅛ miles to Coleorton with a 2½ mile extension to Cloud Hill.

In July an agreement was made with Robert Whitworth that he should be joint engineer with his son Robert, the older man to give three months in the year and the younger his whole time.

Cutting began in the autumn on the section of canal from Ashby Woulds to Marston, and by October 1796 it was clear from what had been spent and Whitworth's estimate of what was still needed that the section from Ashby Woulds to Marston would cost about £100,000 against the original estimate of £27,317. It was in the light of this fact that the company soon afterwards decided, if the landowners were agreeable, to substitute tramroads for the branch canals to Ticknall and Cloud Hill, 'which it is now apprehended would be dangerous, and too expensive to be executed, with any hope of final success'.[14]

The year 1796 was an exciting one for the Ashby company, because the Commercial Canal project offered it the best chance it would ever have to become part of a through line of barge canal from London to the Mersey. This project had been surveyed by Whitworth, who must have been influenced by his interest with the Ashby company. It was, however, defeated by the close alliance of the Grand Junction and the Trent & Mersey—against the long-term interests of the former, one thinks—and the Ashby then turned for some months in early 1797 to considering whether, instead of their projected branch canals or tramroads to Ticknall and Breedon, it would be more sensible to extend their canal from Ashby Woulds to the Trent, and also to build tramroads from the limeworks to that river. Lime traffic could still be carried via the Trent, and wider prospects for both lines would also open.

Discussions between the Ashby company and the Earl of Ux-

bridge, the owner of the Trent (Burton) Navigation, and his
lessees, the Burton Boat Company, made easier because Joseph
Wilkes, a colliery owner at Measham, was prominent in the Ashby
Canal Company and a principal of the Boat Company, got so far
that in April the Trent (Burton) Navigation offered to amalgamate
with the Ashby. However, the latter company had by then too
much else to think of and too little money, and nothing more
happened for a time, though contacts were maintained. In June
1800 the Ashby committee did inquire whether Lord Uxbridge
would be willing to negotiate upon the transfer of the Trent
(Burton) Navigation to the Ashby company in exchange for
shares, and in January 1801 suggested a meeting with him, the
Burton Boat company and the Trent & Mersey company. By this
time, however, the Trent & Mersey was negotiating with the
Burton Boat Co for their lease.

Meanwhile an editorial of October 1796 had congratulated the
Ashby company on the progress of its works, and said, presumably
referring to the Trent & Mersey, that this refuted

'the CALUMNIES which have been circulated from the emis-
saries of a certain (universally allowed to be) most arbitrary,
avaricious, and monopolizing canal company, to discredit this
undertaking and its finances',

and referred to its proposed

'junction with one of the greatest undertakings that was ever
projected, "THE INTENDED COMMERCIAL CANAL"
(against which the jealousy of the DETRACTORS above
alluded to, is particularly excited . . .'.[15]

They had many troubles. In May 1797 the younger Whitworth
was reported ill, and at the end of June the services of both father
and son were terminated, though it was agreed that they might be
employed on a day-to-day basis. Thomas Newbold succeeded to
the job. By early March 1798 the canal was open from Ashby
Woulds to Market Bosworth, but before then the Committee had
had another shock. In early 1797 they had commissioned an in-
quiry into 'the State of the several Coalworks on Ashby Woulds
and the neighbourhood and the prospect of those works from
their present State being capable of supplying the Country with
Coals agreeable to the expectations entertained by the public in
that respect'.[16] The result was not satisfactory. There was 'delay
likely to happen by the Trials making for Coal on the Woulds, and
the probability of the Company being, for a very long period,
deprived of all hopes of receiving Interest for their Money, from

a want of that Article to pass along the Canal';[17] they therefore
wrote to Lord Moira, Colonel Hastings, and Wilkes of Measham,
the three big proprietors, asking them to hurry up and open new
collieries and prospect for more. Finally, the financial pressure of
the times meant that calls were far in arrear—in April 1798
£112,500 had been called but only £82,363 received, and a number
of shareholders had to be prosecuted for their arrears.

In June 1798 it was at last decided to build tramroads to Ticknall and Cloud Hill instead of canals, and in August Benjamin
Outram was asked to advise. In October his report in favour of
tramroads was agreed, and he was told to make detailed surveys
and estimates. In mid-1799 construction began. Meanwhile a
reservoir was being built at the head of the canal, and the possibility of tramroads to the collieries at Swadlincote and Church
Gresley investigated. By April 1800 the full call of £150,000 had
been made, though only £115,849 had been received, and a loan
had to be raised from the shareholders, who were told that 'delays
of payment on many of the Shares and the impossibility of collecting speedily those arrears even by compulsory means, have left the
Treasurer for the present destitute of provision for carrying on the
business'.[18] Progress was now made by loans and getting in
arrears; it was hard work, and payments to Outram were often
behindhand.

In November 1800 the Grand Junction was open throughout,
using its tramroad over Blisworth Hill; it much shortened the
water route between London and the Midlands. The capital had,
however, no canal link with Leicester, because the Union Canal
had got no nearer the Grand Junction than Gumley on a route
that was not to be completed until 1814. When the Grand Junction
opened, Pickfords started to carry from London by water as far as
Brownsover wharf near Rugby and thence to Leicester by road. In
January 1802, the Ashby company asked whether they would
consider Hinckley, Market Bosworth or Sutton Cheney wharves
as substitutes for Brownsover, so shortening the land carriage.
Pickfords asked for reduced tolls; the Ashby, Coventry and Oxford companies agreed, and the Ashby therefore hurried on to
complete their line to the junction with the Coventry. An additional inducement was the hope that traffic from Birmingham and
Liverpool would also find it convenient to use Hinckley rather
than the long water route by the Trent & Mersey and the Soar.

The tramroads were probably completed between July and
October 1802,[19] and the canal itself opened on 19 April 1804. By

June £166,322 had been spent on the canal and tramroads, of which £140,285 had been received by calls on the 1,482 shares (£113 on each £100 share) and £21,539 had been borrowed, the rest coming from tolls and miscellaneous receipts. In October 1807, when a reasonably final figure was produced, the total was £184,070. There were no celebrations: it was not a joyous occasion. A few months earlier Joseph Wilkes of Measham had reported that there was not enough coal available along the canal, advising its import from the Warwickshire and Staffordshire collieries in exchange for lime carried to Birmingham. No wonder the shareholders were soon afterwards told that there was 'very little probability of their reaping at present any advantage from the undertaking'.[20] The forecast was correct. It was not until 1826 that the company turned the corner, or until 1828 that the first dividend was paid in respect of the year 1827. The price of the £113 shares fell at one time to £10, but the first dividend pulled them up to £60, and in February 1830 they were £85. A dividend of £2 per £113 share was paid for 1827 and thereafter £4 p.a. to and including 1837, except for 1833, for which only £2 was distributed. Before dividends were declared, however, the loan debt had been paid off, mainly between 1820 and 1827. Here are the receipts from tolls averaged in three-year periods.

Years Y.e. 31 March	Average tolls £
1806–8	2,265*
1809–11	2,591*
1812–14	2,961*
1815–17	3,627*
1818–20	3,510*
1821–3	3,931*
1824–6	5,456
1827–9	7,027
1830–2	7,070
1833–5	7,682
1836–8	8,867

* Figures net, i.e. after deducting drawbacks. Remaining figures gross, before deducting drawbacks.

Pickfords' trade had begun when the canal was opened, though in October 1806 the company complained that they were using Far Coton wharf near Market Bosworth, instead of Hinckley, so getting more miles on the canal than had been agreed for the same

toll. This trade lasted until 1810, and was then probably transferred to the Union line in anticipation of the opening of the
Grand Union.

In 1810 the Grand Junction Canal had tentatively encouraged a
canal across the Peak to link the Cromford and the Peak Forest
Canals as a means of shortening the London–Manchester water
route, and during the first months of the year much was done to
organize support for it. The Trent & Mersey, however, bitterly
opposed it, and won over the Grand Junction by concessions
elsewhere, and by supporting the Grand Union Canal bill of that
year. This situation perhaps led the Ashby shareholders in October
to arrange to 'communicate with the Proprietors of the Old Union
Canal,* on the expediency of an union between each of these
Canals and the Ashby Canal, for the purpose of shortening the
distance of Canal Navigation between Manchester and London'.[21]
This meant the revival of the canal link between Ashby Woulds
and Burton on the Trent & Mersey, and presumably the building
of a new connection from the Ashby above Hinckley to the
Leicestershire & Northamptonshire at Blaby. However, the condition of the Ashby's trade was such that no one got enthusiastic:
indeed, it was difficult to assemble a meeting of the shareholders
or the committee. The idea was briefly revived in 1820.

In 1804 the colliery at Moira was begun and taken down to the
main coal: further pits were sunk a year or two later, and more
again in 1813. In 1812 Lord Moira had been given extended credit
facilities and, apparently, a drawback if a sufficient quantity was
passed down the canal, and by 1815 this coal, to become so well
known as a canal-borne commodity during the nineteenth century,
was introduced to London:

'Those who are curious in the truly English blessing of Coals,
and give some attention to domestic comfort and economy,
would do well at this season to attend to a new quality of Coal
found in LEICESTERSHIRE at Ashby de la Zouch and called
MOIRA COAL . . . it is brought by the Canal to Paddington
at about 47s. per ton. . . . This appears a little higher than good
Newcastle Sea Coals at this cheap time, but on the trial of its
economy in use, burning very slow, clear and bright, without
the aid of a Poker, without smoke or smell, and having no
cinders, it will be found a most agreeable and desirable fuel for

* The Leicestershire & Northamptonshire Canal: so called to distinguish it from
the Grand Union.

the Public Office, the study, bedroom, apartment of the sick, hospital, parlour, and drawing-room; . . .'[22]
It found a market there, and also at Oxford, where it began to be used in the colleges, and at many places in the Midlands, the south, and along the Thames valley. It was largely the development of the Moira group of pits, notably in the eighteen-twenties, that made the Ashby Canal an important waterway.

The principal events of the canal's early history are these. In 1815 the company rented warehouses at Measham, and tried to build up an export in cheese. In 1816 a passenger boat was put on the canal by a private group, who had to pay 3d a mile toll; the horses were forbidden to go faster than a walk, and the boats might not carry merchandise exceeding 50 cwt. In 1819 it was decided to make the regulating lock at the junction with the Coventry Canal a narrow one, and the two canal companies shared the cost of converting it, though broad boats seem to have been used within the Ashby Canal itself, probably on the coal run to Hinckley and other wharves. Then in 1822 the committee made a move that produced a great effect: they sent their engineer William Crossley on a round tour of eight neighbouring canals to find out what their tolls on coal were, and what drawbacks were allowed. He must have come back to recommend an extension of the drawback system, for in October it was decided to allow a drawback of 1s a ton on coal passing over the whole length of the canal (i.e. from Moira) to 'the foreign market'.[23] This subsidy had an immediate effect, for in January 1823 it was reported[24] that there had been an 'increase of the Tonnages the last three months by an extension of the Coal Trade in consequence of the exertions made in that Trade and by the facilities given by the Company thereto'.[25] The policy was most successful. The tonnage entitled to drawback rose from 4,367 in 1824 to 14,293 in 1826 and 22,011 in 1828, and by 1837 had reached 37,316, yet the company was earning about 2s a ton on this coal carried the full length. Their success with Moira coal encouraged the company to build a tramroad from the end of the canal to Gresley Green to join others built privately by colliery owners. This was begun in 1826 and finished in the following year, when coal from Swadlincote and later from Church Gresley also began to earn the drawback, and later contributed much to the tolls earned.

About 1826[26] salt water was found below 300 ft in the Moira pits; it was considered to be valuable medicinally, and baths built at the Bath Hotel near the pits were much patronized till the Royal

Hotel was erected at Ashby, and the water taken there in tanks. Visitors to the baths are said to have travelled by boat on the canal or by coach.[27]

In March 1830 the first word about railways had come to the committee-table, and in 1831 it was agreed to co-operate with the Grand Junction, who were reducing tolls as a precaution against the London & Birmingham project, by allowing a drawback of half the Parliamentary toll (1¼d) on coal passing on to that water-way which fulfilled certain conditions. Thenceforward till 1845, except for a Parliamentary notice in November 1840 for a 6-mile Burton & Moira Canal to link the Ashby and the Trent & Mersey at Burton by way of the Bond End Canal, with a branch to Swad-lincote,[28] the affairs of the canal remained uneventful. (*To continue the history of the Ashby Canal, turn to p. 211.*)

Oxford Canal

For the first eleven years after its completion the Oxford Canal formed part of the shortest water line from the Midlands to London. The opening of the Grand Junction route in November 1800, though it diverted much of the through London trade from the southern half of the Oxford, brought a huge increase to the northern half as the great new waterway sucked trade into itself. When, however, the Warwick line opened from Birmingham to Napton in March 1800, it for a time caused trade on the northern section to fall back as traffic to and from Birmingham was diverted, but so buoyant was business that by 1814 takings on this section had passed those for 1799. In any case, trade on and off the Warwick line not only paid tolls, but also the heavy compensation payments that had been granted as the price of junction.

The tolls taken at the four interchange points tell their own story: here are the figures, averaged in five-year periods:

Dates	Hawkesbury £	Braunston £	Napton £	Oxford £
1793–7	6,802	1,787	—	7,964
1798–1802	7,497	6,178	4,282	10,879
1803–7	5,698	15,664	11,230	11,180
1808–12	5,991	30,566	14,839	14,611
1813–17	9,324	32,281	13,457	13,595
1818–22	10,799	33,500	12,003	13,041
1823–7	13,058	36,157	11,276	12,641
1828–32	13,843	32,495	12,173	12,720

Hawkesbury was the interchange point with the Coventry Canal, Braunston for the Grand Junction, Napton for the Warwick & Napton. Oxford was partially an interchange point for the Thames, but also a terminus. Little traffic originated there, however, and interchange traffic, together with local trade originating between Napton and Oxford, probably accounts for most of the Oxford figures.

As we have seen, the company strongly opposed the bill for the Grand Junction, and unsuccessfully promoted the rival Hampton Gay or London & Western Canal. The price of acquiescence was a guarantee embodied in the Grand Junction's Act, which ensured from the beginning of 1804 £10,000 p.a. in tolls to the Oxford company from traffic to or from the Grand Junction, and also an authorization to the Oxford company to increase certain tolls, e.g. it was now empowered to charge 2s 9d a ton for all coal off the Oxford on to the Grand Junction, irrespective of distance.

The guarantee of revenue was never required, but the Oxford company for many years collected large sums from compensation tolls levied at Napton and Braunston, receiving perhaps a higher proportion of its revenue in this way than any other company.

Though the Grand Junction line took most of the London traffic, except that in cheese which continued to use the river, and even attracted some trade from Oxford itself, there was local traffic, mainly in coal, to be developed up and down the Thames. Therefore the Oxford company opened a wharf on the Chil Brook at Eynsham in early 1792; coal was handled here for Eynsham and Witney as well as stone and agricultural produce. They leased it in 1807, bought it back in 1849, and maintained it till after the First World War; indeed, the Docks & Inland Waterways Executive inherited the Talbot Inn, which the company had also built, and sold it in 1948.[29] The growth of the river trade also led the Duke of Marlborough to build about 1800 the first portion (11 chains) of the private Cassington Cut from the Thames below Eynsham, and to continue it at some time before 1814 for a further 45 chains to the Cassington–Eynsham road. It had one lock similar in size to those on the upper Thames. The cut ceased to be used about 1870.[30]

In 1793 the company introduced a scale of drawbacks for coal passing down river, the most generous relating to large cargoes passing Caversham (Reading) lock; in 1794 these were adjusted and the most favourable rate was brought back to Benson lock. Such drawbacks were given not only on cargoes by water from

Oxford but also on loads by road to Abingdon, Witney and even Lechlade. In 1795 wharf premises were bought at Reading and then let, and a trade seems to have been encouraged, probably short-lived and connected with the presence of the owner of the Kennet Navigation on the Oxford's committee, with the southern seaports via the Kennet and land carriage to the Andover Canal. In 1800 a wharf was opened at Wallingford, and in January 1801 up to six barges were ordered to be bought to promote the river trade. In the same year a fourth river wharf and buildings were leased at Abingdon. However, by no means all the trade onwards from Oxford went by river: Rushet's *Directory* of 1812 for Banbury tells us that: 'The boats are met at Oxford by regular land Carriers to and from Reading, Newbury, Winchester, Salisbury, Southampton, Portsmouth and all intermediate places.'

After 1810 the company began to feel competition along the Thames from coal carried on the Wilts & Berks Canal to Abingdon and the Kennet & Avon to Reading.[31] Standing shoulder to shoulder with the Thames Commissioners, however, they had successfully defeated the Western Junction bill of 1811, and prevented a second reading for that for the Severn Junction, later the North Wilts,[32] a victory that was considered important enough for the company to give their chairman, the Rev David Durell, £2,000, partly 'as an acknowledgement of the permanent and substantial benefit derived from his late unwearied assiduity in defending and supporting the interests of the Canal'.[33] In 1813, with competition getting more intense, they wrote to the Staffordshire coalowners to complain that the cargoes they were sending were of mixed quality: the coals 'on the outside of the Cargo are good, but those withinside are bad'.[34] They emphasized that quality had better improve if they were to compete, and that they would not give drawbacks on fraudulent cargoes. They also firmly maintained a policy of refusing to allow coal brought to Oxford by other canals connecting with the Thames to enter their basins, but insisted that the craft use the public wharves on the river.

In August 1795 the company became involved in the semi-famine conditions of the time. The Vice-Chancellor of the University wrote to the chairman, fearing that the high price of wheat might 'be made a handle for evil-designing persons, to stir up and commit much Mischief', and said that 'much sourness has arisen, and now exists, amongst the lower Class of People of the place, on account of the great Quantities of Corn which have lately been sent off from your wharf'[35] to Warwickshire and Staffordshire, some believing it to be going to Liverpool for export. It seems that some violence followed, for when Dr Durell the chairman wrote to the Under Secretary of State asking if it were practicable to find out what corn could properly be spared, and then to protect its transport, he referred to a disturbance which had intimidated those who used to supply Birmingham and Dudley. The Government replied that no corn had been exported for some time, and that it was wrong in law and policy to prevent the free circulation of corn in times of distress.

The company was financially prudent. Very soon after the canal had been completed, the shareholders created a reserve fund and began steadily to pay off debt. Their annual charge for loan interest, which was £6,506 in 1800, was down to £2,003 for 1829, by which time they had a reserve fund of £40,000. It rose again, because of borrowing to shorten the northern section, to £5,199 in 1835. Once again the shareholders set themselves to reduce it, and got it down to £2,198 p.a. in 1846, the first year in which they experienced a serious fall in revenue because of railway competition. Making a great effort, and reducing their dividend, they paid off all the remaining debt in three years. It was an admirable achievement. Here are some figures, averaged in three-year periods:

Years	Gross tolls* £	Dividends per cent
1791–3	18,478	2
1794–6	24,238	4⅓
1797–9	33,423	6
1800–2	39,598	10½
1803–5	50,686	13¾
1806–8	63,257	20⅔
1809–11	79,679	27
1812–14	85,699	31
1815–17	77,938	31
1818–20	81,018	32½
1821–3	82,671	32
1824–6	87,529	33⅓
1827–9	90,446	32
1830–2	85,457	32
1833–5	73,314	32
1836–8	84,779	30
1839–41	85,315	30

* Before drawbacks.

There had been many discussions with the Grand Junction and Coventry companies about widening and shortening the northern part of the Oxford Canal, but the notice in *Aris's Birmingham Gazette* of 12 November 1829 for a new canal from the Stratford line to Braunston demanded action. A committee meeting on 19 November thought the proposal 'highly injurious'[36] to their interests, and decided to oppose it. The company was, however, clear-headed enough to see that they had better put their house in order, and modernize a line which Rees's *Cyclopaedia* had thirty years earlier described as 'particularly ill-adapted to the great thoroughfare or communication which it forms with other canals'.[37] They at once called in Sir Marc Brunel, who recommended a shortened and improved line, and sent a bill for £512 19s 7d. He was followed by Charles Vignoles who surveyed it, and in 1829 a bill to authorize the shortening was introduced and passed. Within eighteen months of the original *Gazette* notice the company had its Act.[38]

The estimated cost was £131,877. Power was given to raise this sum, so that the capital would be in 1,786 48/100 shares. But the Act also laid down a new rates structure, which reduced tolls to a maximum of 1d per mile on coal and 1½d on everything else, but provided that on the new line they should be charged on the mileage of the old, to compensate the company for building it. The compensation tolls off the Warwick & Napton were substantially reduced to give that line an equivalent benefit, and the liability of the Grand Junction to provide traffic worth £10,000 p.a. was repealed. Finally, the compensation toll of 2s 9d a ton on coal which by the Grand Union Act of 1810 had to be paid by the Leicestershire & Northamptonshire Union to the Grand Union, and, when it passed to the Oxford, by the Grand Union to the Oxford company, was reduced to 1s 6d. These changes were to come into force from 31 March 1832, and their (largely temporary) effect can be seen in the figures quoted.

The scheme involved the shortening of the canal from 91 miles to 77⅜ miles by building a virtually new waterway over much of the ground between Hawkesbury and Wolfhampcote near Braunston. The alterations included a new tunnel, 250 yd long with double towing paths, at Newbold, the abandonment of the old Newbold tunnel and the short one at Wolfhampcote, the building of an embankment along one side of the Brinklow aqueduct to widen it, and of an iron aqueduct over the Rugby–Lutterworth road. The old curves were abandoned, graceful iron towing path bridges being built over them as they cut across the new line. Sections of them were turned into branches to points that had previously been on the main line: for instance, Stretton wharf branch ($\frac{1}{8}$ mile), now a cruiser station, Brinklow wharf branch ($\frac{1}{8}$ mile) and the Braunston branch ($\frac{1}{2}$ mile) from the new main line to the Grand Junction, a small part of the old line becoming a dock to serve Pickfords' premises there. The Brinklow branch got a new name in a newspaper report of 1857, when an 'aquatic party, per canal, from Coventry' with a brass band, ended their day thus: 'as the sun sank in the far West, the happy couples wended their way to the "Fair Rosamund" which was moored off "Brinklow Bay".'[39]

John Ferguson was appointed resident under the company's engineer, Frederick Wood, with William Cubitt as consultant, and work began in the year of the Act. The Coventry company now suggested a new junction with their canal as part of the improved line, by a cut from Ansty on the Oxford to near Bedworth, which involved a long embankment and a $1\frac{1}{2}$ mile tunnel, to be built at joint expense, the Oxford north of Ansty being abandoned. The latter company did not like the course chosen, thinking it expensive and difficult to maintain, and commissioned Cubitt to find an alternative. Meanwhile the Coventry were threatening to make the cut themselves, which would have deprived the Oxford of tolls, when they were stopped short by Peel.

The new line was opened on 13 February 1834 at a cost of £167,172. Then in early 1836 the Coventry's representative came to ask the Oxford's sanction to a new junction at Hawkesbury, to which the Oxford agreed so long as their tolls were protected. The junction was probably then made, the old line to Longford being retained for traffic to Coventry. The toll-clerk at the time of the change was Richard Sutton, who had first been appointed to the post in 1807; there was a Sutton in the job till 1876, and even now Hawkesbury turn is known to boatmen as Sutton Stop. The last branch on the line, the Wyken colliery company's $\frac{1}{4}$ mile long private canal to Wyken New Colliery from the Wyken loop of the original line, was probably built in 1840 as a result of an agreement of 13 November 1839. In 1840 the existing flight of three locks at Hillmorton was duplicated. The new locks, which were fitted with iron gates as the result of earlier experiments with the material on the Napton and Claydon flights, were expensive, because running sand was met with during their construction.

Doubtless the notices that had been issued early in January 1831

L

for a London and Birmingham railway had their influence upon the revised tolls embodied in the canal's Act of that year. While the line was building the company made considerable rate reductions, but were reluctant to parallel the toll cuts of other companies on the grounds of the reductions that had been made in the 1831 Act and the cost of the new improvements. Happily on one occasion, after reciting their views, they made an exception, and remitted 'one-third of the present tolls upon Burton Ale to London, and the same upon Staves and raw Cotton from London to Burton'.[40]

In 1838 the canal had carried 520,000 tons; of about this total in 1840, 345,407 had been interchange traffic with the Grand Junction, 50,790 ex-G.J.C. to Longford and 169,220 ex-Longford to the G.J.C., 93,754 ex-Warwick canals to G.J.C. and 31,643 ex-G.J.C. to the Warwick canals. In this year the tolls were £84,159 and the dividend 30 per cent. In 1842, again, 20,859 boats passed through Hillmorton locks, 9,900 over Claydon summit, and 14,515 to and from the Warwick & Napton. The Oxford clerics who controlled the company could reflect that they might be worldly, but they were certainly not incompetent. (*To continue the history of the Oxford Canal, turn to p. 214.*)

CHAPTER VIII

The Warwick
and Stratford Lines

++++++++++++++++++++++++++++++++++◆++++++++++++++++++++++++++++++++++

IN December 1789 the first connected water route—though it involved transhipment—was opened between Birmingham and London by way of the Staffs & Worcs Canal, the Severn, the Stroudwater and Thames & Severn Canals, and the Thames. It was followed, a few months later, in July 1790, by a much shorter line, still with transhipment, through Fazeley, the Coventry and Oxford Canals and the Thames. In 1791 the Worcester & Birmingham Canal was authorized to link Birmingham to the Severn by a new route less roundabout than that through Wolverhampton and Stourport. Handicapped by a physical bar between its water and the Birmingham Canal, and loaded with guarantees, the Worcester & Birmingham was, nevertheless, the first successful attempt to break the monopoly of the Birmingham company. In the early part of 1792 the ideas that became the Grand Junction and its unsuccessful rival the London & Western were being actively promoted. In the autumn of 1792 the Dudley Canal company were planning an extension of their line eastwards to join the Worcester & Birmingham at Selly Oak, which promised them a route to London independent of the Birmingham company.

The opening of the Fazeley line had seriously affected the trade of the Warwick market, which had been accustomed to sell corn to the Coventry area, sending it in waggons that brought coal back. Stratford was similarly affected, and therefore the two towns became interested in the possibilities of canals. The first plan, which a committee was promoting in August 1792, was for a line from either the Digbeth branch of the Birmingham or from the Worcester & Birmingham to Stratford, with a branch to Warwick. When this committee learned of the interest of the Dudley company in an extension to the Worcester & Birmingham, however, they realized at once the value of having alternative sources of coal supplies on the Dudley and the Birmingham canals, and therefore they also chose a connection with the Worcester & Birmingham.

By this time it was clear to the Birmingham company that the Grand Junction or the London & Western, and probably the former, would be authorized in 1793. If so, it was essential that they, and not the Dudley company, should be behind any concern with a line of canal to Warwick, since an extension to Braunston or Napton on the Oxford Canal would enable a junction to be made with a project that promised great things. Stratford was less important, for a canal there could only conveniently connect with the old-fashioned Upper Avon Navigation leading towards the Severn, a route already prospectively shared with the Worcester & Birmingham. The influence of the Birmingham company was exerted; the result was a split in the project. Part became the Warwick & Birmingham Canal, authorized in 1793 from the Digbeth branch of the Birmingham to Warwick, the rest the Stratford-upon-Avon Canal, also authorized in 1793 to that town but not, however, yet to join the river.

The Birmingham company had been right, for in 1794 the gap was filled by the Warwick & Braunston's Act for a canal from Warwick to the Oxford Canal at Braunston and so to the Grand Junction—a line later altered, together with the name of the company, so that a junction was made instead with the Oxford Canal at Napton, 5½ miles from Braunston. Both Warwick lines were opened to traffic on 19 March 1800; in November goods could pass the whole length of the Grand Junction, and once more the Birmingham to London canal route had been shortened. Thereafter the history of the Warwick line is mainly a tale of competition with the Coventry company, rivals in the trade from Birmingham, and of efforts to persuade the Oxford to mitigate its compensation tolls and supply much-needed water.

The Stratford Canal went through more vicissitudes[1] before it was opened on 24 June 1816 on a changed course to a junction with the Upper Avon Navigation. The most important intermediate date was 24 May 1802, when the first section, from King's Norton on the Worcester & Birmingham to Lapworth, together with a short branch to connect it with the Warwick & Birmingham, was finished. It was then possible for coal and other trade from the Dudley Canal, itself connected with the Stourbridge

Canal with access to Stourport and the Severn, to pass into the Warwick & Birmingham on its way to Midland destinations or London without touching the Birmingham company's canals, though the Warwick concerns put some difficulties in the way of this trade lest it should compete too severely with their own from Birmingham itself. To the Stratford company, however, this transit trade was most important. They tried also to build up traffic onwards from Stratford itself, by river down to Evesham, and by the Stratford & Moreton Tramway after its opening in September 1826. To some extent they succeeded, but neither became part of a through route, for the Avon was never a good enough navigation, and William James's hopes for an extension of the Stratford & Moreton towards London came to nothing.

Warwick & Birmingham Canal

The Warwick & Birmingham Canal was built with the benevolent help of the Birmingham company. At the first committee meeting of the new concern, they were thanked for 'their great Civility in assisting with their Surveyors this Canal Company',[2] for Samuel Bull, the Birmingham's engineer, had taken charge of the survey and produced an estimate of £95,000. William Felkin, who now became the company's engineer, did so from the Birmingham service. However, only two of the Warwick & Birmingham's committee were also on that of their powerful neighbour; the weight of influence came from Warwick, the first shareholders meeting was held there, and the Earl of Warwick strongly supported the project: 'the obtaining the Act . . . was owing to his Lordship's great Exertions in support of it', and he was asked whether he would allow his arms to be incorporated in the design of the company's seal 'with such other Device as his Lordship shall think most proper'.

The Act[3] was passed in March 1793; it authorized a canal from the Digbeth branch of the Birmingham, where there was to be a stop-lock, for 22⅝ miles to Warwick. From Digbeth the line rose by the six Camp Hill locks at Bordesley to its summit, which it maintained for some ten miles to Knowle, where there were six falling locks. Thence the canal ran through Shrewley tunnel (433 yd) to the top of the Hatton flight of 21 locks, not far from the bottom of which was its end at Saltisford wharf, Warwick. Tunnels were intended also at Rowington and at Yardley in Birmingham, but during construction changes in plans made them unnecessary. The authorized toll structure was peculiar. For coal and most commodities it was on the basis of 2d per mile with 1s minimum, falling to 1½d for distances over 16 miles, with a heavy additional charge for passing either of the locks at each end of the summit (2s 3d a ton), and for passing Hatton top-lock (2s 9d). Clearly, water supply difficulties were forecast. In addition, 6d a ton compensation toll was payable to the Birmingham company for outward traffic passing Digbeth stop-lock.

The company began by renting a house in Birmingham and instructed the clerk to 'put a skirting Board round the Room appropriated to the use of the Committee, and to put a Hearth stone, and Chimney piece to the same. To build a Brewhouse, Privy and Wall, to make the yard and Garden private and entire. To sink a Well and put down a pump—to glaze the windows in the room to be occupied as an Office', and later, to buy 'twelve Chairs, a Table, Window Blinds and Curtains'.[4] Moving into a new office was even more troublesome in those days than now.

Work began quickly. The original intention had been 'that the Bridges and Locks and Tunnels' should be 'of a sufficient Space for to admit Boats only to pass under them and not Barges',[5] but perhaps influenced by the starting of work on the Grand Junction, intended as a barge canal, the committee in April 1794 ordered that the tunnel should be built 16 ft wide, and in May that bridges should be made with 21 ft of space beneath them. The main source of water was a reservoir at Olton, but in 1796 a Boulton & Watt engine started work at Bowyer Street, Bordesley, to pump water from the bottom to the top of Camp Hill locks. By the autumn of 1795 £81,000 had been spent, and it was obvious that more than the £100,000 authorized would be needed. A further Act[6] was therefore passed in 1796 to enable £50,000 more to be raised in £50 half-shares as well as an extra £30,000 under the original Act. These half-shares were mostly subscribed for by the original share-holders at the rate of one for each full share held.

The company shared the financial troubles of the time. At the end of 1795 interest on calls was ended; in June 1796 the number of men employed had to be reduced while arrears were chased; in the autumn of 1797, most of the new shares having been issued, the committee were finding it hard to borrow £30,000, and in January 1798 a shareholders' meeting was called to 'determine whether the Workmen now employed shall be discharged and the Works stopped, the Money at present agreed to be lent being totally insufficient'.[7] However, sufficient loans were raised to let work go on, so that the opening could be simultaneous with that of the Warwick & Napton. This took place ceremonially for both canals on 19 December 1799, but more work clearly had to be done, for trading began on 19 March 1800. The cost had been about £160,000.

There had been some engineering vicissitudes, starting with the collapse of the aqueduct over the River Blyth in late 1795. The company then advertised for a new engineer, but in fact made no change, and in May 1796 the first nine miles from Birmingham to Henwood were opened. There was more criticism of the engineer, and in November William Felkin was dismissed, only to be taken on again when his successor failed to take up the job. He left finally at the end of 1797, his accounts having been investigated because he seemed to be paying contractors more than was due to them. He was replaced by Philip Henry Witton, who added engineering to his existing job of clerk-accountant, and finished the canal. He in turn left in October 1800, and after two short stayers the job was taken by Thomas Sheasby, who had helped to engineer the Swansea, Neath and Glamorganshire Canals;[8] owing to ill-health he was replaced in 1804 by Thomas Green.

Two of the matters which most affected the company will be dealt with elsewhere, the junction with the Stratford at Kingswood under that canal, and the compensation tolls at Napton and the competition with the Coventry line in the account of the Warwick & Napton. The other main events of the company's early life can be quickly told.

In 1805, coincident with the full opening of the Grand Junction, that company proposed to raise its tolls. This was strongly opposed by the Warwick & Birmingham, 'which was cut and opened into the Grand Junction Canal in full dependence of the tonnages on that Canal remaining unaltered',[9] and they got the bill satisfactorily amended. Ten years later the company successfully negotiated with the Birmingham an agreement to give them reductions equivalent to those to be made when Worcester Bar was removed on 21 July 1815.

In 1820 the annual resolution of the shareholders empowering the committee to take necessary action on any bills of other canal companies that might affect their interests for the first time included the ominous word 'railway'. In 1824 there was much talk of such round Birmingham and in 1825, when the Warwick & Birmingham had a delegation in London opposing them, the company were taking a gloomy view. Already, they said, the prices of coal and iron had increased alarmingly. Much land would be used, horses and cattle would be destroyed, residents would be annoyed, and 'the Engines, moving with a high pressure, will occasionally burst and cause the loss of many lives'.[10]

Like the Oxford company, the Warwick & Birmingham were greatly taken aback when they first heard of the proposed London & Birmingham Junction project, which proposed to cut across their line from the Stratford Canal to Braunston. While affirming that the country was 'already amply provided with Water communication by the existing Canals made at great risque and expense upon the faith of Parliament',[11] they hurried to mobilize canal companies as far away as the Ellesmere in their support (including, oddly enough, the Birmingham & Liverpool Junction); to get landowners to resist; and to engage an engineer to give evidence against the new proposal. They continued to oppose the later manifestations of the idea, and after 1831 added the London & Birmingham Railway. This same year also saw the beginnings of general toll reductions on the Birmingham & Fazeley, Coventry and Oxford lines, as well as on the Warwick canals, and a growth in drawbacks and bounties, which reflected increased inter-canal competition, falling road carriage rates, reductions due to the abolition of the coastwise duties on coal, and precautionary moves against railway promotion. Symptoms of increasing competition were anxiety to get more water, which caused the company in 1833 to contribute £1,500 to the cost of enlarging Boddington reservoir on the Oxford Canal, and their later decision to participate in the building of the Birmingham & Warwick Junction Canal (see p. 176).

In the late 1830s about 250,000 tons passed on to or off the canal at the junction with the Birmingham at Digbeth. The company's dividend record was as follows, averaged in three-year periods:

Years Y.e. 31 March	Average dividend per cent
1803–5	$1\frac{1}{2}$
1806–8	$5\frac{1}{6}$
1809–11	$8\frac{1}{3}$
1812–14	12
1815–17	12
1818–20	$10\frac{2}{3}$
1821–3	$10\frac{2}{3}$
1824–6	11

Years *Y.e. 31 March*	*Average dividend* *per cent*
1827–9	$11\frac{5}{6}$
1830–2	$12\frac{1}{2}$
1833–5	$14\frac{1}{2}$
1836–8	$15\frac{1}{2}$
1839–41	$16\frac{1}{2}$

In these figures can be read the jump in dividend when the Grand Junction was fully opened in March 1805; the favourable effect of the ending of rate-cutting with the Coventry Canal in 1810; the sudden fall in 1815 and 1816 when the opening of the Leicester line brought Derbyshire and Nottinghamshire coal to compete with that from Staffordshire; and the effect of the improvements made to the Birmingham Canal main line between 1829 and April 1838, and of the completion of the Birmingham & Liverpool Junction in March 1835. The dividend reached its highest point of 18 per cent for the year ending 31 March 1839, the year in which the London & Birmingham Railway was opened; seven years later it was down to 3 per cent. (*To continue the history of the Warwick & Birmingham Canal, turn to p. 229.*)

Warwick & Napton Canal

The Warwick & Braunston Canal (as it was first called) was promoted in the autumn of 1792 by those who were shareholders in the Warwick & Birmingham, and surveyed early in 1793 'to Braunston and Napton'[12] before that company had got its Act. Though many Birmingham banking and other names appear on the shareholders' register, again the main driving force seems to have come from Warwick. Dr Walter Landor, the father of Walter Savage Landor, who had married an heiress and lived at Warwick, was frequently chairman in the early days, the company's bankers and solicitor were there, and perhaps the most energetic man behind the company, John Tomes, was a Warwick solicitor who later became the town's Member; he was present at the first meeting, and was chairman from 1807 to 1841, as well as being a committeeman of the Warwick & Birmingham. Others who had great influence over it were John Towers Lawrence, who joined the committee in 1825 in his father's place—he was also on the committees of the Warwick & Birmingham and the Dudley—and Kelynge Greenway, treasurer from 1806 of both the Warwick canals, a member of the committee of the Napton from 1818 and of the Warwick & Birmingham from 1824.

In the middle of 1793 the promoting committee were uncertain whether to join the Oxford Canal or the Grand Junction direct. William Felkin, the engineer of the Warwick & Birmingham, James Sheriff, Charles Handley and Samuel Bull, the engineer of the Birmingham, were all concerned in surveying and estimating and out of their efforts came proposals for two lines, one from the Warwick & Birmingham at Warwick to the Oxford Canal at Braunston, the other a branch from Warwick to the Oxford at Fenny Compton, the first to connect immediately with the Grand Junction, the second to serve places at the southern end of the Oxford Canal.

The Stratford company had already projected a branch from their canal to the Oxford at Fenny Compton, to which the new proposal was a counter; neither plan was acceptable to the Oxford company once the London & Western scheme had been defeated and the Grand Junction authorized, for either would seriously have interfered with the Oxford's own long-distance trade down its own canal. The Oxford company therefore asked for compensation terms so high as to be prohibitive, and when in October a delegation went to talk further to them, the Warwick & Braunston representatives were kept waiting for a considerable time in the next room to the Oxford committee, had to pass notes backwards and forwards, and in the end never met them that day. Approaches were also made to the Stratford company for a junction with their line at Lapworth, and to the Worcester & Birmingham and Dudley to support it, but the Stratford, foolishly as it turned out, overplayed their hand and asked for compensation. The Warwick & Braunston then suggested that both proposed branches to Fenny Compton should be postponed, and that later, when they were better able, the two companies should judge 'whether the proposed Communication between the Warwick and the Stratford Canals will be immediately beneficial to the two Concerns or in any and what degree detrimental to either of them'.[13] They then dropped their own Fenny Compton project.

The company's Act[14] of 1794 therefore provided for a canal $17\frac{7}{8}$ miles long to join the Oxford at Braunston, at a cost estimated by William Felkin at £82,444. The capital authorized was £100,000, with power to raise £30,000 more. Since the Warwick & Braunston, like the later Grand Union, was to be a linking canal with little local trade, the tolls were favourable to long-distance traffic.

Since it was likely that much of the Birmingham trade to Oxford and on to the newly authorized Grand Junction would in future pass by the Warwick & Birmingham and the new canal rather than by Hawkesbury, the Oxford company insisted on substantial compensation tolls. Coal out of the Warwick & Braunston was to pay 2s 9d per ton, and other goods (except lime, limestone and manure) to or from the Warwick & Braunston 4s 4d, rates equivalent to those charged on the northern section of the Oxford. Lime and limestone out of the new canal were to pay 6d. These payments were to include tolls on the Oxford to the Grand Junction or north as far as the Coventry Canal, but not south, and were to be counted towards the guarantee of annual receipts already given by the Grand Junction. Since it was foreseen that intelligent men might try to avoid these high compensation tolls by carrying goods round from the Oxford to the Grand Junction by land carriage, this was forbidden under penalties.

The company gave themselves the same clerk and treasurer as the Warwick & Birmingham, and had an interlocking committee. In 1794 thirteen of the Warwick & Birmingham's committee of fifteen were also on that of the Warwick & Braunston, while thirteen of the latter's twenty were also on the former's committee. Shareholders in the older canal were entitled to preference in subscribing for three shares each in the newer.

William Felkin was appointed engineer, and work began in 1795. Then, in August, Charles Handley, one of the appointed valuers, who was described as a yeoman of Barford in Warwickshire and who must have been a substantial man, suggested that £50,000 would be saved if the authorized line were varied from the Fosse Way at Offchurch onwards so that the canal joined the Oxford at Napton instead of at Braunston. The engineer agreed, Handley was asked to accept 300 guineas for 'his Indefatigable attention and perseverance in exploring . . . the Line of Canal between the Fosse Road and Napton, and the practicability of executing the same',[15] and in September it was decided to seek an Act for the varied line. We may, however, guess at controversy from the rule adopted by the committee in November 'that when the Chairman calls to Order every Member of the Committee shall immediately be silent'.[16] The cause seems to have been that the decision to change the line was taken without telling Lord Warwick, although he was a member of the committee.

The Grand Junction seized the opportunity to try to persuade the Warwick & Braunston to build their canal broad, for if theirs and the Warwick & Birmingham as far as Kingswood could be made so, the Grand Junction foresaw a barge communication to Worcester and the Severn, since at that time the Worcester & Birmingham was intended to be a barge canal, and was indeed built with broad tunnels. Otherwise it was feared that goods would have to be transhipped at Braunston between wide and narrow craft. The company was unmoved by the Grand Junction's plea, for its main hopes of trade lay in the Birmingham's and Dudley's narrow canal network, and got its Act[17] in May 1796. It explained that the original line through Bascote, Long Itchington, Birdingbury, Leamington Hastings, Broadwell, Grandborough, Woolscott and Willoughby was 'incommodious for Navigation', and would involve a tunnel over 800 yd long that could be avoided by the new line. The compensation tolls to the Oxford company were raised to take account of the greater distance from Braunston, to 3s 4d on coal not going to the Grand Junction, and 5s 2½d on other goods, and to the Grand Junction 2s 9d on coal and 4s 4d on other goods as before. In addition compensation of 6d a ton now had to be paid to the Grand Junction on interchange traffic between the Warwick & Napton (as its name now became) and the Oxford to the south.

In March 1796 the company decided to replace Felkin by an engineer who was not also employed elsewhere, and after a false start with John Turpin of Wisbech they chose their own Charles Handley at 350 guineas a year including valuation fees, plus five free shares should the work be completed satisfactorily.

Work now went on. A tunnel was avoided at Leamington by paying compensation to be allowed to deviate the line; instead of a reservoir the company decided to buy its water from the Oxford at a charge of 2s per boat passing the junction at Napton; there was the usual trouble with arrears of calls. In the spring of 1799, after a difference of opinion with the Earl of Warwick, who had helped to get the canal Act and had been on the committee from the beginning, it was resolved: 'That for the purpose of having an effective Gentleman upon the Committee, and without any disrespect towards the Earl of Warwick, his Lordship be discontinued as one of the Committee.'[18] Then in September they were so short of money that £4,000 had to be borrowed 'under circumstances of peculiar embarrassment to the Company'[19] with an option to convert to shares at par after two years—£2,900 of it from John Tomes—and then on Tuesday 17 December it was resolved 'that Three Shillings per head be allowed for each of the men employed on the Canal, to be expended on Thursday next for Dinner and Beer at the Black Swan, George, and Kings Head Inns in Warwick'.[20] As with the Warwick & Birmingham, the opening on the 19th was formal, the canal being advertised as open to traders on 19 March 1800.[21] Charles Handley was given his five free shares 'for the faithful and able manner in which he has discharged the Duties of Engineer',[22] and retained at £150 p.a.

The canal was 14¼ miles long from its junction with the Warwick & Birmingham at Budbrooke to Napton. The line fell by two locks to the Avon, which was crossed by a three-arched aqueduct that Henry Couchman, a long-standing member of the committee, had helped to design, and then rose by 23 locks to Napton junction; all were built narrow. Construction of the canal had cost about £75,000.

The company then decided to build a reservoir at Napton, instead of buying water from the Oxford. Later again, between 1807 and 1815, Boddington reservoir was built by the Oxford company on its own line, but at the cost of the Warwick & Napton, and enlarged in 1833 at the joint cost of the two Warwick canals. Napton reservoir was duplicated in 1814.

With the Grand Junction open towards the end of 1800, an effort had to be made by the two Warwick companies to divert traffic from the Coventry line in face of the keen competition of that company and the Birmingham's preference for the northern route, since they owned the canal as far as Fazeley and therefore got better tolls upon it than they made from the 6d compensation payment at Digbeth. In September the two concerns, who worked closely together and held regular unofficial meetings, agreed that they would jointly pay the Oxford Canal 1s 5d a ton on coal going towards the Grand Junction, and 1s 3d if going towards Oxford, to reduce the compensation tolls that would otherwise have to be paid by the carriers; three-fifths of the cost would be paid by the Warwick & Birmingham and two-fifths by the Napton. A year later price-cutting with the Coventry began, and payments to the Oxford were raised in two stages to 2s 5d and 2s 3d. The pace was hot, and in May 1803 negotiations were opened with the Coventry for an agreement. It took till 1810 to make it, to enable markets to be shared, tolls raised, and the bounty paid to the Oxford to be reduced by 6d. Such a move may have been necessary in their own interests, but Staffordshire coal, on which both the Coventry and the Warwick lines mainly relied, was feeling competition from Gloucestershire and from seaborne coal from the Tyne which, because it had cheapened, was penetrating up rivers like the Nene into Staffordshire markets, and the higher tolls, unpopular with the coalmasters, lessened its sales.

The sudden irruption of Derbyshire coal into this existing competition by the opening of the Grand Union caused the company to restore the bounty to its former level, though the reason was now to maintain its coal trade, not against that carried on the Coventry, but against that of the Leicester line. Not till about 1842 was the agreement with the Coventry abandoned, and by then Leicestershire as well as Derbyshire coal had obtained a share of the market.

In 1816 the Birmingham company granted a drawback on iron passing by the Fazeley route which removed the trade from the Warwick line, and caused the two companies to give another bounty to the Oxford to reduce the compensation tolls. This helped, but the Warwick & Birmingham was still complaining in 1820. A similar bounty was given on salt. There was no real answer to the Birmingham's natural tendency to favour its own line. In 1824, for instance, the Warwick & Birmingham complained that whereas the Birmingham & Fazeley line was open day and night, Ashted locks leading to Digbeth were often closed. The Birmingham company blandly replied that the Fazeley line was open for the dispatch of urgent Liverpool goods, and that when the Warwick line was equally busy, they would provide equal facilities.

However, the company was doing very well, as the following figures show:

Years Y.e. 28 Feb.	Average dividend per cent	Years Y.e. 28 Feb.	Average dividend per cent
1800–2	$\frac{1}{2}$	1821–3	$9\frac{2}{3}$
1803–5	3	1824–6	$11\frac{1}{6}$
1806–8	$5\frac{1}{3}$	1827–9	$11\frac{1}{6}$
1809–11	$10\frac{2}{3}$	1830–2	11
1812–14	13	1833–5	$9\frac{2}{3}$
1815–17	$9\frac{1}{6}$	1836–8	$13\frac{2}{3}$
1818–20	$10\frac{1}{2}$	1839–41	$11\frac{1}{3}$

A first dividend of $1\frac{1}{2}$ per cent was paid in 1802, by 1810 the rate had reached 10 and in 1814 15 per cent before the opening of the Leicester line and the competition of Derbyshire coal brought it back to about 10 per cent thereafter.

Considering all change as for the worse, the Warwick & Napton

opposed almost every canal bill in sight; the Grand Union because
it would bring competing coal from the north of the Trent, the
North Wilts because it would make easier the passage of Staffordshire and Forest coal to the Oxford area via Abingdon, the Central
Junction link between the Stratford Canal and the Wilts & Berks[23]
because it might decrease trade off the Stratford line at Kingswood, and the first Birmingham proposal for what later became
the Tame Valley line, because this would tend to divert trade via
Fazeley and the Coventry line.

In 1819 the company had agreed to a private cut being made by
Charles Handley and John Tomes from the canal near Long
Itchington; probably that now running south from near the
bottom of Stockton locks to limeworks and a quarry, and known
as Kaye's Arm. As early as 1815 a plan had been made and deposited for a level branch 2½ miles long to Southam. The project
was revived in 1819, when delegates attended a Warwick &
Napton committee meeting and were promised £500. A bill seems
to have been introduced in March, but not proceeded with.

In 1820 the records contain the first mention of railway bills.
The company naturally opposed them, but also worked to improve
its own efficiency, by providing assistance to lock-keepers so that
the locks could be kept open for longer hours, by trying to keep
traffic moving during frosts, and by enlarging Boddington reservoir 'to remove every apprehension of want of an ample supply of
water to carry on the Trade, and to defeat the interested statements
put forth, that the Trade of the Country cannot be carried on by
water communications and Canals'.[24] At the same time inter-canal
rivalry continued. They tried to get their lock-keepers to work
boats faster in order to attract Manchester–London traffic from
the Coventry line, and, to counteract the threat of the proposed
London & Birmingham Junction, sought the alliance of the Stratford company by at last granting them the full bounty on coal they
had wanted for so long, while pressing the Oxford to reduce its
compensation payments. This was achieved by the Oxford Canal
Act of 1829, that which authorized the shortenings of that company's line. The Act reduced payments to the Oxford for coal
passing towards London from 2s 9d to 1s 6d; for iron from 4s 4d
to 1s 2d, for grain from 4s 4d to 1s 6d, and merchandise from 4s
to 3s. Those for goods passing towards Oxford were reduced still
further.

In 1831, along with other canals on the Warwick and Fazeley
lines to London, the company reduced its tolls, to ward off the

combined threats of the London & Birmingham canal project and
of the railway. The latter, they considered, would injure 'the
Landed Interest generally without any corresponding or permanent advantage to the Country',[25] but all the same they refused
to contribute £10 towards the publication of Mr Cort's writings
exposing 'the ruinous projects of Railways'.[26] In 1838 the London
& Birmingham Railway was opened throughout, and in 1839
price-cutting began. The good days were over. (*To continue the
history of the Warwick & Napton Canal, turn to p. 229.*)

Birmingham & Warwick Junction Canal

The improvements to the main line of the Birmingham Canal,
completed in 1829, caused greater congestion than ever at Farmer's
Bridge locks leading to Aston junction, whence the Ashted locks
gave access to the Warwick & Birmingham and the Aston flight
to the Birmingham & Fazeley. Relief had been promised by the
western section of the proposed London & Birmingham Junction,
connecting the Worcester & Birmingham with the Warwick &
Birmingham on its way to the Oxford Canal. When this collapsed
ignominiously in the spring of 1830, a substitute, the Union Canal,
was late the same year advertised by Joseph Parkes, the solicitor
to the Warwick & Birmingham, to join the Worcester & Birmingham near Upper Gough Street to the Warwick & Birmingham
near Camp Hill locks. It was to be nearly two miles long, with two
short tunnels and eight locks, Francis Giles being named engineer.
Ostensibly the case for it seemed good, but probably an important reason for its promotion was that the Stratford Canal was
trying to get the Warwick & Birmingham's compensation tolls at
Kingswood reduced, and the Union project, which provided an
alternative route for Dudley Canal traffic going towards London,
provided a convincing counter-argument. It convinced the Stratford company, who dropped their demands for a revision of the
Kingswood tolls in exchange for a withdrawal of the bill.
In 1836 the Birmingham company, now engaged on the last
stages of their main line improvements, and faced with the additional traffic that had been coming off the Birmingham & Liverpool Junction since that canal had been opened in 1835, were
planning what was to be authorized in 1839 and 1840 as the Tame
Valley line from Danks branch to Salford Bridge junction on the
Birmingham & Fazeley, on to which line the traffic would go

Birmingham & Warwick Junction Canal.

Notice is hereby given, that the Birmingham and Warwick Junction Canal, leading from the Warwick and Birmingham Canal, to the Tame Valley Canal, at Salford Bridge, will be Opened for the use of the Public, on **WEDNESDAY** Morning, the 14th February instant.

CHARLES LLOYD,
Clerk to the Company.

Navigation Office, Birmingham,
1st February, 1844.

M

unless it were offered an alternative. A meeting in November at
Warwick therefore thought it to the interest of the Warwick &
Birmingham to revive a plan, attributed to Giles, for a canal from
Salford Bridge to Camp Hill near Bordesley on the Warwick &
Birmingham, and Frederick Wood, engineer of the Oxford, was
asked to survey and estimate for it. As surveyed, it much re-
sembled the 1830 plan. A line was proposed from the Birmingham
and the Worcester & Birmingham to the Warwick & Birmingham
and then, not to Salford Bridge, but to Aston locks. However, the
Worcester & Birmingham disliked the project, its financial prospects were dubious, and nothing was done.

In 1839, when the first Tame Valley Act was passed, the Salford
Bridge–Bordesley section of the earlier proposal was revived with
Warwick & Birmingham support. It was re-surveyed by Frederick
Wood, and in 1840 a bill[27] was introduced, and passed on the same
day as the second Tame Valley Act.

The Birmingham & Warwick Junction was the creature of the
two Warwick canals, who provided its officers, and in September
agreed to finance it because of its likely advantages 'in preserving
and maintaining the Warwick and Birmingham and Warwick and
Napton Canals in the enjoyment of their present Trade'.[28] James
Potter was the engineer, Clarkson and Hall the contractors; the
line, 2⅜ miles long with six falling locks from Bordesley to Salford,
was opened on Wednesday 14 February 1844, on the same day as
the Tame Valley line itself, and brought the possibility of new
traffic to the Warwick line. The water from the canal's locks was
led into Saltley reservoir, whence a new engine that had replaced
the Boulton & Watt raised it to the top of Camp Hill locks. About
1936 centrifugal pumps were installed, driven by diesels, later
replaced by electric motors. The Warwick & Birmingham held
335 of the 600 £100 shares, the Napton company the rest, and
between them the two companies provided £52,579 of loans also
in the same proportions. The total cost was therefore £112,579.[29]
Subsequently the loans were repaid, and the profits of the B. &
W.J. were then divided between the two parents in the proportions of twenty-two thirty-sevenths to the Warwick & Birmingham and the balance to the Napton.

No separate minute books seem to have been kept after 1845,
the canal being managed by the Warwick & Birmingham in the
joint interest of the two Warwick companies. (*To continue the
history of the Birmingham & Warwick Junction, turn to p. 229.*)

Stratford-upon-Avon Canal

The Warwick line having become a separate project, the Stratford Canal was planned from King's Norton on the Worcester & Birmingham past Lapworth, where the line ran within two miles of the Warwick & Birmingham, to a terminus in the town of Stratford, but not communicating with the River Avon.[30] The Act[31] was passed in March 1793, a capital of £120,000 being authorized, with power to raise £60,000 more.

Two connections with other lines were at once considered. After rather trying negotiations with the Oxford company, the idea of an extension to Fenny Compton on that canal was dropped, but in 1795 a supplementary Act[32] authorized a junction line, 1¾ miles long, between the Stratford and the Warwick & Birmingham Canals at Lapworth, and £10,000 more capital. The latter company exacted a substantial compensation toll of 11d on coal and 11d or 1s on other commodities, but the Stratford, supported by the Dudley company which was building its Selly Oak extension, hoped that in spite of them a good trade in coal off the Dudley's line towards the Grand Junction could be built up.

Construction of the main line began in November 1793 from King's Norton, the engineer being Josiah Clowes, who was also building the Dudley extension. It was completed to Hockley Heath on 25 May 1796, by which time Clowes was dead, and most of the authorized capital had already been spent. For a time the company rested, short of money and without incentive to continue. When, however, the Lappal tunnel of the Dudley extension was completed early in 1798 and allowed that line to be opened and to make coal supplies available, and when progress in the building of the two Warwick canals and of the Grand Junction itself made it evident that the whole line would be open within a year or two, the Stratford company awoke, and in 1799 obtained a third Act to authorize further capital, to vary their line to bring it much nearer to the Warwick & Birmingham and so reduce the length of the proposed connection to ⅛ mile, and to give the latter a further ½d a ton in compensation tolls.

In 1799 cutting began again, with Samuel Porter, who had been Clowes's assistant, as engineer. He took the canal to Harborough Banks near Kingswood, and built the short branch into the Warwick & Birmingham, opened on 24 May 1802. There work stopped once more, after £153,771 had been raised, and £150 called on each active share. Trade was mainly from the Dudley Canal through to the Oxford line, but the Warwick companies refused to let it qualify for the toll rebates they gave their own traffic, which to some extent offset the heavy compensation tolls of the Oxford company at Napton, and so forced the Stratford company to reduce its own tolls to a very low figure in order to get business.

It was not till 1812, after financial false starts and the making of many alternative plans, that cutting once more began, with William James in charge. In 1813 he personally bought the Upper Avon Navigation; in 1815 a Stratford Act authorized the canal company to join the river (and also make the Earlswood reservoirs) and on 24 June 1816 the line was completed to the Avon, at a total cost of about £297,000. It was 25⅝ miles long, level from King's Norton to Lapworth, and then falling by 54 narrow locks, 25 of them in the Lapworth flight, to the basins at Stratford, and then by a barge lock to the river. Notable features were the 352 yd broad tunnel at King's Norton, the brick aqueduct over the Cole, and the three iron aqueducts at Bearley, Wootton Wawen and Yarningale near Preston Bagot.

A good trade built up along the section of canal between King's Norton and Lapworth (Kingswood), though much of it had to be carried at low tolls. To Stratford itself the main traffic was coal, for the town and neighbourhood, the Upper Avon down to Evesham, and carriage along the Stratford & Moreton Tramway after that line had been opened in 1826, with a branch to Shipston in 1836. More money had had to be borrowed, however, and not till 1824 was a first dividend of £1 paid. The rate was not to exceed £2 per £150 share during the canal's independent life. For the year 1838* the total revenue was £13,646, the profit £6,835, dividend £2, and traffic carried 181,708 tons.

From 1827 to about 1836 hopes of greater prosperity were created in the hearts and pockets of the Stratford's shareholders by varying plans for the proposed London & Birmingham Junction Canal, which was planned to start from points along the Stratford's line between King's Norton and Lapworth and which, if it had been built, might have attracted to itself much of the through traffic to London. But nothing came of it.

In 1842 the company agreed to lease the Upper Avon to Evesham for five years at £400 p.a. rising to £450 to protect, and if

* Year ending 31 May.

possible increase, its Avon trade. And so, having reasonably justified the traffic, but not the financial, hopes of its original promoters, the company entered the railway mania year of 1845. (*To
continue the history of the Stratford-upon-Avon Canal, turn to p.
208.*)

PART THREE—1845–1947

CHAPTER IX

Round about the Trent

❖❖

BETWEEN 1840, when the Midland Counties Railway was opened to Leicester, and 1910, the canal line between Cromford and its union with the Grand Junction at Norton carried coal at lessening tolls against increasing railway competition. In that year the closing of the Foxton inclined plane marked the end of the struggle.

Except for the Cromford Canal itself, from which only part of the supplies came, the line never fell under railway control. All the same, competition was unequal, for on one side were ranged the Midland Railway,* the greatest coal-carrying line in the kingdom, and the London & North-Western; on the other five small canal companies on the 78 miles of waterway between Langley Mill and Norton, each continually adjusting its own tolls, granting its own drawbacks or boatage charges, to get the best slice it could from the diminishing cake. Sometimes they all reached an agreement on tolls, but by the time five committees exchanging correspondence to be read at infrequent meetings had at last made a decision, the situation with which it was meant to deal had changed, and the laborious and lagging negotiations began again. This situation did improve a little. The Erewash and Loughborough companies had always shared officials and worked closely together, and later in the century the Leicester moved closer to them. Farther south necessity drove the Leicestershire & Northamptonshire Union and the Grand Union to a similar collaboration.

The five dancers all faced one way, towards the Grand Junction, the sixth and greatest, which did most of the long-distance carrying, and could never be ignored. It did not, however, dominate until 1894, when it bought the Grand Union and the old Union and extended its line to Leicester, as a preliminary to a last great

---

* Formed in May 1844 by amalgamation of the North Midland, Midland Counties and Birmingham & Derby Junction Railways.

effort to compete in the Nottinghamshire and Derbyshire coal trade. One common factor was that none of the small companies was a carrier. When Pickfords left the canals at Christmas 1846, the Grand Junction's new carrying department was given low maximum tolls over the five lines, operating there until 1876 when Fellows, Morton & Clayton replaced it.

The railway mania year of 1845 saw abortive amalgamation talks between the Erewash, Loughborough and Leicester companies, proposals from the promoters of a railway from Nottingham to Ambergate to join the Cromford, Erewash and Nottingham canals in one concern, and eventually a pledge by four companies 'not to sell or dispose of their several Lines of Canal to any Railroad Company, or otherwise, whereby the line of communication by Canal as at present existing, may be broken or interrupted'.[1] The old Union refused to pledge itself, but instead offered a lease of its line to the Leicester, Loughborough and Erewash companies for 21 years at £8,581 10s 0d p.a. or £4 10s 0d a share. These three then got in touch with the Grand Union and the Grand Junction, but soon afterwards, as a result of opposition by canal companies to the sale of the Oakham Canal to the Midland Railway, Parliament decided to consider the whole subject of railway and canal amalgamation, and the offer dropped.

The Cromford company, whose dividends the wind of change had already halved, flirted with two suitors before in November choosing the Manchester, Buxton, Matlock & Midlands Junction Railway, a line projected from the Birmingham–Manchester line at Cheadle to the Midland Railway at Ambergate. The price was £103,500, and the purchase was completed on 30 August 1852. The effect of railway competition can be seen from these figures: typically, a small fall in tonnage was accompanied by a much larger fall in receipts from tolls.

Date	Dividends £120 shares £	Tons carried	Tolls £
1841	24	320,571¾	12,086
1843	15½	297,296¼	10,409
1845	12	258,052¼	8,788
1847	10	302,486	9,159
1849	10	300,639¾	9,138
1850	10	284,889¼	7,588

Under the pressure of opposition from several canal companies, a clause was included in the Act authorizing the sale similar to that in the Ashby's Act, to give the connecting canals the right to call for a reduction of tolls if they reduced them on their own lines. Immediately before the purchase was completed, the railway company was leased jointly to the Midland and L.N.W.R. for nineteen years; in 1870 the Midland bought both it and the canal.

Traffic fell away steadily, for in addition to the disadvantages of railway ownership, the canal had the M.R. line alongside it the whole way, and the G.N.R. also from Pinxton to Langley Mill. The 284,889 tons of 1850 fell to 145,814 in 1870, 84,990 in 1880 and 45,799 in 1888, trade becoming at the same time more local.

Below Langley Mill the effect on the canals of railway expansion and competition can be seen in the following summarized figures:

	Erewash	Lough-borough	Revenue Leicester	L. & N.U.	Grand Union
	£	£	£	£	£
1842–4	7,808		6,411	11,771	
1845–7	7,292		8,625	12,327	
1848–50	6,976		6,221	11,355	7,551 (1848 only)
1851–3	5,132		4,766	7,227	
1854–6	4,353		3,843	6,146	
1857–9	3,699		3,308	3,995	3,108 (1858 only)
1860–2	3,539		3,364	3,113	
1863–5	3,636		3,404	2,800	2,924 (1865 only)
1866–8	3,562		3,355	2,769	2,653
1869–71	3,363		3,221	2,520	2,246

			Dividends per cent		
1842–4	39·7	61·7	18·9	4·2	1·6
1845–7	32·7	61·1	18·6	4·75	1·9
1848–50	34·0	48·6	12·6	4·5	1·7
1851–3	23·3	38·9	9·8	2·5	1·1
1854–6	20·7	30·3	7·0	2·0	0·8
1857–9	13·3	22·2	5·9	1·1	0·7
1860–2	12·0	22·8	6·0	0·9	0·45
1863–5	13·0	18·9	6·8	0·75	0·5
1866–8	11·7	22·5	6·2	0·7	0·35
1869–71	11·3	20·8	6·0	0·6	0·3

In 1845 the Erewash Valley Railway had been authorized from Long Eaton junction to Codnor Park after determined canal opposition; it was opened in 1847, and competition increased. Toll reductions were made and drawbacks multiplied in an effort to

keep the long-distance trade: on coal, for instance, to the Trent &
Mersey, to the Melton Mowbray, to the Grand Junction in
general, to the Buckingham and Aylesbury arms in particular. In
1847 the Erewash company allowed boats through its locks at all
times, except for a few hours on Sundays, but they had to complain of 'the great falling off of the Tonnage upon Derbyshire
Coal',[2] and 'how difficult it is to get three or four Companies to
agree on any plan for the benefit of all'.[3] In addition to the through
canal trade, however, they could pick up a small toll from coal
brought by rail to Long Eaton basin to be transhipped for the
short run down the canal and then on to the Trent. The company's
only departure from normal was when in 1881 they suddenly built
the Midland Hotel at Langley Mill,* and then sold it in 1890 for
almost twice its cost; the profits paid for a number of improvements.

Once the Erewash Valley Railway had been opened, branch
lines followed to collieries such as Nutbrook and Shipley which
were sending their coal by the Nutbrook Canal, or by tramroads
to the Erewash. Some new business came, however, when in 1846
Benjamin Smith and his son Josiah (the family had formerly had
ironworks at Chesterfield and elsewhere) were granted a lease in
the parishes of Dale and Stanton-by-Dale. They built three small
blast-furnaces and a general foundry, using local deposits of ironstone, coal and limestone brought by canal, which took the pig-
iron away. In 1858 the concern was re-formed under new management as the Stanton ironworks. The company was later to buy the
Nutbrook Canal.[4]

South of the Trent the Loughborough and Leicester companies
were carrying Derbyshire coal towards London in competition
with rail-borne supplies and with cargoes going by the Trent and
coastal ships, Warwickshire coal carried on the Coventry Canal,
and Leicestershire coal coming on to the canal line from the
Leicester & Swannington Railway. In 1846 there was a proposal
from George Stephenson to the two companies that they should
join him in building a mineral railway from Derby to Rugby along
the Soar valley, but they seem not to have taken it seriously.

The Leicester Canal and its neighbours to the south did well out
of carrying stone from the great quarries at Mountsorrel and
Quorndon, and when in 1858 the Midland Railway gave notice of
a bill for a branch to the quarries, the stone company at once got

* As far back as 1791 they had built, and they still owned, the Erewash Navigation
Inn at Trent Lock, now the Fisherman's Rest.

a reduction in canal tolls. The Leicester was persuaded not to oppose the bill by a guarantee of £200 p.a. in tolls from Mountsorrel for twenty years. The authorizing Act was obtained in 1859, and the line, a private one, was opened in 1860 by the Earl of Lanesborough.

At the end of 1860 the Midland proposed to the canal companies that they should all raise coal tolls to an economic level and not cut them against each other on the trade to Market Harborough and Northampton. The arrangement seems only to have worked for Market Harborough, the Grand Junction refusing to cooperate on the Northampton trade unless the L.N.W.R., with which it had its own rates agreement, was brought in.

The recorded history of the Leicester company is one of perpetual negotiations on through tolls and participation in opposition to railway bills affecting canals. Because it considered itself different in position and prospects from the other companies on the line, it did not support a Grand Junction scheme of 1863 for amalgamations on the Leicester line, but instead hoped for 'greater unity and promptitude in action by the Canal Companies'.[5]

After negotiations with the Leicester and old Union companies, considerable alterations were made to the River Soar and the navigation through Leicester by the Corporation under Improvements Acts of 1868 to 1881, in order to control flooding. The Leicester Navigation was given a new lock, Limekiln, near the public wharf; the levels of North and Belgrave locks were altered, and the channel widened and deepened between Belgrave lock and the wharf, and between North lock and West bridge. On the old Union line, a new canal channel was cut for 1¼ miles from near West bridge to the Midland Railway viaduct on the Burton branch. Two locks on the old line were replaced by one (No. 41) on the new. The company's committee reported in the spring of 1890, when it was opened, that they 'consider the new Cut a decided improvement'.[6]

The Leicester company owned a good deal of land in the town. In 1872 they had laid out a new street* from Belgrave Gate to the public wharf; in 1874 they sold some compulsorily to the corporation in connection with the flood prevention works, and more went to the gas company and the Midland Railway. These sales enabled a cash distribution of £15 per £140 share to be made, and also provided a considerable increase in investment income to balance falling toll receipts.

* I assume this to be Memory Lane.

When in November 1844 the Oakham company was invited to join a meeting of canal concerns threatened by the proposed Syston & Stamford (later the Syston & Peterborough) railway, the shareholders empowered the committee to negotiate with the railway company for purchase or amalgamation, and only in the last resort to oppose. On 11 October George Hudson himself came to Oakham to announce that plans were to be deposited, and that the Midland would meet the canal shareholders on amicable terms. The Midland's own surveys were at this time being enlivened by those conflicts between their men and the Earl of Harborough's servants that are called the 'battles of Saxby'; though the canal company must have sympathized with the Earl, they took no active part. On other occasions they too had been troubled by that pugnacious nobleman.

On 19 April 1845 the canal company agreed to sell its business to the Midland Railway for £26,000 and 200 new Midland £40 shares, fully paid up, subject to authorization of the Syston–Peterborough line. For the year ending 31 March 1845 it had carried 31,182 tons, of which 22,498 were coal, much of it for Stamford and its neighbourhood and 4,564 merchandise upwards, and 4,120 tons wool and grain downwards. Receipts were £2,903, and the dividend £3 per £130 share. Enthusiasm for the canal had been lessened by the dry summer of 1844, during which it had been unnavigable for five months, so that land carriage had had to be used.[7] The railway Act passed, and that[8] to authorize the sale of the canal and its abandonment followed on 27 July 1846 in spite of opposition by a number of canal companies. The sale was completed on 29 October 1847, the proceeds being enough to return £44 7s od of his capital to each shareholder.

The railway was opened from Syston to Melton on 1 September 1846, and to Oakham on 1 May 1848. It affected traffic on the Melton Mowbray Navigation directly, and through the loss of the Oakham canal trade. In the latter year the tonnage carried was 30,879 and the receipts only £1,401, against 40,421 and £4,001 ten years before; 3½ per cent was paid in dividends, against 10 per cent. In June 1848 the clerk wrote to the Loughborough company to say that 'unless something is done to compete with our Rivals this canal will not receive sufficient to keep it open'.[9] Tolls to Melton were reduced from 2s 6d to 2s, then to 1s, 10d, 8d and finally 6d in 1849, 'the very lowest that we can reduce to pay even expences (without any Dividend)'.[10] The other canal companies helped with drawbacks on their own lines upon coal for Melton, but in 1858 the tonnage was down to 14,654 and the receipts to £437, out of which the company managed to pay £275 in dividends.

In December 1862 the navigation was offered to the Loughborough Navigation, who were warned that if they refused, the Melton would 'try what they could do with the Midland'.[11] They did, but so did the Midland 'decline treating for the Purchase of the Melton Canal',[12] and the company struggled on, with tonnage in 1868 down to 11,169, receipts to £327, and dividend to ¼ per cent. Early in 1877 they decided to give up, and as a last hope asked the Midland Railway whether, in their proposed abandonment bill, there was any point in giving the railway power to buy. Again the railway was uninterested, and the Act[13] was passed. Its preamble said that traffic had greatly diminished, receipts being so reduced as to be insufficient to maintain the waterway and yield a profit. The navigation was closed from 1 August 1877.

By 1845 about 80,000 tons a year of coal from the Leicester & Swannington Railway were being delivered to the old Union company for points along their line or for the Grand Junction. In 1847, to get retail coal prices reduced, they themselves began to trade in it at Market Harborough, and in 1849 at Kilby bridge also, business that seems to have continued to about 1860 at Harborough and 1872 at Kilby. In 1848 Charles Robinson the chairman, who had been on the committee since 1834, retired, and was given a piece of plate because 'his exertions on behalf of the interest of the Company have mainly contributed to the flourishing condition of its finances'.[14] He retired just in time; 1851 saw a catastrophic fall in the revenue, and by 1855 it was down to less than half that of 1848, while the dividend had fallen from 5½ to 2⅜ per cent. By 1862 revenue was below £3,000; by 1873 below £2,000, and the dividend to 10s per cent.

Few notable events broke the gloom. In the autumn of 1865 the embankment at Smeeton Westerby gave way in heavy rain, but was restored in a fortnight; in May 1872 the company sold land and premises at West Bridge wharf, Leicester, to the Midland Railway for £5,000, reducing wharfage receipts but increasing interest received, so that thenceforward only about half their receipts were tolls and wharfages, the rest being interest and rents.

In the autumn of 1889 the committee sadly reported that 'The trade of the Canal is . . . in anything but a flourishing state, as is apparent by the falling off of the profits. Your Committee hope, however, that the future will be brighter for Canals generally and that from the working of the Railway and Canal Traffic Act of 1888 and the attention Canals are now receiving, some benefit may accrue to this Company'.[15]

Farther south the Grand Union was also hard pressed. In 1851 the company sought to economize 'under the circumstances of the reduced Traffic',[16] and in 1856 they agreed to reduce coal tolls to the Grand Junction rate of ¼d per ton per mile for traffic carried ten miles or more. By 1858 toll receipts at £3,108 were less than half the £7,551 of ten years earlier. By 1861 the dividend was down to 9s per cent, and the company began to negotiate with the old Union for every kind of joint working short of amalgamation. In 1863 the meetings were transferred to Leicester, and the Leicestershire Banking Company were made joint bankers with Praeds: two years later all three of the Praeds had left the Committee.

Thenceforward the canal's fortunes declined with its tolls and dividends: these fell from £2,053 and 10s per cent in 1865 to £1,024 and 2s 11d per cent in 1875 and £742 and 1s per cent in 1885. The company struggled on, doing considerable repairs to Crick and Husbands Bosworth tunnels and badly interrupting traffic while they did so, economizing on staff till they had only one combined toll-collector and lock-keeper, negotiating fruitlessly with Northampton and other towns for the sale of water, and yet building an ice-boat, even though the cost turned the year's profit into a loss, and a dredger. But by 1884 the canal was in bad condition, and the company almost penniless. Then, for the old Union and themselves, a new prospect opened (see p. 225).

Meanwhile, beyond the Trent, the Nutbrook Canal paid its last dividend in 1885. Money was spent to counteract mining subsidence, but after 1 June 1895 traffic ceased altogether. An abandonment bill was introduced in 1896, but lost after opposition by a number of canal companies. In 1899 and 1900, the Grand Junction considered taking the canal over, but even the most enthusiastic of the colliery companies, the Manners, was lukewarm. Then the Grand Junction's decision not to buy the Erewash (see p. 226) ruled out the Nutbrook too. The lowermost half-mile was used for some time by the Stanton company, but by 1928 this also was disused. No formal abandonment seems ever to have taken place.

Meanwhile, the lease of 1852 having expired, the Cromford and its railway owner had together been vested in the Midland Railway under an Act of 1870. Traffic had fallen badly, for the railway had taken the long-distance part, leaving the waterway only local busi-

XIII. Braunston, the old arm that was formerly part of the Oxford Canal before it was straightened: (*above*) in 1926, showing the Fellows, Morton & Clayton depot; (*below*) a picture taken from the same position in 1956, showing the Blue Line Cruisers base

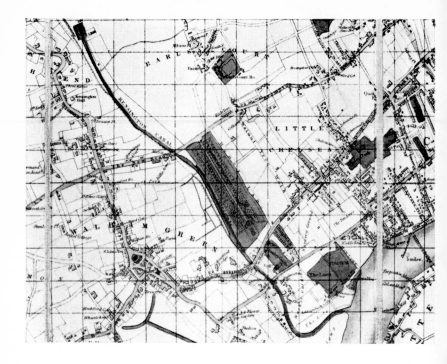

XIV. London canals in 1843: (*above*) the Kensington; (*below*) the Grosvenor. Victoria station now occupies the basin of the latter

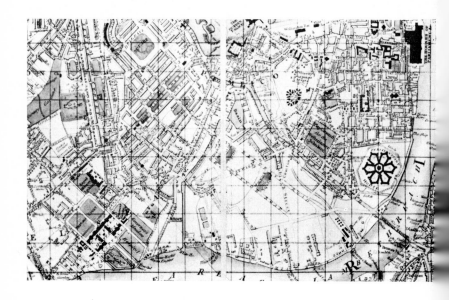

ness. A tonnage of 284,889 in 1850, 145,814 in 1870 and 84,990 in 1880 was down to 45,799 in 1888. Then, in 1889, a bad subsidence occurred in Butterley tunnel. It was closed, £7,364 was spent on it, and it was reopened in May 1893; thereafter an average of 178 boats a year used it, carrying about 3,000–4,000 tons a year of coal upwards, and some hundreds of tons a year of stone from Whatstandwell downwards to the Erewash and Nottingham Canals. On 5 July 1900 a worse subsidence occurred, due, it was alleged, to the working of a colliery beneath the tunnel; it was now impassable, and even cut off some of their water from the Erewash and Nottingham.* The railway's engineer reported that if anything were to be done, the tunnel would have to be completely reconstructed once the ground had settled. The company therefore decided to close it. The Erewash pressed strongly for reopening, to which the Midland Railway replied that this was useless when the Butterley company was mining under it, but that they would carry stone from Whatstandwell to the Erewash at no extra cost. Unmollified, the company obtained a Board of Trade inspection of the Cromford, and with others opposed the railway bill and compelled the clauses to close Butterley tunnel to be withdrawn pending the report of the Royal Commission which was then sitting. This body, however, reporting in 1909, said that the interests of trade did not call for the reinstatement of the tunnel or the maintenance of navigation above it.

Some traffic remained on the upper portion, mainly coal to Cromford and lead from the Lea Wood branch to High Peak wharf. Below the tunnel there was 39,000 tons of traffic in 1905, which brought in £875. The Lea Wood cut closed in March 1936, and on 14 July 1937 the L.M.S.R. gave notice that it intended to seek a warrant of abandonment for the upper section. Because of objections (though not on navigation grounds) this was not granted. At the initiative of Frank Pick the whole canal was then offered free to the (new) Grand Union, but refused, and, except for the lowermost half-mile, which was still in use, was abandoned in 1944.[17] This remaining half-mile followed in 1962.

Railway pressure on the Derby Canal caused the company in March 1840 to make drastic cuts in tolls, notably from 1s 5d to 10d a ton upon coal on the Little Eaton line, which were matched by reductions elsewhere on cargoes coming to Derby, for instance, from the Cromford Canal. In June 1845 the Little Eaton tolls were again reduced to 8d.

* A further collapse took place in February 1907.

N

In September the Derby & Gainsborough Railway company*
showed interest in buying the Little Eaton line of canal and the
gangway; they were quoted £30,000, of which £3,000 would be
a non-returnable deposit in case the railway failed to get an Act.
An agreement was ratified at the Derby's meeting of June 1846,
but the deposit was never paid. In May 1847 the Midland Railway
was quoted the same price. Instead of buying, they decided instead
to build their own branch up the same valley as the gangway to
Ripley; it was authorized in 1848 and opened in September 1855.

Receipts, which had been £8,180 in 1838, had fallen to £4,932
in 1848, £3,461 in 1858, and £2,556 in 1868. Dividends in the same
years were 10½, 6¾, 4½, and 4 per cent. In 1872 the company
offered the canal to the Midland Railway for £90,000, but though
Allport, the general manager, made an appointment with the
Committee, he did not keep it. An offer to the L.N.W.R. also
brought no response.

Trade slowly declined and was considerably affected when Butterley tunnel on the Cromford became impassable. In 1898 the
company were considering closing the gangway. The last loads of
coal were carried down it in July 1908.[18] In the eighties the Trent
company had seriously considered plans to help develop the line
from Derwent Mouth to Derby, but nothing had come of their
plans. In 1927 their committee was told that traffic had almost
ceased on the Derby Canal, and that the company had informed
Fellows, Morton & Clayton that they intended to apply for
authority to close. The Little Eaton branch was abandoned by
warrant of 4 July 1935, and in 1937 the company proposed also to
abandon the Sandiacre line, but failed owing to the objections of
Imperial Chemical Industries. They again proposed to do so in
1945, and finally succeeded in abandoning the whole canal by
warrant in 1964.

On the Nottingham Canal railway competition began seriously
to affect canal revenue from 1842 onwards. Receipts of £12,184 in
that year† fell to £10,761 in 1843 and £9,443 in 1844. Early in
1844, after an economy investigation, wages were reduced, four
men were dismissed, a charge was made for houses previously
provided free, and—a serious blow—no free ale was to be provided for the men unless it was absolutely necessary, and then
never more than a quart a day.

Tolls were reduced from 1840 onwards. In 1844 the company,

* It later called itself the Derby, Gainsborough & Great Grimsby.
† Year ending 30 April.

with others, opposed the Erewash Valley Railway scheme, but in May 1845 authorized its committee to negotiate for amalgamation either with other canal companies connected with their line, or with the projected Nottingham, Erewash Valley, Ambergate and Manchester Railway, which had Nottingham and also Cromford Canal directors on its board. The committee was even empowered to advance money 'for the purpose of the said Railway', out of canal funds, to be repaid from the first call.[19]

The Nottingham company asked its contact for £240 a share in cash, or ten railway shares of £25. By September the railway company had amalgamated with two others, the Nottingham, Vale of Belvoir & Grantham, and the Nottingham & Boston, to become the Ambergate, Nottingham, Boston & Eastern Junction, which had as chairman, W. F. N. Norton, who had recently joined the committees of the Nottingham and Grantham canals, and on its board several canal shareholders and committeemen. Railway representatives then attended a Nottingham Canal committee meeting, and offered £220 a share in cash, or nine £25 railway shares, payable within six months of the opening of the railway from Ambergate to Grantham. Relations were friendly, agreement was reached at £212 10s od per share cash, the railway got its Act, and the canal company was left for the time being to manage the canal and take the profits. Toll reductions and economies followed, and it was therefore with relief that the canal company served notice on the railway to pay the £112,500 they owed on 15 January 1851, six months after the opening of their line to Grantham, and take over the canal. But nothing happened, as the Grantham Canal company had already found out. That concern had in 1845 authorized its committee to negotiate for an amalgamation with the Nottingham, Vale of Belvoir & Grantham Railway, and to advance it up to £500. After absorption the combined Ambergate company offered £160 per Grantham share or six £25 railway shares, also payable six months after the opening of the line from Ambergate to Grantham. This offer, too, was accepted.

The railway was opened on 15 July 1850 from Nottingham to Grantham, the company having by then abandoned the rest of their proposed line, and soon afterwards its competition caused the canal to reduce its tolls. The cause of the railway's failure to pay up on the agreed date seems partly to have been scarcity of funds, and partly that the company hoped to link itself with the Great Northern, which had no wish to take over the canals.

The Grantham Canal company, supported by the Nottingham,

now took legal action. Case after case was fought for three years, the last being in the House of Lords, while the canal companies added to the pressure by successfully opposing various Ambergate bills. Finally the railway capitulated, and on 1 June 1854 an agreement was made, by which £45 per canal share was to be paid in cash for Grantham and £50 for Nottingham shares, the balance being in railway mortgages, together with £3,000 towards legal costs. On 20 December the Grantham Canal was transferred, and on 2 January 1855 the Nottingham.

In October 1854, in anticipation of the transfer, the railway company altered its name to the Ambergate, Nottingham and Boston & Eastern Junction Railway & Canal Co, and on 30 March 1855 agreed that the Great Northern should work their line for ten years. In May 1860 the company again changed its name, to the Nottingham & Grantham Railway & Canal Co, and on 1 August 1861 leased itself to the Great Northern for 999 years, remaining in existence up to the end of 1922 only to receive dividends.

By 1905 traffic on the Grantham was down to 18,802 tons, mainly in manure (8,256), roadstone (3,466), plaster and coal on short hauls, and tolls to £242. On the Nottingham traffic was 123,488 tons in 1916, most of it from the Trent to the Nottingham wharves or through to the Beeston cut. Tolls were £1,028. Merchandise headed the traffic (31,887 tons), followed by coal (17,133), gravel (16,819), roadstone (16,116) and manure (14,731). Then and later the Trent company often complained of short water in the canal, mainly in the Trent lock—Lenton section, but got little satisfaction from the G.N.R. Commercial traffic other than to the Beeston cut ended in 1928.

The Grantham was abandoned in 1936, and the Nottingham in 1937, except for the section from Trent lock to Lenton, which was transferred to the Trent Navigation Company.

The Chesterfield Canal faced the railway mania somewhat differently, for canal proprietors took the principal part in forming a Manchester & Lincoln Union Railway company, which in October 1845 issued a prospectus that included in its objects the partial conversion of the canal to a railway as part of a through line from Liverpool to Great Grimsby.[20] A line was to run from Staveley through Worksop to Gainsborough, with a branch to Lincoln, and another from Worksop to the Midland Railway at Beighton near Norwood. These lines were intended as a counterbalance to the Sheffield & Lincolnshire Junction, projected in

1844 to connect Sheffield and Gainsborough, and supported by the Sheffield, Ashton-under-Lyne & Manchester Railway. The S. & L.J. and the M. & L.U. proprietors then met to set up a joint committee, and by the time of the second reading of their bill the M. & L.U. had agreed to future amalgamation.

In exchange for retaining their canal, the M. & L.U. withdrew all their intended lines except one. The Act[21] of 7 August 1846 authorized a line from the M.R. at Staveley to the canal at Worksop, the canal and railway amalgamating as the Manchester & Lincoln Union Railway & Chesterfield & Gainsborough Canal. Power was given to amalgamate with the S. & L.J. The canal shareholders could exchange their shares for fully paid new shares or be repaid in cash, the purchase being later valued in the railway books at £147,912. The canal company was to be dissolved, but the new body was not to dispose of any part of the canal, but to keep it in good order, preserve its water supplies, and maintain just tolls.

The company now gave notice to the S. & L.J. to amalgamate, but that having already been absorbed by the Manchester, Sheffield & Lincolnshire, the Manchester & Lincoln Union was also amalgamated with that company on 9 July 1847. A week earlier, an amending Act had provided for a deviation of the Staveley-Worksop line to join the S. & L.J. at Worksop, but this was never built.

For 1848 the canal revenue had been £12,636. In this year the railway company put the canal in order, 'in consequence of the ordinary repairs having been for many years grossly neglected, and the canal becoming almost impassable in many places, but it is satisfactory to find that this outlay is already being returned by means of the increasing trade'.[22] About now the railway started a small carrying business, which in 1854 carried 7,811 tons out of a total of 118,946 in 1854. In 1856 the reservoirs at Chesterfield were being enlarged, and in 1858 the owning company reported that traffic on the canal had kept up well in spite of the commercial panic of the time and the 'ruinous competition on the part of the L.N.W.R.'.[23] In 1872, 1873 and 1884, however, the M.S. & L.R. prepared schemes to convert the canal into a railway (particularly the section from Kiveton Park to Chesterfield), but withdrew them all. In 1888, out of a canal revenue of £4,734, £2,793 was attributable to freight as carriers; in this year 62,075 tons was carried, of which 11,705 tons was off the Trent, and 11,385 on to it, the rest being internal traffic.

The following year an Act was obtained to divert the canal for the company's own new railways between Beighton, Staveley and

Chesterfield. At Killamarsh and Renishaw a new line along the edge of the Park was substituted for over a mile of curving canal and with two small deviations at Whittington and Chesterfield reduced the length of the canal by half a mile. An extension into a loop, authorized in 1890, accompanied a deviation of the section already authorized between Staveley and Whittington, with another alteration of the canal through the ironworks. The railways concerned were opened between Beighton and Staveley Works on 1 December 1891 and onwards to Chesterfield on 4 June 1892. The company then gave up carrying on all its canals, and by 1905 the tonnage figures had fallen to 45,177, of which 7,174 were from the Trent, and 11,638 tons to it; the main traffics were coal (15,000) and bricks (11,000). About 40 boats were working. Receipts were £1,837 and expenses £3,883. By this time the upper part of the canal had been seriously affected by subsidence. A short length between Staveley and Chesterfield was unnavigable, after £21,000 had been spent on Norwood tunnel between 1871 and 1905 in repairing damage and raising the roof. In 1908 a further collapse caused the tunnel to be closed, which virtually ended traffic above it, and below as far down as Worksop. In 1955, when the Stockwith–Walkeringham trade ceased, all commercial traffic ended.

A 1¼ mile private branch was built privately about 1840 by the Barrows of Staveley ironworks from the Chesterfield Canal across the Norbriggs road at Netherthorpe to their Speedwell colliery. It had been converted to a railway by 1860.

The Trent company, which had earlier thought enlargement of its waterway unnecessary, in September 1844 refused to reduce its tolls. It learned quickly, for early in 1845 those on iron and salt had to be reduced from 1s to 6d, and were soon followed by timber charges. By September they had appointed a sub-committee to receive proposals 'from any railway or Canal company which may desire to confer with the Trent Company in reference to any proposed amalgamation of their interests'[24] and by December, when eighteen railway lines across the river were being planned, they received an offer of £100 a share from the Nottingham & Gainsborough Railway. They rejected it. By December 1846 all tolls were down to a maximum of 6d for the whole length; in 1847 wages had to be raised to stop men transferring to railway employment, and locks kept open at all hours for fly-boats. Cheap through tolls to Manchester were negotiated in 1850, and in 1855 there were staff economies.

Receipts had fallen steadily from £11,344 in 1839 and £8,011 in

1845 to £3,111 in 1855, and reserves were being drawn upon to pay the dividends. Some selective toll increases then improved the position, but the original company's tolls were never again to exceed £5,000. Here are averaged figures from 1826:

Years	Average tolls £	Years	Average tolls £
1826-8	7,940	1853-5	3,698
1829-31	7,953	1856-8	4,245
1832-4	7,613	1859-61	4,711
1835-7	9,103	1862-4	4,631
1838-40	11,193	1865-7	4,103
1841-3	9,132	1868-70	4,173
1844-6	8,119	1871-3	3,900
1847-9	5,813	1874-6	3,386
1850-2	4,618	1876-9	2,918

For the two years ending November 1856 we get an interesting picture of the trade of the river at a time when carryings had been far less affected by railways than receipts:

Commodity	2-year average tons	Commodity	2-year average tons
Coal and coke	77,006	Stone	4,211
Timber	30,384	Flour	4,052
Manure*	30,292	Malt	2,377
Gravel*	26,477	Flints	1,683
Iron	20,413	Cheese	301
Lime, plaster	18,370	Earthenware	216
Grain	16,988	Spelter	189
Domestic salt	11,014	Sundries	23,030

Total 267,003 tons

* Carried toll-free.

As with the Grantham Canal and others, the Trent was losing heavily on carrying large quantities of gravel and manure toll-free, a burden competing railways did not have to bear, and which was made worse because many new kinds of manure, such as salt, ground bones, and guano, had been introduced since the Acts of 1783 and 1794.

By now the Trent was hemmed in by railway-controlled water-ways. The Trent & Mersey, the Cromford, Nottingham and Grantham, the Fossdyke and Witham, the Chesterfield and the Stainforth & Keadby were all such. Only the Erewash and the Soar line remained independent. From now on the company was to experience not only direct railway competition, but also the slow decay of many connecting waterways. An instance of this occurred in 1873, when it was reported that wide boats could not be used on the Nottingham and Grantham for lack of dredging, and protests were made to the Great Northern Railway. There was an exception: the Trent & Mersey was heavily worked by the North Staffordshire Railway.

In 1858 a new Trent Act gave power to raise more money by shares and borrowing, to increase the permitted tolls, and to charge for commodities previously exempt. However, traffic, especially long-distance, still tended downwards, and the higher tolls could not be sustained: in 1869 most were reduced to two-thirds of the 1858 Act's maxima. In this year also W. E. Hopkin was appointed engineer-surveyor, succeeding his father; in 1846 he himself had succeeded John Hopkin, who, after having been toll-keeper at Beeston, was appointed superintendent of works under Jessop in 1806.

By the end of 1873 the company was in a bad way. A decision to find out whether anyone was prepared to run a steam tug between Newark and Gainsborough developed into discussions of what might be done to improve the river. These went on for years, during which the dividend, which had stood at 7 per cent since the previous century, dropped in 1876 to 5 per cent, a rate which could only be maintained by drawing on reserves. In 1878 the company noted that more traffic would only be obtained by 'giving such facilities as will enable the river to compete for some part of the traffic now carried by the Railways and by keeping down to the lowest limit the expenditure',[25] and proposed to install a rope from Gainsborough to Nottingham or Wilden Ferry.

This system, by which a tug hauled itself along a wire rope laid in a river-bed, had been proposed for the Severn as long ago as 1852, and was already in action on several Continental rivers. The line on the Neckar was indeed opened in this same year of 1878, and F. J. Meyer, one of the patentees, attended a Trent meeting to explain it.[26] The shareholders agreed that some form of steam haulage was necessary, bought a steam dredger in order to make a start on getting a depth of 3 ft, encouraged the chairman, J. W. Leavers, to put on a steam tug, and in 1881, the first year without a dividend, appointed traffic agents, got some new people on to the committee, and made Henry Rofe engineer and general manager. In 1882 they decided to hire craft from Fellows, Morton and from Farley & Co of Hull and Gainsborough, and, having issued £8,300 of debentures, to buy the steam tugs and other equipment belonging to Leavers. By October they had a traffic manager in Nottingham, a fleet engineer in charge of the tugs and dredger, small depots at Nottingham and Newark, and were operating 16 keels and nine lighters; soon afterwards they ordered three more craft on hire purchase.

The financing of the changes needed to improve the river trade were, however, beyond the financial capacity of the old company. Some proprietors therefore in November 1883 formed a limited company, the Trent Navigation & Carrying Co, to acquire the old business and then promote a statutory company with additional powers. A bill was prepared, but meanwhile Nottingham Corporation favoured taking over the navigation, so that it was agreed that the limited company's bill should be allowed to pass, but that its operation should be suspended until in the following session the Corporation would seek a bill to carry out its terms themselves. The bill then went ahead, and was passed in May 1884.[27] Under it both the old and limited companies were dissolved and amalgamated into the Trent Navigation Company, with powers to issue £26,000 of fully paid shares, taking over the debt of the old company, and £100,000 of ordinary shares as well. The new company raised £11,250 of new capital, but, the Corporation having paid a deposit of £2,000 upon its purchase, they then waited to be taken over. However, Nottingham changed its mind, and having introduced a bill in 1885, withdrew it and sacrificed the deposit.

The river went on getting worse—the depth was down to 20 in. on some occasions, with much lightening of craft—and ideas of improvement larger. In 1887 a further Act[28] was obtained to form yet another company, the Trent (Burton-upon-Trent and Humber) Navigation Co, with greatly enlarged capital powers. This concern did not intend to build additional locks, but to dredge the river to a depth of 6 ft, enlarge those already built, and reconstruct the Trent & Mersey Canal up to Branston lock near Burton to take large Trent craft. The Trent company was to spend not less than £30,000 on enlarging this section of canal, and to pay a rent to the North Staffordshire Railway rising from £250 in the first year to £1,000 in the third and subsequent years, in exchange for which their traffic would be toll-free. Goods going beyond Burton other than by canal would transfer there to rail. The N.S.R. were to appoint two directors to the Trent company. For the rest, the 1884 company was to be given £37,250 in fully paid shares and £30,000 in cash to pay off its £11,000 bank overdraft and liquidate its other debts, while the new shareholders under the 1884 Act got new £10 shares, £3 paid up. Another agreement gave the company the lease of the Newark Navigation for 99 years at a rent of £243 17s 0d p.a. No power was taken to increase tolls.

The new company was led by E. M. Hutton Riddell, a banker from Newark, as chairman, and J. W. Leavers as vice-chairman. A dredger was bought, and calls were made on the existing share-holders. An attempt to issue further shares was, however, a failure, only 65 being subscribed, and at the end of 1888 £25,000 worth of debentures were placed instead. By early 1889 the plans to enlarge the Trent & Mersey Canal had been dropped with the consent of the railway company, and it was apparent that none of the other envisaged improvements could be carried out unless long-term capital could be raised. In late 1891, therefore, a pro-visional agreement was made with contractors to carry out im-provement works, and a further Act[29] granting capital powers was passed in 1892. This also once more changed the name of the concern, this time back to Trent Navigation Company. In 1894 tolls were put on a ton-mile basis.

In March 1894 a town's meeting in Nottingham agreed that if a 'waterway could be made so as to admit a regular service of boats of from 100 to 200 tons burden, great pecuniary gain would accrue to manufacturers, colliery proprietors and consumers'. The Corporation agreed to inquire and report in consultation with other local authorities, but only Lindsey County Council were interested.

The energetic Frank Rayner took over as engineer in 1896 (later also as general manager), and some improvements were made, such as the deepening of Cranfleet lock, and one or two new craft launched. By now, however, Riddell had been appointed receiver for the debenture holders, whose interest was in arrears, and prospects were poor. By 1900 the company's liabilities were £53,563. Two years later the share and debenture holders agreed to a scheme by which most of the existing debentures, arrears of interest and other debts were exchanged for Preference shares, while £6,950 of new debentures were issued to pay off a loan on the security of the fleet. The Newark Commissioners also agreed to take £100 p.a. in rent, as indeed they had been doing for some years past.

At this time the river traffic amounted to 350,000–400,000 tons a year, 60,000–70,000 tons of which was carried by the company, using their own tugs between Nottingham and Torksey, and those hired from Hull for the run beyond.

The future looked better, and the company decided that, to improve the river satisfactorily, dredging was not sufficient, but that new locks would have to be built. Sir Edward Leader Williams, who had engineered the Manchester Ship Canal, was called in and surveyed the river, and an agreement was made with the North Staffordshire Railway, still anxious to support the Trent in order to penetrate into other companies' territory, to repeal the relevant clauses of the 1887 Act. Instead, the Trent company would provide boats for traffic on the Trent & Mersey and pay ordinary tolls; the railway company would appoint two directors and subscribe for £2,000 in shares, though they politely declined to take any debentures. A new Act was passed in 1906 to authorize new capital, and give powers to build locks and weirs at Cromwell, Newark Nether, Hazelford, Gunthorpe, Stoke Bardolph and Holme, and to dredge from Cromwell to Holme to get 5 ft of depth and 60 ft of width. These proposals were accepted by the Royal Commission in their report, and became their recommended standards for the Trent.

Debentures proved difficult to place, but thanks to the enthusiasm and willingness to subscribe of the banker chairman, Sir Henry Robson, and his partner the vice-chairman Ernest Jardine, £20,100 had been raised by late 1908, and a decision was taken soon afterwards to proceed with Cromwell lock, the Newark Commissioners at the same time agreeing to advance £1,500 to deepen the Town lock and basin there. By September Newark Town had been deepened and its sills lowered to give 6 ft 6 in., and a programme of gravel dredging begun to improve the channel while at the same time recovering most of the cost by selling the gravel. On 22 May 1911 traffic first passed through the new lock, 188 ft long by 30 ft wide, big enough to take a tug and three barges. By this time nearly 400,000 tons of gravel had been dredged.

No effort was made before the war to do more, though dredging continued, and improvements were made to the carrying services. In 1913, too, a new traffic, petroleum, started to be carried by water, and was soon to be a great help to the company's finances. A pamphlet of 1912, *The Trent in the Service of the Trader*, tells us that there was a daily service of boats between the Humber ports and Newark, Nottingham, Loughborough and Leicester, with delivery services by the company's horses and drays at those towns and at Hull. There were warehouses at Newark, Nottingham, Loughborough and Leicester. The services to Loughborough and Leicester, and agreements for premises there, dated from 1903, and were profitable. In 1910 the company decided to extend its warehousing side, and bought the Wilford Street property. The building was started with money borrowed from a company controlled by Ernest Jardine, chairman since Sir Henry Robson's death in 1911. It was completed in 1915. At this time the company had about 20 Hull boats and one motor barge, other towing being done by a contractor.

It was clear the company could not itself finance the building of further locks, but contacts made in 1914 with Nottingham Corporation led to negotiations, which were encouraged by the news that the Development Commissioners, set up to assist works that would find employment for those affected by the war, might help with the cost. The Commissioners were favourable, but pointed out that they could not lend money to companies working for profit, and it was suggested that the Newark–Nottingham section of the river should be transferred to the Corporation, who would be toll-takers, but not carriers, upon it.

By the end of December Rayner had been called up, and the hope of money from the Commissioners had disappeared. However, Nottingham Corporation itself now agreed to find the £150,000 necessary to make the waterway able to take 100-ton barges and in 1915 an Act authorized the transfer to them of the river between Nottingham and Averham Weir above Newark. But the war stopped such plans, and instead of locks being built, the company saw an acetylene searchlight placed on the roof of Wilford Street warehouse.

In October 1919 Rayner came back from military service to find that the government subsidy paid during the war was to end on 31 August 1920. No power existed to raise tolls once that happened to take account of increased costs, and there seemed only two alternatives, either to close down or to ask the Ministry of Transport for control, as a means to getting tolls raised under temporary powers. The Ministry agreed and temporarily took over on 24 September, the government having lent the company enough money to carry on from 31 August. Tolls were raised, and the company began to do better. The Chamberlain Committee[30] had been appointed to study the canal question, and was encouraged to report quickly on the Trent, which it did in February 1921, recommending immediate action on the lines of the 1915

Act, and following this with a proposal to form a trust to include the Trent and its connections.

The recommendations were among the reasons that decided Nottingham Corporation to start work on Holme lock on 28 September, and Stoke Bardolph lock shortly after, followed by the others. Meanwhile the company itself rebuilt Newark Nether lock with a grant from the Unemployment Grants Committee and a loan from Nottingham Corporation. This was opened on 12 April 1926, and on 25 June the last of the river locks to be built by the Corporation, Hazelford, was opened by Neville Chamberlain. Only dredging remained to complete the works authorized in 1906, and this was done during the next few months. On 1 April 1927 the Corporation, having spent about £450,000, took over the section of river allotted to them, and employed the company as managers. A year later Col Rayner resigned owing to ill-health, but was appointed consulting engineer and given a seat on the Board.

In 1930 finance was sought, unsuccessfully, from the Newark Commissioners and from Nottingham Corporation for the re-building of Newark Town lock. At the same time the company were considering the improvement of the line to Leicester to about the same standard to which the Grand Union was working on the Braunston–Birmingham reconstruction. As a result, talks took place with the L.N.E.R. upon the enlargement of the Trent lock–Lenton section of the Nottingham Canal and with W. H. Curtis of the Grand Union upon possible co-operation. This interest in the river above Nottingham led to the purchase of an old brewery of Offiler's below Shardlow bridge, which was converted into Shardlow depot, working by the beginning of 1932. In that year plans were deposited and a bill introduced for new locks at Beeston and Wilford to be ultimately of the 1906 dimensions (though powers were to be sought to build them of single-boat size and enlarge them afterwards), as well as for rebuilding Newark Town lock to 1906 dimensions. The new locks above Nottingham had to be withdrawn from the bill because of opposition from the Trent Catchment Board, though authority was obtained for Newark lock. Later, in 1934, the Catchment Board paid for the sills of Sawley locks to be lowered.

In spite of this setback, the company hastened to assure W. H. Curtis that they were still interested in development above Nottingham, and invited him to join the Trent board; he was too busy himself, but he suggested C. K. Tatham, one of the Grand Union directors, who was appointed. All the same, no further up-river changes took place, though in 1934 the company briefly considered an extension from Shardlow to Burton, involving four new locks and the rebuilding of that at Kings Mills at a cost of about £130,000. In 1936 they themselves started to carry from Newark to Leicester by road, while the Grand Union decided that they were not prepared to deepen from Leicester to the Trent unless they could be assured of 135,000 tons of new traffic, an assurance the Trent company could not give.

In 1933 negotiations were begun with Nottingham Corporation to re-purchase their section of the navigation. They went on for years, but were never completed. Other developments were the building of an additional pair of gates below Cromwell lock to form a second lock holding two boats, and giving an additional depth of 3 ft 6 in., which could be used when water was low. This was opened in 1935. In 1936 the L.N.E.R. agreed to let the Trent lock–Lenton section of the Nottingham Canal to the company, with an option to purchase which was exercised in 1946. In 1939 there were also talks with the L.N.E.R. upon leasing the Fossdyke; these were in abeyance during the war, but afterwards a site for a depot was bought at Lincoln, and negotiations began for lengthening Torksey lock, where the Fossdyke joins the Trent.

For these years profits, small but increasing, had been ploughed back:

	£		£
1930	7,808	1936	5,863
1931	13,658	1937	9,244
1932	5,783	1938	8,253
1933	7,270	1939	11,176
1934	7,874	1940	11,600
1935	7,901	1941	20,080

In December 1945 Col Frank Rayner died, having joined the company in 1887 as junior engineer. In that same year interest payments were at last begun on the preference shares. In 1947 Sir Ernest Jardine, who had led the company through so many vicissitudes, also died—only a few months before nationalization brought it to an end. In December, at their last meeting, the Board wrote: 'It is the sincere desire of the Directors that the Trent may continue to play an important part in the transport system of this country.' A first and last dividend of 7½ per cent on the ordinary shares was paid in 1950 out of the final assets.

The Transport Commission built a larger Newark Town lock

in 1952, while the small flood-lock at Holme was eliminated as part of the Trent River Board's Nottingham flood prevention scheme. Above Nottingham, however, traffic to Shardlow or Leicester travelled in 40-ton barges. In 1955 extensions to the depots at Nottingham were begun. In 1957 a further programme of improvements was announced, under which more bank protection work was done, dredging plant and workshops were improved, some locks were mechanized, and Cromwell was enlarged by taking the extension lock built in 1935 into the main chamber, and reopened in 1960, to take eight instead of four standard Trent barges. Traffic in 1893, before the first new lock had been built, was 199,500 tons. In 1910 it was 391,965 tons; in 1937, 616,882 tons; in 1951, 620,000 tons; and in 1964, 1,017,356 tons.

By 1948, the Grantham, Nottingham and almost all the Cromford Canal had been abandoned, and the Nutbrook was disused. Except for the Derby Canal which remained in the possession of its shareholders, the other waterways described in this chapter passed on nationalization to the British Transport Commission, and in 1963 to the British Waterways Board. The Newark Navigation Commissioners still, however, remain in existence, and lease their waterway to the British Waterways Board at a rent of £150 p.a. until 31 May 1966, and thereafter at £243 7s od p.a. Except for the Trent upwards to Nottingham, the decade of the fifties saw very nearly the end of commercial traffic upon them all, side by side with a growth in pleasure cruising and increased sales of water.

CHAPTER X

Stratford, Coventry and Oxford

++++++++++++++++++++++++++++++++++++++◆++++++++++++++++++++++++++++++++++++++

Stratford-upon-Avon Canal

In early 1845 the promoters of the Oxford, Worcester & Wolver-hampton Railway offered to buy the Stratford-upon-Avon Canal and lease its feeder, the Stratford & Moreton Tramway. Both companies accepted the offer, the canal concern agreeing to sell for £30 per share on 3,611 shares, the railway to assume all liabilities. The tangled story of the purchase has been told else-where;[1] it was not completed until 1 January 1856, or the canal worked by the O.W.W.R. until 1 May 1857.

Thenceforward receipts fell steadily as the century moved on, and by the end of it most of the traffic was upon the King's Norton–Kingswood section, with perhaps some 8,500 tons a year moving down towards Stratford itself. The portion south of Kingswood ceased to be navigable about the end of World War II, and in 1958 the Warwickshire County Council decided to apply for a warrant of abandonment. This led to public protests, in which the Inland Waterways Association took a prominent part, and to a British Transport Commission Act of 1960 authorizing a five-year lease to the National Trust, and payments by the Govern-ment or the Commission totalling £27,500. With a donation also of £10,000 from the Pilgrim Trust, and contributions from the public, the canal was restored and reopened in 1964. It was trans-ferred in 1965, the National Trust having exercised their option to take over the freehold. The upper section remains with the British Waterways Board.

Coventry Canal

Farther north lay the Coventry; its committee were in 1845 and remained for a hundred years businesslike men, who faced a

7. Regent's Canal: (*above*) King's Cross granary, showing its connection with the canal; (*below*) legging through Maida Hill tunnel about 1885

XVI. The Regent's Canal in 1828: (*above*) the City Road basin; (*below*) the entrance to Regent's Canal dock

changing world efficiently and made the best of their ancient waterway. Though the company's dividend had fallen from 48 per cent in 1836 and 40 per cent in 1839 to 24 per cent in 1845 and 14¼ in 1853, it was still 14 per cent in 1870, 8 in 1890, 6¼ in 1910, 6 in 1920, and the same in 1947.

The late 1840s were a time of necessary toll reductions, many of which were included in agreements made in 1847 with the Oxford and Grand Junction companies. These limited certain Oxford and Grand Junction tolls, and insured that the former did not favour the Warwick or the latter the Leicester line at the expense of the Coventry; they supplemented heavy reductions already made on Ashby Canal coal to the Grand Junction, from 11½d to 6d a ton on the Coventry, and from 2s 9d to 1s 6d on the Oxford.

Further cuts followed, and a joint approach with the Oxford company to the L.N.W.R. for a rates agreement was unsuccessful. Fortunately, the company had accumulated a comfortable reserve fund, which was used to finance improvements which otherwise the shareholders might have been reluctant to make, because the cost would have come out of the year's dividend; it was replenished from drafts on profits and from capital sales. One use of the fund, after the judgment (see p. 212) allowing steam boats on the Ashby, was to buy a tug, the *Volunteer*, jointly with the Moira Colliery Co. It was working in 1860, and was considered 'highly satisfactory and greatly calculated to improve the property of the Company'.[2] A second, the *Harrison*, was bought in 1861, the original *Pioneer* of the lawsuit, presumably now transferred from the Moira company, being taken out of service in 1870.

In 1880 the company decided to negotiate with the B.C.N. to buy or lease the Fazeley–Whittington section of the canal and so restore their continuous line, and to seek powers to charge tolls on roadstone, hitherto carried free. The B.C.N., however, firmly refused to negotiate, on the grounds that L.N.W.R. interests might be endangered, and the Coventry company, having included compulsory powers to acquire the section in their bill of 1881, thought better of it, and removed them. Roadstone charges were authorized, however, and improved the toll revenue by some £1,000 p.a. Later, in 1894, they reached a useful rates agreement with the Warwick canals on coal tolls.

Thenceforward the company's aim was to offset falling tolls by seeking other sources of revenue. They went in extensively for developing the wharf and other property they owned, and also for selling water for industrial purposes and to local authorities. One

o

COVENTRY CANAL NAVIGATION.

CAUTION.

On FRIDAY, the 17th day of MAY inst., HENRY WOODWARD, the Steerer of a Boat, was brought before the County Magistrates, at Coventry, charged with endeavouring to

EVADE THE TOLL

PAYABLE TO THE

COVENTRY CANAL COMPANY,

In respect of several Cases of Pipes which he had secreted in his Boat laden with Road Stone, on the 1st instant, and was CONVICTED of the offence, and fined in the mitigated

Penalty of 1s., and £1. 0s. 6d. expenses.

THIS IS TO GIVE NOTICE

That all Persons offending in a similar manner will be proceeded against under the Bye-Laws of the above Company, and the whole PENALTY OF FIVE POUNDS prescribed by the same sued for, and in addition

THE WHOLE OF THE CARGO IN THE BOAT,

Although partly consisting of Road Stone will be

Charged with Tonnage.

BY ORDER,

CHARLES WOODCOCK,

CLERK TO THE COVENTRY CANAL COMPANY.

Coventry, May 25th, 1861.

agreement, both for property and water, encouraged an early example of what was to become a famous Coventry industry: it was made in April 1897 with The Great Horseless Carriage Company Ltd. On a smaller scale they sought revenue from agreements with fishing clubs and from granting wayleaves to public utilities.

So the company survived two wars, maintained revenue and paid reasonable dividends until nationalization.

Ashby-de-la-Zouch Canal

The first outside railway with which the Ashby company were concerned was the Coleorton, authorized in 1833 from Worthington Rough on the canal tramroad past the colliery area to the Leicester & Swannington Railway and the Leicester canals. In order that Joseph Bostock, lessee of the Cloud Hill limeworks, could send lime to Leicester without transhipment, combined tramplates and edge-rails were laid on the 2-mile section of the Ashby company's tramroad between Cloud Hill and Worthington, the connections being completed in 1840.[3]

In 1845 the Midland Railway was anxious to keep potential competitors away from the Leicestershire coalfields: among them the projected Leicester & Bedford, and also an Atherstone, Ashby-de-la-Zouch and Burton-on-Trent Railway, which would have served the collieries at Moira, the mineral districts round Ticknall and Breedon, and places along the Ashby Canal such as Market Bosworth and Hinckley. George Hudson, the chairman of the Midland, therefore agreed with the Ashby company to buy their canal for £110,000, after the canal company had flown the usual kite of 'taking into consideration the propriety of adopting such measures as may be deemed advisable for substituting a railway in lieu of the present canal'.[4] The Midland engaged to make a railway by way of Hinckley and Moira to their line near Burton, and to convert the canal tramroad to Gresley Common, and a clause of the agreement said: 'The Midland Company to keep the Canal intact, and in good repair for the purposes of trade, until the completion of the Railway and as long after as may be deemed expedient.'[5] Payment was to be made within six months of an authorizing Act.

The wording of this clause makes it clear that the local interests controlling the Ashby Canal were prepared to see it superseded by a railway. The Oxford and Coventry Canal companies took a different view; they strongly opposed the bill, which threatened the loss to their waterways of a very considerable long-haul coal tonnage,* and only agreed to it after compelling the Midland to make amendments.

The Act as agreed stated that the canal was to be kept in good order, with its water supply unaffected. If the Midland Railway did not do so, the Coventry company could undertake the work and charge the railway company with the cost. The maximum tolls to be charged in the future were not to exceed those levied by the canal company at the time of sale, nor were they to be greater than those charged by the railway on the competing line. Again, the Oxford company having foreseen that the Moira coal trade might be diverted to rail, the Act provided that if because of such diversion coal tolls were lowered on the Oxford, a proportionate lowering of those on the Ashby should take place, so long as they did not fall below ¼d per ton per mile. Lastly, the Board of Trade were given special powers of investigation.

The result was, of course, that the collieries along the line were put in an excellent position to compete. Moira used rail to some extent, but also owned its own fleet of boats well into this century, while Measham did not have rail connection till 1902. The railway contemplated by the Midland in 1846 had not been built, and serious rail competition was not offered until the Midland and the L.N.W.R. jointly opened the line from Overseal on the Leicester–Burton line to Nuneaton in 1873. Much of the tramroad line between Ashby and Worthington was also used for a Midland line opened in 1874.[7] The result (helped by the provisions of the 1846 Act) was that canal tonnages held up well. In 1862 138,117 tons were carried, in 1872, 116,853, in 1882 113,659. The real falls occurred in 1886, when traffic dropped to 74,604 from the previous year's 104,238, and again in 1893, when it fell to 33,329 from 58,092.

In 1856 a steam tug, the *Pioneer*, with twin propellers turning opposite ways to minimize wash, designed by John Inshaw of Birmingham and able to pull four loaded boats at 3 m.p.h., was bought by the manager of the Moira colliery to haul coal-boats towards London. The Grand Junction, Coventry and Oxford companies agreed to its use, but the Midland Railway as owners of the Ashby objected. The colliery company then employed the Coventry solicitors, Woodcock & Twist (Charles Woodcock being clerk to the Coventry Canal Company), to file a bill in Chancery for an injunction to restrain the railway company from

* In 1845 79,929 tons of coal from the Ashby passed on to the Oxford Canal.[6]

preventing the tug from working on the Ashby. The case was heard in 1859 before the Master of the Rolls who, after practical experiments had been made, decided that tugs of similar construction to the *Pioneer* should be allowed to navigate the canal at speeds not exceeding 3 m.p.h., costs being awarded against the railway company. The *Pioneer* and a similar tug the *Volunteer* seem then to have worked trains of boats on the comparatively lock-free stretches from Moira to Coventry, Rugby and Braunston.[8]

In 1875 a curious scheme, probably part of L. & N.W. Railway politics against the Leicester–Burton line, got as far as deposited plans. This was for a canal from Grendon north of Atherstone on the Coventry Canal to Congerstone on the Ashby, and from Shackerstone on the Ashby through Ravenstone near Coalville to Swannington, altogether about 20 miles of new waterway. In addition, a 6-mile branch was proposed from the Ashby near Market Bosworth to Ellistown colliery near Ibstock.

By the 1890s the railway was taking a pessimistic view of the canal. Maintenance was allowed to fall off, since it was known that the Coventry Canal was in an equally bad state,[9] and therefore in no condition to take action under the Act, even if it were financially strong enough for the battle. The Midland was probably encouraged by the failure of the Board of Trade to take action when appealed to by the Measham colliery company,[10] who thereupon put in a rail siding. By 1906, as envisaged in the 1846 Act, the coal tolls on the Ashby were down to ¼d, but the tonnage was by then only 38,130.

On 2 January 1918 a serious breach occurred in the embankment two miles from Moira, which necessitated the building of a section of new canal at a cost of £9,864. The line was reopened to Moira on 23 July 1919. In 1944 subsidence was increasingly affecting the upper section. This was used only by the Moira Colliery Co, who in 1943 had sent 20,807 tons of coal along it out of a total of 43,733 tons carried. At the initiative of Frank Pick, the whole canal was offered free by the L.M.S.R. to the Coventry Canal company, who refused it unless 'they received a substantial monetary consideration to cover the liability that they would incur'. The colliery company, anxious to mine beneath the canal, raised no objection, and in 1944 the upper 2½ miles from Moira to Donisthorpe were abandoned and dewatered.[11] In 1957 a further section of 4¾ miles from Donisthorpe to Ilott wharf, Measham, was closed under a British Transport Commission Act.

Oxford Canal

The year 1842 saw the first, and sudden, fall in the Oxford's gross receipts, from £86,217 in 1841 to £73,120, the result of toll reductions. The opening of the G.W.R. branch from Didcot to Oxford on 12 June 1844 affected the canal's river trade to Reading, and reduced takings from £76,211 in 1845 to £66,574 in 1846. Worse was the opening of the Great Western line to Banbury on 2 September 1850 and its extension to Birmingham on 1 October 1852, worse still the Buckinghamshire Railway from the L.N.W.R. at Bletchley to Banbury, opened for goods on 15 May 1850, and its branch to Oxford from Verney junction on 20 May 1851.

When the line to Banbury was about to open, the coal dealers there were nervous of stocking canal coal lest they be undersold. The canal wharfinger was therefore authorized to stock coal for sale to the public, and this move enabled the company to make a new agreement with the traders. However, in June coal dealing had also to be started at Wallingford, and cuts made in tolls to Banbury and places to Oxford, followed by others to points above and below Banbury in December. Then an effort was made to agree with the L.N.W.R. 'for equalizing the charges on the transit of Coals to Oxford and Banbury by Railway and Canal, and dividing the traffic between the two routes',[12] but this failed, and further reductions had to be made. The result was that between 26 June 1850 and 17 March 1852 the coal toll over the whole length from Longford to Oxford came down from 5s 11d to 2s 7d a ton, and proportionately for other distances. The effect was to reduce the company's takings from £46,198 in 1850 to £26,312 in 1853, at about which level they remained for over twenty years. The dividend, 30 per cent in 1844, had fallen to 20 in 1850, 11½ in 1853 and 9 per cent in 1855; it did not fall below 8 per cent till 1878.

The worst falls in receipts took place, as we might expect, on the Warwick line. Comparing 1861 with 1841, receipts at the Hawkesbury toll-house fell to 29·9 per cent of their former level, at Braunston to 36·3, but at Napton junction to 9·2 per cent. At a country wharf like Enslow they fell to 34·4 per cent. These did not, of course, connote corresponding falls in the tonnage carried. In 1838 the canal handled 520,000 tons, in 1868 482,000.

In 1865 the company decided to open the southern section of Fenny Compton tunnel 'in consequence of the representations made by Traders of the inconvenience it causes the Traffic'.[13] A year later they were offered the land over the northern section, and decided to open that too. The southern part was ready on 13 June 1868, and the northern about the beginning of August 1870. The feeder to Wormleighton reservoir had crossed the southern section. When the tunnel was opened the feeder was taken over the cutting in a rectangular open-topped wrought-iron channel on brick piers, which still exists.

Presumably because of the number of clergymen on its Board, the canal company was inclined to give donations towards the building or alteration of churches along the line that were attended by canal staff, and to the Boatmen's Chapel Fund. Because the clergy were mostly university dons, the company also consistently contributed to the many parish school buildings and enlargements that followed the Education Act of 1870, and then to maintain them. They did, however, jib when asked to contribute to the golden jubilee festivities of the villages on the canal. The company seem, incidentally, to have been outstandingly good employers. Even at the worst time of railway competition they made no wage reductions, but waited for retirements to make economies, and also had a liberal pension policy.

In 1876, when the Grand Junction carrying department closed down, the company received a notice from the Warwick canals requiring certain traffic to be forwarded over the Oxford Canal at through rates, about which they had not been consulted. The Oxford, together with the Regent's, was only of secondary importance, the main target being the L.N.W.R.-controlled Birmingham Canal Navigations, whose policy was to encourage local but not long-distance canal traffic. An example of their tolls was the Wolverhampton–London rate for iron, 4s 7d for 156 miles, of which the B.C.N. took 1s 8d for 12 miles. The Oxford refused to agree to the Warwick canals' demand, and were taken with the Birmingham to the Railway Commissioners; the Regent's never actually refused, but right to the end took up a discouraging attitude. These ruled in June 1877 that the B.C.N. through tolls should be considerably reduced, and the Oxford's to more than the Warwick canals had offered them, but less than their previous rate. The Oxford now agreed, supported the other canal companies against the B.C.N. when the latter appealed, and relieved their feelings by promptly refusing to allow the L.N.W.R. to take engine water at Newbold; they did not relent till 1896, when the railway agreed to pay 3d per 1,000 gallons for a minimum of 120,000 gallons a day. The Railway Commission then seems to have referred the dispute to the Board of Trade under s. 28 of the Act of 1846 which authorized the lease of the B.C.N. to the L.N.W.R., and which gave the Treasury or the Board power to take action 'to proceed forthwith to the Correction or Prevention of any Inconveniences or Evils' specified by them. 'Forthwith' was perhaps optimistic; the Board called a meeting in 1881, eventually an agreement on through tolls from south Staffordshire and east Worcestershire to London and the Thames was reached in December 1883, and came into force at the beginning of 1885. It gave the B.C.N. a considerably higher toll per mile than other canals, but it was something gained, and even the Grand Junction did not dare to disturb it.

From 1868 to 1892 dividends were well maintained, having fallen only from 8½ per cent in the former year to 6½ in the latter. Thereafter, however, the combined effect of increased railway competition, the lower tolls under the Railway & Canal Traffic Act schedules, and those of the inter-company through rates, brought the dividend down to 4½ per cent by 1899, from which it recovered to 5 per cent in 1931 and 7 per cent in 1938. Tolls, which had been £23,632 in 1870, were still £15,431 in 1913. After a fall during the war they rose to £19,654 in 1922, and then fell away to £13,514 in 1933. Thenceforward a slight recovery took place to £15,513 in 1938, probably the result of the enlarged Grand Union. Here, as with so many, we have a company whose dividend increasingly depended upon receipts other than from tolls: in 1938, for instance, when these yielded £15,513, other receipts produced £10,761.

The basin, which contained the principal wharves at Oxford, was sold in 1937, and Nuffield College now stands upon it.

CHAPTER XI

The Grand Union

✦

FROM 1845 the Grand Junction company's affairs passed through four phases. Until 1876 they worked hard to compete with the railways mainly through their own carrying department. Then, discouraged by the Regent's Park explosion and its inability to make profits, they gave it up, to rely upon the independent carriers who, earlier, they had not thought able to maintain the canal trade. The third began when Fellows, Morton & Clayton, the biggest of the carriers, persuaded them that it would be possible to regain the Derbyshire coal trade to London: the old Union and Grand Union were bought, options obtained on other canals on the Derbyshire and Birmingham lines, and the Foxton inclined plane built. But within twenty years the company realized that their hopes would not be fulfilled; the expansion ended, and a fourth period began, given to making the best of the canal while building up their property interests.

The initiative for a fifth phase of reconstruction came, indeed, partly from the Regent's. That company had spent much of the latter part of the nineteenth century trying to become a railway or part of a railway system, and in developing its dock. In the twentieth railway ambitions ended, and were replaced by a scheme, planned and carried out in the 1920s and 1930s, to amalgamate the canal companies from London to Langley Mill and Birmingham, and to base it upon the Regent's Canal Dock. This created the Grand Union, whose achievements and vicissitudes take us to nationalization.

The Grand Junction

From the opening of the London & Birmingham Railway in 1838 until 1857, when a rates agreement was made, railway* and

* From 1846 the London & North-Western Railway.

canal competed against each other. During that time carriers' charges and canal tolls alike fell greatly, though the tonnage carried by water increased. Here are figures for the Grand Junction:

	1838	1858
Receipts (tolls)	£152,657	£67,634
Tonnage carried	948,481	1,142,450
Average toll received per ton	3·2s	0·93d
Dividend	10 per cent	3½ per cent

Toll reductions were as far as possible carried through by agreement with the companies on the Leicester, Manchester and Birmingham routes, but on the last two they were hampered till 1846 by bitterness between the Grand Junction and the Oxford.

The Grand Junction's case was that the Oxford was taking advantage of its central position on the second and third routes to overcharge and so force other companies to make unreasonable reductions. For instance, in May 1841, just before price cuts by the railways, the canal tolls[1] between Manchester and London were as follows:

Canal	miles	tolls	
		s	d
Duke of Bridgewater's	25	1	0
Trent & Mersey	67	2	9½
Coventry (Fradley section)	5½		2¾
Birmingham (Fazeley section)	5½		5½
Coventry	21¼		11
Oxford	23⅝	2	11
Grand Junction	101	4	2½

In 1845, again, the Grand Junction alleged that the Oxford were charging 1¾d per ton per mile for coal to London against ¼d on the Grand Junction, and 3d for other goods against ½d, 'by which exactions the Oxford Canal Company had been and were still enabled to Share a Dividend of 30 per Cent, while the Grand Junction Canal Company were sharing one of only seven per Cent'.[2]

The Oxford based its case on three arguments: that the mileage of their canal was quoted as reduced by their shortening of 1834, for which convenience they made no charge other than their previous tolls for the more circuitous course; that whereas Oxford charges related to all traffic entering the Grand Junction, the latter's cheap rates were only for through trade to London; and that the Grand Junction favoured the Leicester line because of its special relationship to the Grand Union company. 'Should the proprietors of this Canal be at a loss', their committee said, '. . . to account for this marked partiality towards another Canal, and would enquire into the amount of the increased trade thereby thrown into the Union line, and who are among the parties deriving the profits of such increase, they might probably find a more satisfactory solution of such management than is furnished by the imputed high charges of the Oxford Canal.'[3]

It was perhaps an approach in May 1846 by the Grand Junction to the Warwick canals for 'a general amalgamation of their common interests',[4] which would have isolated the Oxford, that finally caused the latter to give way and make a comprehensive toll agreement in August.

In 1853, when the Grand Junction called a meeting of canal companies to consider policy on railway and canal amalgamations, and especially on the proposed union of the L.N.W.R., Midland and North Staffordshire railways, all of which controlled canals, the Oxford maintained its reputation for uncooperativeness, its broad view being that it disliked the Grand Junction much more than the railways. It suggested that the canals, both railway-owned and independent, in the area covered by the proposed amalgamation should be linked, 'so that the Railway Companies might have an interest in using the whole line of Canals in their district for the heavy traffic of the country, thereby relieving their Railways of a traffic which at present encumbers them, and is a fertile source of danger to their passenger trains'.[5] But 'the Grand Junction . . . having a monopoly of the carrying trade, a reduction of tolls on any of the canals upon which the Company carries would not necessarily involve any reduction to the public', and therefore the Oxford company 'cannot be parties in inducing the Committee of the House of Commons on Railway and Canal Amalgamation to report in favour of a principle of legislation, which in its application would benefit one Canal Company at the expense of the others'.

Price cutting continued; both tolls and freight rates had been driven to low levels when a rates agreement for maintaining differential charges was reached with the L.N.W.R. and G.W.R. in 1857. This agreement worked satisfactorily, so much so that a small rise in tolls in 1859 discussed with other canals was agreed to only after the Grand Junction had warned the others that 'any decided combination between the Railway and the Canals may materially affect the interest of the Canals with the Board of

Trade'.[6] Thenceforward long-distance tolls were held steady. About 1856 transhipment began from the G.W.R. at Bulls Bridge to the canal for destinations towards Paddington and down the Regent's.

The Grand Junction notably failed to hold, still less to increase, the carriage of coal to London against competition from the railways, notably the L.N.W.R. and the Great Northern. The following figures,[7] taken at five-yearly intervals, of coal imports to London paying the coal duties, must be read against an import by sea that remained fairly constant at about 3 million tons annually.

Year	By Canal tons	By Rail tons
1845	60,311	8,377
1850	29,479	55,096
1855	23,251	1,137,835
1860	19,593	1,477,546
1865	8,532	2,733,057

In addition, of course, the canal carried large quantities of coal to points near, but short of, the coal duties' boundary, such as Aylesbury, Leighton Buzzard, and points from Tring to King's Langley. But so, of course, did the railways.

Pickfords having left the canal at Christmas 1847, the Grand Junction decided in 1848 to enter the business; it raised £114,550 in preference shares and soon afterwards began operations that were to continue on a large scale till 1876. We have noted the agreements they made with the companies on the Leicester line to Langley Mill. A railway journal made this comment on the enterprise in August 1848:

'Grand Junction Canal and the London & North Western Railway
We understand that this Company having suffered much in their traffic from the London and North Western Railway, have determined to expend £100,000 in stations, better horses, &c., to go more rapidly and compete with the railway. They talk of having eight or ten-mile stages, and travelling ten miles an hour. We expect the fruit of this competition will be something like those of the labour of trying to wash poor blackie white.'[8]
One result was to set up Grand Junction carrying depots well away from that canal: for instance, at Stourbridge and Derby.

Unlike the Shropshire Union, which after experimenting with steam tugs went back to horse-haulage, the Grand Junction carrying department went in for steam cargo-carrying boats usually

hauling a butty. These seem to have been managed somewhat
haphazardly, for in 1864 the Leicester company complained of
'repeated injuries to the works of the Navigation caused by the
improper Navigation of the Steam Boats belonging to the Grand
Junction Company',[9] and received back a letter that 'Our Carrying
Establishment has never been a source of profit to ourselves although our neighbours have benefitted from it' . . . and went on
to say in allusion to their guarantee that if others complained also,
'the question will soon arise, how much longer are we to continue
paying our neighbours at a loss to ourselves'. In 1867 the Leicester
again complained of the 'improper and reckless Navigation of the
Grand Junction Company's Steamers',[10] and the Erewash added
that they had suffered loss 'from the negligence of the Men working these Boats both by damaging the Locks and injuring the
Banks by excessive speed'.[11]

In 1861 a curious accident took place with one of these steamers
in Blisworth tunnel:

'A barge, called the *Wasp* . . . was on its journey from Birmingham to London, having another boat in tow. In the first
boat were two men, named Gower and Jones, engine drivers,
and one or two other men employed on the canal. They were
passing through the tunnel at about three miles per hour, and
stopped at a place called a "stanks", which is a number of piles
driven in to afford a standing place for some workmen who
were engaged in repairing the tunnel. Here they took a carpenter
named Edward Webb, who lived at Stoke Bruerne. They proceeded on their way, and soon afterwards met in the tunnel two
boats, which were being worked by "leggers". They became
entangled, but by some exertion . . . set free. The boat which
the steamer was towing was, however, unloosed and was left
behind. The smoke from the engine-flue became very dense and
very much affected the "leggers", so much so that they could
not work. On board the steamboat the effect was such that it
suffocated two men, one of whom fell into the water, and was
not found till some hours afterwards, when the canal was
dragged. A third man in the company's employ was so overpowered that, on arriving at the mouth of the tunnel, he too
fell overboard; the water, however, restored him to conscious-
ness, and he managed to climb on board the boat again and
instinctively shut off the steam. The boat could only proceed a
short distance, and on arriving at the lock the awful catastrophe
was at once revealed. The young carpenter was lying dead in

the hold, one of the boatmen was missing, and the two engine-men were lying near the furnace awfully burned. They were at once removed to the *Boat* Inn, adjoining the lock, and medical men were immediately sent for from Towcester and Blisworth. They attended to the sufferers, who are now progressing favourably.'[12]

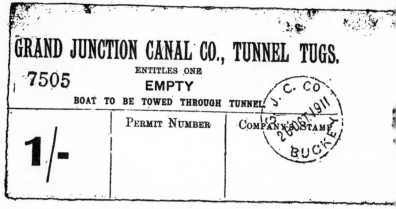

12. Grand Junction Canal tunnel tug permit

About 1869 endless wire ropes to which craft attached them-selves, and driven by steam engines, were installed in Blisworth and Braunston tunnels, to avoid the delays caused by slow 'legging'. They were replaced soon after 1871 by steam tunnel tugs to tow boats through, a service that lasted until 1936. These tugs were 49 ft long, with the boiler and engine in the middle.[13] After the 1861 accident the four existing ventilation shafts were supple-mented by a fifth; two more were opened in 1881.

In 1861 the engineer of the Regent's Canal had complained that 'Gunpowder was frequently conveyed upon the Canal by the Grand Junction Canal Company, in non-fire-proof vessels',[14] and his memorandum was sent to the Grand Junction with a note saying that they would 'be held responsible for any damage or loss that may result'. On 2 October 1874 one of the Grand Junc-tion's boats, laden with gunpowder and petroleum, blew up on the Regent's Canal in Regents Park, under Macclesfield bridge,* closing the canal till the 6th. As a result, 632 claims were made against the company, who had to pay out about £80,000. The

* See the account and illustration in my *British Canals*, 2nd ed., 1959, pp. 60-1, 76.

carrying business was not paying, and this disaster probably decided the company to give it up in 1876, leaving the field mainly
to Fellows, Morton & Clayton; it also encouraged the passing in
1875 of the Explosives Act, under which canal and other companies had to make by-laws to regulate the carriage of explosives.†

In 1838 the tonnage of through, as differentiated from local,
traffic on the Grand Junction had been 202,134 tons; in 1845 it had
risen to 294,257 tons. The figure dropped to 229,000 tons in 1846,
rose to 253,141 tons when the company started carrying, and then
fell slowly back to only 135,657 tons in 1870. The control of some
canals by railway companies, delays due to stoppages and frost,
attractive railway rates, and the gradual decline of canalside works
and collieries, were among the causes of the decline.

Meanwhile in 1863 the company had approached all the other
canals on the Birmingham, Coventry and Leicester lines (including
the Erewash, Nottingham and Derby companies) 'as to the expediency of a general Amalgamation of Canal interests'.[15] At first
the two Warwick canals, the Grand Union, old Union, Leicester,
Coventry and Regent's companies took interest in the idea, but
later all fell out except the two Warwick concerns. Finally, these
also stood aside on the grounds that the others had not supported
it.

During the nineteenth century the demand for bricks for London's housing caused a great development of brick and other
works along the canal in Middlesex, and a number of small private
branches totalling about 4½ miles were built, which can be traced
on early editions of the Ordnance plans and in many cases on the
ground. One, Otter Dock, a mile long, left the canal to the north
near Yiewsley & West Drayton station; it was built about 1822,
and extended about 1880 and 1895. Another feature not far away
was the Ordnance works at Wentworth Road, Southall, which
was served by a ring canal, the Hanwell loop. The Board of Ordnance had first suggested building this on 11 November 1813. A
final expansion, authorized by an Act of 1879, was the 5-mile
branch to Slough, which was opened in 1882 at a cost of about
£107,000.

At the end of 1886 Fellows, Morton & Clayton, already the
largest carriers, took over the London traffic of the London &
Midland Counties Carrying Co and negotiated even more favourable tolls. Probably at their instigation, the Grand Junction in-

† The gunpowder and ammunition boats to the Weedon arm had to be legged
through the tunnels after the steam tugs had tied up. They finished in 1920.

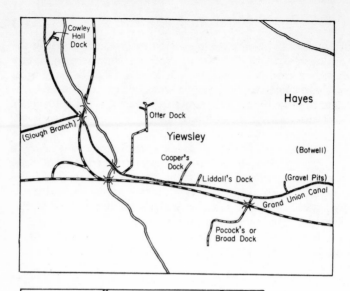

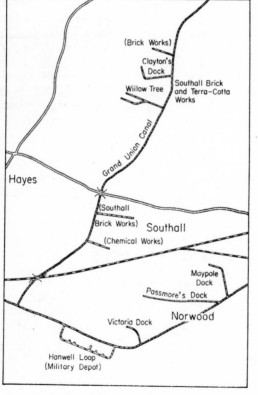

13. Plan of private branches from the Grand Junction Canal in Middlesex

spected the condition of the Grand Union and old Union canals, and then wrote to each clerk to ask if 'any arrangement could be entered into for improving and increasing the traffic on the respective Canals'.[16] They having replied offering to sell, the Grand Junction suggested £5,000 for the two. A counter-offer of £25,000 from the canals, who had an asset in their water supplies, was laid on one side by the bigger concern.

In February 1893 the Grand Union's engineer reported to his committee that the canal might do better if 'more energy were thrown into the matter of Boat accommodation, expedition and canvassing for trade, particularly on the part of the principal Carriers, Messrs. Fellows, Morton and Clayton Ltd.'.[17] The company then met Mr Fellows, who told them that trading under existing conditions was impossible, but that if the company would widen their two flights of narrow locks at Foxton and Watford and dredge the waterway to take 'wider boats with a heavier carrying capacity', Fellows, Morton would run large steamers which would enable them to compete with other forms of transport.

Immediately after this meeting Fellows wrote to the Grand Junction asking for a reduction in the guaranteed minimum of tolls he had to produce to get his 25 per cent drawback and suggesting that they should buy and improve the Leicester line. Shortly afterwards the carriers themselves asked the two companies for a selling price and were quoted £20,000; Fellows passed this information to the Grand Junction and was authorized to buy as their agent. On 12 July 1893 he reported that he had obtained the Grand Union for £10,500 and the old Union for £6,500, plus £250 compensation to their joint clerk.* The winding-up meetings were held on 16 November, the transfer Act[18] was passed in 1894, and the purchase was completed on 29 September of that year.

The Grand Junction started to dredge its new purchases, and also moved on to negotiate agreements for low through tolls, made under the powers of s. 43 of the Railway & Canal Traffic Act 1888, with the Leicester (£350 p.a.), the Loughborough (£200 p.a.) and the Erewash (£150 p.a.), though they failed to do so with the Regent's. Early in 1897, also, options to purchase all three were obtained at £38,075, £26,250 and £21,000 respectively. With toll agreements and prospective control over the whole canal line to the Derbyshire coalfields, the Grand Junction could now con-

---

* Subsequently increased to £17,400 in all to include winding-up costs.

P

sider seriously the proposal made to them by Fellows, Morton & Clayton in a letter of February 1896 to widen the locks at Foxton and Watford 'to enable them to work wide boats which they anticipated would decrease the cost of haulage and enable them to increase the traffic from the Leicester and Nottingham districts to London',[19] one that probably only confirmed an idea that had already been discussed. The company was certainly facing a calamitous situation, for in 1850 125,000 tons of Derbyshire coal had reached the Grand Junction; in 1855, 73,000 tons; and in 1894 only 4,700 tons. In July they decided in principle to go ahead with the building of an inclined plane at Foxton capable of taking 70-ton barges, while leaving Watford locks for later consideration, Fellows, Morton agreeing to put extra narrow boats on to the Leicester line while the incline was being built.

The plane was designed by the canal's engineer, G. C. Thomas, and his brother, to raise two narrow boats or one barge a vertical height of 75 ft 2 in. Tenders were received in November 1897, and that of J. & H. Gwynne & Co of Hammersmith for £14,130 was accepted. Construction began early in 1898, and the plane was opened for traffic on 10 July 1900, at a cost of £39,224 including the land. It was of counterbalanced type, using a steam-driven winch to overcome friction. The two caissons, connected by a wire rope, each ran sideways on eight sets of wheels carried on four pairs of rails. The time taken to exchange a pair of boats was said to be twelve minutes instead of seventy by the locks, and the cost of working to be £1 4s 6d a day, which, we may notice, was more than the net profit of the Grand Union for its last year of independent working.[20]

Even before the incline was at work, Thomas seems to have recommended against a second one, and early in the year the company authorized the widening of Watford locks for £17,000, though in March this order was countermanded 'till the Foxton lift is working satisfactorily'.[21] In August the company wrote to Fellows, Morton that 'the results from traffic are not at all encouraging, the through trade, especially Coal, of which we had great hopes, has decreased considerably',[22] and the options to buy the northern canals were allowed to lapse. In May 1901, in reply to an offer from the three northern canals to sell for a total of £50,000, the Grand Junction wrote that they had spent a large sum that was unremunerative, and were disappointed at abandoning 'a much cherished scheme of Canal amalgamation with the hope of developing the Coal traffic from the Nottingham district

to points on their Canal to London';[23] and in 1902 they added that
they feared the acquisition of the three northern canals would
'from past experience . . . simply be a burden to their existing
undertaking'.[24] Payments to the three northern companies had
regularly to be made under their guarantees. Between November
1901 and February 1902 Watford locks were completely rebuilt as
narrow locks at a cost of £5,545. The experiment had failed.

Thomas himself, who of course had an interest in showing that
responsibility for failure lay outside the Grand Junction, blamed
the bad condition of the railway-owned Cromford, and also of the
Erewash, the desuetude of the Nutbrook, and the high tolls of
the railway-owned Nottingham, in his evidence before the Royal
Commission.[25] The plane itself was not at fault, for both Thomas
and the company were sufficiently impressed with its usefulness to
suggest to the Royal Commission in 1906 the building of a number
of others as part of a plan to enlarge several canals to 80-ton
standard.

The Watford widening was therefore dropped. In November
1908 it was decided to reinstate the Foxton locks to pass traffic at
night when the incline was not working; on 26 October 1910
instructions were given to cease working the incline after a fortnight, and to revert to the locks for all traffic,* and finally, in
January 1911 the company told Fellows, Morton, who were reported to be preparing to use engined and horse-hauled wide
boats between Braunston and London, that these would cause a
serious inconvenience in the tunnels and could only be used south
of Stoke Bruerne. So ended the Grand Junction's efforts to improve the Leicester line. The machinery of the incline was dis-
mantled in 1926, and sold in 1928 for £250.

In 1897 we get a glimpse of the trouble canals experienced from
insufficient means of getting rid of sewage. An engineer, E. Bailey
Denton, went over the River Brent, and reported:

'At the present time masses of sewage sludge are visible floating
on the canal above the Tumbling Bay,† and are being continually carried over into the backwater only some thirty yards
above the effluent outlet from the Hanwell works. Each laden
barge that passes up the canal stirs up the filthy deposit in the
bed, and barge-men state that the condition of the waterway
above the Hanwell outfall is such that they are unable to eat

* In fact, the incline was used occasionally in 1912, and perhaps later, probably
when the locks were being repaired.
† Where the canal joined the Brent.

their meals until they get above the London Colney Asylum locks.'[26]

In the autumn of 1902 there was a severe drought which for three months hindered canal traffic, especially over Tring summit. 'Heroic exertions on the part of the Grand Junction Company's engineer and servants do not enable more than 80 or 90 barges a week to pass over the Tring summit, whereas in times of plentiful water 130 pass. . . . An extraordinary meeting of boatmen stretches three miles along the bank and never adjourns. Their horses lie down and go to sleep, their wives sit knitting and gossip, their children playing in the fields. . . . A pumping station at Cow Roast . . . is labouring with a reduced head of water. . . . It is the pumping station, brought into use two months ago, that has saved the traffic from cessation.'[27]

By this time the toll on long-distance traffic had fallen to a very low figure. In 1905 the through toll from Birmingham to London gave an average of ·158d per ton per mile; within this figure, the Oxford was taking ·363d, the Birmingham Canal Navigations ·357d, the Warwick canals ·21d, and the Grand Junction only ·101d. The possession of a long line was not necessarily an advantage.

It was not until 1906 that the name of Praed ceased to appear in the list of directors of the company, an association that had lasted from its foundation. In 1913 R. F. de Salis became chairman, and remained so until the formation of the Grand Union, one of a family whose name had appeared intermittently in the minute books since Peter de Salis was recorded as a shareholder in 1795.

From 1850 until 1928, when the company was absorbed by the Regent's, the dividend had been maintained at or near 4 per cent, but as the years had passed a greater proportion of the receipts had come from income other than tolls, mainly from property developed near the canal in London.

Newport Pagnell Canal

In 1845 the L.N.W.R. applied for authority to take the canal and make a branch from their main line at Wolverton to Newport Pagnell, but were refused. However in 1862 the canal company agreed to sell itself to the Newport Pagnell Railway for £9,000, the line to be worked by the L.N.W.R. After opposition from the Grand Junction, Oxford and other canal companies, who went so far as to send a deputation to the Board of Trade, and also from the Moira and Shipley collieries as the main suppliers of water-borne coal, the Act[28] was passed in 1863. The canal was finally closed on Monday, 29 August 1864,[29] and the railway partially built on its site.

The Warwick Canals

The full weight of railway competition, mainly from the London & Birmingham, fell upon the Warwick canals, with their predominantly through trade. For such traffic the tolls on the Warwick & Napton, in 1838 mostly at or near Parliamentary levels, were in 1839 reduced to 20 per cent below, in 1840 to one-third below, and in 1844 to two-thirds below. A casualty of 1841 was the old rates agreement with the Coventry company, whose competition was thenceforth added to that of the railways. Dividends came down with a run, on the Warwick & Napton from 15½ per cent in 1838 to 8 per cent in 1843 and 2 per cent in 1845, around which figure it was maintained till 1850; ¾ per cent for 1851 and nothing for many years thereafter. The Warwick & Birmingham paid 16½ per cent in 1838, 11 in 1843, 9 in 1845, 4 in 1850, 2 per cent in 1853, and then nothing.

In 1845 signs of the times were the departure of the Warwick & Napton's clerk to be clerk to a railway company, and the refusal of their bankers to grant an overdraft to pay the dividends, upon which they at once switched their account to another bank. They also received an offer from the London & Birmingham Extension & Northampton, Daventry, Leamington & Warwick Railway to buy theirs and the other two Warwick canals. They agreed, at the same time giving the usual notices of intention to build their own railway should the agreement fall through. The railway promoters paid over a total of £10,000 in deposits, and then came back to say that they were unlikely to get an Act authorizing conversion, and suggested instead the formation of a separate company to convert the Warwick & Birmingham and Warwick & Napton, which would be bought for £545,000. These terms were refused, the canal concerns trying instead to enforce the original contract. No more was heard of the scheme, but the companies thankfully kept the deposits.

The Warwick & Napton was now in a bad way, the Warwick & Birmingham not much better. Many of their bondholders, feeling nervous, asked for repayment. Only a little cash could be found, replacement loans could not be negotiated, and they had to promise that most of their profits would be put to debt redemption; the Napton company also raised its interest rate. For a time the companies struggled on against falling revenues, having negotiated with the Grand Junction's carrying department similar agreements for maximum through tolls to those already made on the Leicester line. But the bondholders' pressure was too great, and on 28 July a receiver was appointed for the Warwick & Napton, and on 2 November for the Warwick & Birmingham.

It seems that both companies were then reconstructed, with capital much written down. Small dividends were resumed on the Warwick & Birmingham in 1859, on the Napton not till 1871, but never thereafter exceeded 3 per cent on the former or 1¾ per cent on the latter. How greatly the companies' revenues had been affected by competition can be seen from the following figures:

| | *Warwick & Birmingham* | | *Warwick & Napton* | |
	tons carried	receipts £	tons carried	receipts £
1838	319,927	33,700	308,045	19,092
1848	226,084	15,788	219,643	9,055
1858	208,071	7,240	201,789	4,742
1868	243,373	7,216	212,948	4,240

Thereafter their life was unexciting until in 1895 both made a conditional agreement to amalgamate with the Grand Junction, but the bill had to be withdrawn on rating grounds. Three years later the latter company agreed to charge and collect the whole of the through tolls between Birmingham and London. Then in 1903 Fellows, Morton & Clayton offered to lease both canals 'with a view to providing Electric traction along the same',[30] but instead for a time acted as the Grand Junction's carrying agents on the London and Birmingham run, they guaranteeing 100,000 tons of traffic a year, reduced in 1904 to 70,000 tons.

In 1917 the three Warwick canals put themselves under the management of a joint committee consisting of four members of the Warwick & Birmingham's board and three of the Napton's, the rest attending only on formal occasions; it was increased to nine, split five and four, in 1919. Finally, the three Warwick canals were sold to the Regent's and on 1 January 1929 became part of the new Grand Union.

Regent's Canal

The position of the Regent's Canal, running as it did from near

Paddington station across the tracks of the northern railway termini to the river not far from the India docks, made it an obvious site for a railway linking the termini. In 1845, after two such outside suggestions had been put forward, the company's engineer, William Radford, suggested that they themselves should build 'a Railway (as far as practicable along the Canal) from a point near the City Road Basin, to the London & Birmingham Railway; and from thence to the Great Western Railway'.[31] Immediately afterwards the company were approached by an outside group to sell for conversion, and after turning down an offer of £725,000, settled for a million in September, the projectors of the London Junction, later the Regent's Canal, Railway, agreeing to deposit £5,000, to be forfeited if the subscription were not filled by the end of the year. It was not, and the deposit remained with the canal company. A line that threatened competition, however, was the East & West India Docks and Birmingham Junction, later the North London; it was authorized in 1846 from the L.N.W.R. at Camden to the docks, and paid the Regent's £8,000 in compensation.

In July 1846, after the City Termini Commission had reported, the company again became interested in taking action before someone else did, and referred a proposal for railway conversion to the engineer James Rendel, who estimated £685,000 for building a line from Paddington station to the Regent's Canal Dock, as far as possible along the canal, with a branch to the West India Dock. However, there was opposition from the new East & West India Docks railway company and from those who objected to a railway through Regent's Park, and the bill was withdrawn.

The rail-water transhipment facilities already arranged with the L.N.W.R. were supplemented when in 1850 transfers started from the Great Northern, who had built a goods yard and warehouses near Maiden Lane just north of Kings Cross. *The Observer* of 5 December 1850 wrote: 'The Great Northern Railway commences carrying ... on Thursday next, and from its cheaper tariff, shorter distance and facilities for loading and unloading barges under cover of the warehouse at Kings Cross, it is likely to divert a large portion of goods traffic from the London and North-Western and Midland lines.'

Eventually the canal had rail-water transfer facilities also with the Great Western, Eastern Counties, Midland & Great Central. The line to Euston had passed over the canal, as did that later to

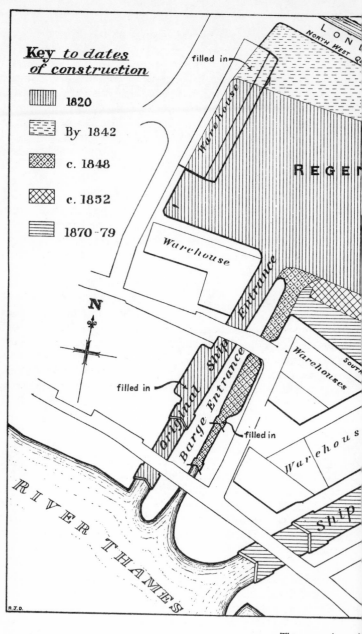

Key *to dates of construction*

▦	1820
▦	By 1842
▦	c. 1848
▦	c. 1852
▦	1870-79

filled in

Warehouse

REGEN

Warehouse

Entrance

N

filled in

Original Ship Entrance

Barge Entrance

filled in

Warehouses

Sou

Warehous

Ship

R I V E R   T H A M E S

LON

NORTH WEST Q

R.J.D.

14. The successive enl

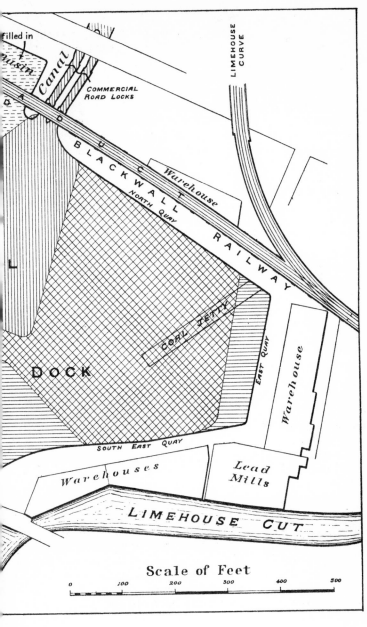

Scale of Feet

0   100   200   300   400   500

t's Canal dock

St Pancras;* an aqueduct had, however, to be built to take the canal over the Kings Cross line; water was turned into the first half on 27 October 1851, and completely about March 1852.

In 1847, exceptionally for a canal company, the Regent's took over all horse towing except on the trade to the Lee, the charge being added to the toll and the work put under a Superintendent of Towing Horses. A bad start was made when some drivers struck only a month after the scheme had been introduced. They were dismissed, pleas from the traders for their reinstatement were rejected, and there seems to have been no further trouble. In 1850, when tenders for towage by contract were sought, the lowest was £5,973 p.a. more than the cost to the company.

Throughout the nineteenth century the Limehouse basin, or Regent's Canal Dock as it was later called, was steadily improved. In 1836, the year that the London & Blackwall Railway was authorized to run along part of the north side of the dock, an agreement was made with that company whereby a quay wall was built, and a barge basin excavated under and to the north of the railway and eastwards of the canal entrance, much of it at railway expense. The work, which also included a northwards extension of the dock itself, was completed by 1842. On 30 May 1849 a barge entrance, east of the older ship entrance, with a lock 79 ft by 14 ft 6 in., was opened which, with further extensions of the dock to the east and south, cost £30,000. In July 1848 a new idea developed, when the committee met that of the Lee Navigation to propose a level junction between the Limehouse Cut and the dock through a short cut, with two stop-locks, the Bromley and the Britannia, at each end of the Cut to protect it and the dock against changes in the water levels. The Regent's was to pay part of the cost, to maintain the junction, and to levy tolls for its use by Lee traffic. Agreement was reached in December 1852, and the connection was built soon afterwards.

In 1852 the company also hoped to build 'an additional Ship Entrance from the Thames into the Limehouse Basin, so as to receive the new Screw Steam Colliers now used for the transit of Coals from the North . . . having regard to the present deficiency of Dock accommodation for the increased and increasing Trade of the port of London, and to the peculiar capabilities offered by the Limehouse Dock and the property adjoining for that purpose'.[32] However, the cost proved too great, but hydraulic cranes and new sheds and equipment were installed.

* Though a branch from St Pancras to the Metropolitan lines was carried beneath it.

In 1863 it was agreed to build a new ship entrance to the east of the old entrances, buy more land, widen and deepen a portion of the dock, and build a river wharf outside it. To do so, the land occupied by the connection to the Limehouse Cut had to be used, and an agreement of November 1864 with that navigation provided for a separate entrance and channel for Lee traffic. Once more the dock was separated from the Cut, the Limehouse lock from the Cut into the Thames being at the same time widened from 16 ft to 20 ft. An Act was obtained in 1865, and on 2 August 1869 the new dock entrance, its lock 350 ft by 60 ft to take 3,000-ton craft, was opened. One more enlargement, which took the dock to the south and west, and a little to the east also, of the new ship entrance, was completed between 1877 and 1879.

A portion of the old barge basin under the railway had been filled in before 1873, and the whole by 1926, when the quay wall was extended across it. The old ship entrance was partially filled in by 1897, wholly by 1922, and the old barge lock closed in 1924, though part of it was visible until recently. The dock is still a busy one, serving regular steamer services to Belgium, Denmark, Germany, Norway, Sweden and Spain. In 1965 the British Waterways Board obtained an Act to close the river entrance of the Limehouse Cut, and once more to make a connection between the Cut and the dock.

Schemes in connection with railways continued in the fifties. In 1859 the canal company agreed to sell for conversion to the promoters of the Central London Railway & Dock Co* for £803,040. However, after opposition from the Grand Junction and others, the bill was lost. The canal's engineer and John Fowler then prepared a plan for a line beside the canal from Kings Cross station to the Dock with an extension to Copenhagen Fields, which would not have affected the waterway, but this got no further than a prospectus and draft bill.

The capital structure of the company was now cleared up. In 1869 the company began to issue debentures to replace the mortgage debt, which in 1867 had stood at £131,050, and in 1874 decided to convert the 36,018 shares, nominal value £996,625, into new £25 shares totalling £900,450. Trade was very large: for the year 1876–7 the tonnage handled was 2,240,274, of which 1,427,047 passed on the canal, the rest being handled only at the dock. Receipts were £92,877, net profit £46,559, and dividend £4 17s 6d per cent.

* This was long before the Central London underground line.

Still another agreement with an outside group was made in 1875, and an Act for the 'Purchase and Improvement of the Regent's Canal and Dock, and the connection of the Limehouse Dock and Basin with the existing Railway systems' was passed to incorporate the Regent's Canal & Dock Co, and transfer the undertaking to them. But the new promoters did not follow up the authority, and the Act lapsed.

So busy was the company that between 1877 and 1882 it opposed the granting of through tolls on certain commodities between Birmingham and London (see p. 215) on the grounds that 'the Traffic on important Sections of this navigation, is already so great, that the introduction of a large Trade in Boats . . . would at times be detrimental to the interests of the Public'.[33] This large trade used great quantities of water. In 1833 the company had taken over powers obtained earlier by the Grand Junction to build a reservoir at the Welsh Harp, Hendon. This was opened in June 1835 as an addition to its other reservoirs at Ruislip and Aldenham. About 1853 the Welsh Harp was enlarged, and in 1861 Aldenham was given up. Then, from 1865 onwards, pumps were installed to pump back to the summit from the dock level. These were replaced at the turn of the century by a 38 in. main and five pumping stations, and after that the canal had no more water difficulties.

In September 1880, soon after the Islington tunnel tug had caught fire and sunk, and the Superintendent of the Zoo had been given permission to catch fish in the canal to feed the rare birds, an offer of £1,170,585 in cash was received and accepted, an Act was passed in 1882 to authorize numerous lines of railway, and on 31 March 1883 the sale was completed and the old canal board met for the last time. The company was now the Regent's Canal City and Docks Railway Co, a new board taking office under the chairmanship of J. S. Forbes, the chairman also of the District Railway.

Various railway lines had been authorized, but no action followed until in 1889 a committee of shareholders asked to meet the Board to discuss the 'great advantages they would derive from the carrying out of the Railway undertaking'. A special meeting in August then decided that some of the lines should be proceeded with as a separate undertaking with a capital of £2½ million. Still nothing happened, till in 1892 an Act was passed to abandon certain lines, extend the period for others, and change the name of the company to the North Metropolitan Railway & Canal Co until 1900, when it became the Regent's Canal & Dock Co.

No lines were ever built. In 1905 the Regent's Canal, apart from the dock, carried 1,045,184 tons of goods, about two-thirds of it upwards traffic from the dock, including 234,000 tons of sea-borne coal mostly bound for canalside gasworks, and a great deal of timber for furniture and box-making industries, carried in barges of up to 100 tons. Almost alone of those who gave evidence before the Royal Commission, the company said that they would be willing to enlarge to 400-ton standard at their own expense if the adjoining waterways would do the same. The revenue in 1905 was £92,000, of which £29,000 came from warehouse and wharf rents.

The extensive Birmingham and Midlands traffic of earlier years had largely been lost to rail. Only about one-ninth of the Regent's tonnage was exchanged, mostly with the Grand Junction, a little with the Lee. The bulk was local, and some of it was threatened by the increasing size of Thames lighters working for instance to Westminster, combined with better cartage services from Thames wharves to places formerly served from the canal. Four-fifths of the towing was still done by the company, using horses, which were considered to be most economical for working barges through the many locks, and a steam tug working on chain haulage through Islington tunnel. Incidentally, at this early date the company had worked out a plan to build a motor road above their canal and part of the Grand Junction, using its underside to support cables for overhead electric traction of their craft.

In 1908 the company had tried to get their dock and canal included in the bill to set up the Port of London Authority, but had failed. After the strains of World War I, they set about building the Medland and Bergen quays and warehouses (the present Quays B and A in the south-west part) at the dock, raising the money by mortgage. These were opened in 1922. Dividends, which had fallen from 2 per cent in 1908 to 1⅛ per cent in 1913, rose to 1¼ in 1922, and an average of 2 per cent from 1924. Then began the planning of the scheme that was soon to become the Grand Union.

Hertford Union Canal

The better prospects of the early 1840s came to nothing, and by 1848 the canal was unused. Sir George Duckett saw no future for it, and a clay stank was put across it to prevent loss of water by the Regent's.

In May 1851 the canal was advertised for sale. The Regent's company considered buying it, but decided against. In 1855 they changed their minds, and obtained an enabling Act. The purchase was reported complete on 28 October 1857, in which year Sir George disposed of the other navigation he possessed, the River Stort, to Gurney & Co of Norwich.

The Hertford Union has been kept open ever since.

The Grosvenor and the Kensington

The Grosvenor remained in use as a private canal until an Act[34] of 1858 confirmed an agreement between the Victoria Station & Pimlico Railway and the Duke of Westminster, which authorized 'the making of a Station at, in, or near the Grosvenor Basin ... the diverting or narrowing of the Grosvenor Canal and the making of a new Towing-path between or near the Points at which the Grosvenor Canal passes under Ebury Bridge and Eccleston Bridge respectively'. The land was conveyed in 1859, the canal shortened to end by Eccleston Bridge without a basin, and the railway opened to the new Victoria station over the canal site on 1 October 1860. Under a London Brighton & South Coast Railway Act of 1899[35] the canal above Ebury Bridge was to be closed and absorbed into the expanding railway lines: closure probably took place in 1902.

In 1866 the Vestry of St George, Hanover Square, then a local government body, leased premises in Pimlico Road near Ebury Bridge for use, among other purposes, as a depot for barging away house and street refuse by the canal, and receiving road and other materials. The remaining section of the canal was sold by the Duke of Westminster in 1904 to the Westminster City Council, and still enables London's refuse to be barged out to sea.

As we saw, the Kensington Canal was taken over by the West London Railway company in 1839. The line was opened in May 1844 to a terminus at what is now Kensington (Olympia) station, adjoining the canal basin. Passenger services were a failure, and goods were not much better. After only a few months the company was unable to carry on, and in 1845 the line was leased to the London & Birmingham with Great Western support. The canal was not, however, leased, and remained the property of the West London company, which thus found itself in the odd position of operating a canal while their railway was worked by others. Their headquarters now became a room built on to the wharf house near the Warwick road basin. In 1844 traffic on the canal had been 32,519 tons yielding £334; in 1846 45,728 tons yielding £489. It was not a gold-mine.

After various manoeuvres a new railway company, the West London Extension, promoted by several railway companies including the L.N.W.R., was authorized in 1859. The Kensington Canal was transferred to it, and power was given to convert the length between the basin and Kings Road, Chelsea, to a railway opened in March 1863. Part of the rest was filled in, part transferred free to the Imperial Gas Light & Coke Co, and part, less than ½ mile long leading out of Chelsea Creek, remains open, the property of the British Waterways Board, and carries some trade to the gasworks. It is, however, more like a tidal dock than a canal.

Millwall Canal

In 1864 a bill was introduced and passed[36] for a scheme reminiscent of the old Isle of Dogs Canal, to authorize the Millwall Canal Company to build a canal across the Isle of Dogs from Limehouse Reach nearly opposite the Greenland Dock to Blackwall Reach near Cubitt Town pier, and from it a branch north towards the West India Docks. The capital was to be £510,000, and £170,000 more if necessary. The purpose, however, was not a transit canal, but to provide shipping wharves and also accommodation for shipbuilding and other businesses needing waterside premises. In the next few years the plan was much changed, partly because of a railway branch authorized in 1865 from the London & Blackwall; in March 1868 the western half of the original plan and the branch, both much enlarged, were opened as a dock, the concern's name being changed in 1870 to the Millwall Dock Company.

The Grand Union

The first step towards the creation of the Grand Union was taken in 1925, when the Grand Junction sought a report from the engineer of the Warwick canals on the cost of putting them in order and, having had his reply, appointed a special committee to consider purchase or a merger. The possibilities opened up for the future of canals were a number of existing companies to be superseded by one big enough to compete on better terms with other forms of transport were discussed between the Regent's and the

Grand Junction, and led W. H. Curtis, chairman of the Regent's, about the end of the year to suggest purchase of the Grand Junction concern other than its Paddington estates. Negotiations went on throughout 1926, and agreement in principle was reached in November, subject to the Grand Junction in turn acquiring the Warwick canals.

A year later the Grand Junction had agreed to do so, though for convenience the actual purchase was carried out by the Regent's company. In November 1927 the latter suggested the name 'Grand Union' for the united concern, and a few days later the proposed combined board, of four Regent's and three Grand Junction directors, was chosen. Bills were deposited in January 1928.

The Regent's agreed to pay £62,258 15s 0d (£67 per share) for the Warwick & Birmingham, £65,104 for the Birmingham & Warwick Junction, and £8,641 (£35 per share) for the Warwick & Napton, plus £4,000 compensation to an officer and committee members. The total figure, paid in cash, included the purchase of investments that had been valued in 1927 at £87,000. As regards the Grand Junction, it was arranged that after having transferred to the Regent's all its assets other than the Paddington estates, it should continue as a property limited company—as it still does. The successor company was allotted a large block of Grand Union 5½ per cent debentures, and the original shareholders received new Grand Union shares on the approximate basis of £70 18s 6d per £100 of Grand Junction stock.

In August 1928 the Acts were obtained, and the new company came into existence from 1 January 1929. In February they issued a block of preference shares, in August decided to apply for a grant under s. 2 of the Development (Loans, Guarantees and Grants) Act, 1929, for a reconstruction scheme between Braunston and Birmingham, and paid a dividend on their first year's working of 1⅜ per cent. The development plan envisaged an immediate scheme to widen so that craft of 12 ft 6 in. beam and drawing 4 ft 6 in. could navigate to Birmingham, with the ultimate aim of increasing the width to take 14 ft barges. The cost of the immediate scheme was estimated at £881,000, towards which the Government agreed to make a grant of 5 per cent interest on £500,000 for ten years, and 2½ per cent for another five. The enabling Act was passed in 1931, money was raised, mainly by debentures, and work began.

Meanwhile the idea of getting a further grant to help finance the widening of Foxton and Watford locks occurred to the company.

This led to the purchase of the Leicester Canal for £48,126 10s 0d, the Loughborough for £11,595 and the Erewash for £15,702, sums that included considerable property. The authorizing Act, with further capital powers, was passed in 1931. Almost at the same time the Government refused a grant towards the £144,000 estimated cost of widening the two lock flights.

Between early 1928 and 1931 the Coventry company had been sounded, and a series of talks with the Oxford had covered possible arrangements varying from running powers to outright purchase. In 1931 provisional agreement upon buying the Oxford company was reached, only to be broken off probably because a settlement could not be made upon the future of the property owned by that company in Oxford. The 1931 Grand Union Act, however, enabled the latter to carry out certain works between Napton and Braunston at their own expense. In July 1935, W. H. Curtis, addressing the Royal Society of Arts, said: 'The Company was precluded, by circumstances into which I need not enter, from acquiring a further portion of the Oxford Canal and also the Coventry Canal, which would have given a water route under one ownership, thus establishing a direct contact with the Warwickshire coalfields and the industries in that district.'

Between Calcutt and Sampson Road at the top of Camp Hill locks, Birmingham, 52 old narrow locks were converted to weirs, and 51 new broad locks, 83 ft 6 in. by 15 ft, to take a pair of narrow boats or a future barge, built alongside; on the Knowle flight six locks were replaced by five, and at Bascote two separate locks by a staircase pair. Lock sills were dropped or weirs raised to give a depth of 5 ft 6 in. over the sills, and the waterway rebuilt to give a similar dredged depth and a bottom width of 26 ft. Over 26 miles of walling or protection work was also carried out. South of Braunston the lock sills were also dropped as necessary or the weirs raised to give the standard 5 ft 6 in. depth of water over the sills.

The Grand Union intended to encourage the use of 12 ft 6 in. wide barges upwards from Berkhampsted to Birmingham pending the ultimate scheme, which would have involved much bridge reconstruction, and one prototype timber craft, the *Progress*, to carry 66 tons and powered by a British Junkers engine supplied by Peter Brotherhood Ltd, was built by Bushell Bros of Tring at a cost of some £1,158: she remained afloat until 1963. It was in *Progress* that the Duke of Kent worked down Hatton locks to the bridge on his way to lunch at Warwick after having opened the

Q

top lock of the flight on 30 October 1934, to mark the completion of the wide locks. The whole work, however, was not finished until 1937. Because the ultimate scheme of extending the bottom width of the canal was never carried out, there were so many lengths where two such craft as *Progress* could not pass that it soon seemed impractical to use wide craft. The curious can still see near the Rose & Castle Hotel at Braunston the entrance made to a proposed basin where cargoes were to be transhipped from the 12 ft 6 in. barges to narrow boats working up the northern section of the Oxford Canal.

It had been clear to the new company from its formation that traffic would not come to the reconstructed line: it would have to be sought. Even while the 1928 bill was going through, the Regent's had ordered a motor-boat and butty, the *George* and *Mary*, 'suitable for navigation between London and Birmingham'. Then in August 1930 a small firm at Northampton, Associated Canal Carriers Ltd, were found to be owing £609, and were bought for that and £750 more. The Grand Union carried on and modestly expanded this business over the next few years, until by the end of 1934 some £20,000 had been invested in it, though no profits had yet been earned. In January 1932 the Erewash Canal Carrying Company was also formed as another subsidiary—it remained a comparatively small one—to continue and develop after their purchase by the Grand Union the carrying already in existence on the Loughborough and Erewash lines.

After experimenting first with small compartment boats* and then with an improved design of narrow boat, Associated Canal Carriers at the end of 1934 proposed to change its name to the Grand Union Canal Carrying Company Ltd, to increase its fleet from 14 pairs to about a hundred, and to pay for them by issuing debentures. In April 1936 W. H. Curtis, the chairman of both the canal and the carrying companies, reported that this expansion had taken place. 'Never before in the history of Canal Transport has such a programme been embarked upon,' he said, 'the greater number of boats in commission, the more economically and efficiently can we run our concern.' By then Thomas Clayton (Paddington) Ltd, a firm engaged in boating refuse from Paddington, Willesden and Hayes, had been bought, to be operated separately from the carrying company. Orders had been placed by the carry-

---

* Four such welded boats, each 18 ft by 7 ft by 4 ft 6 in., intended to carry 10 tons, to fit together into a narrow lock, and to be towed in series, were ordered from Peter Brotherhood Ltd in 1932.

ing company for a further 62 pairs, to be followed in May by 40 pairs more, a total of some 200 pairs, and in July negotiations were opened to buy the S. E. Barlow fleet also. To pay for the first craft ordered, £120,000 had been borrowed from an investment company in debentures.

By now, however, the main company was doing badly. Tolls and dock dues, instead of rising, had fallen from £160,510 in 1929, the first year after the acquisition of the Grand Junction and Warwick canals, but before the purchase of the Leicester group, to £132,367 in 1936 including that group; water sales also fell, largely because the railways had found other supplies; and the carrying concern was well in the red. Tolls had been affected by heavy competition from rail and quickly growing road transport, and also by developments such as the new Battersea power station, the opening of which had caused the closing of small installations on the Regent's Canal and the loss of some 30,000 tons a year of coal traffic. In 1931 1¼ per cent had been paid on the Ordinary, in 1932 ¾ per cent, in 1933 ⅞ per cent, and since then nothing; after 1936 there were to be no Preference payments either.

Late in 1935 the firm of John Miller (Shipping) Ltd introduced a new trade in iron and steel imported from the Continent to Regent's Canal Dock, and put on canal for Birmingham, a trade that immediately aroused protests from the railway companies associated with the Canal Association in the Rail-Canal Conference set up in 1933. The Grand Union held their position, and in February 1936 the John Miller firm were appointed the company's agents in France, Belgium and the Netherlands. In October Miller was elected a director, a month later a Commercial Manager was appointed, and in January 1937 J. M. Whittington joined the Board. In February E. J. Woolley (who had also joined the Board in January), Miller and Whittington were appointed a committee of investigation, with full power to make staff economies and changes, and to reorganize the business. At the same time the company withdrew from the Canal Association and so from the Rail-Canal Conference, so that its hands would be free to fight for traffic.

In March W. H. Curtis was re-elected chairman, but a month later he resigned to become consultant to the company. Woolley became chairman, and Miller and Whittington a committee of management with Miller in the chair. Other directors soon retired and were replaced, and certain officers also; some years later Miller became chairman and managing director.

The carrying company, with its tremendous existing and poten-

tial debt, was also reorganized. In October 1936 John Miller became a director. At that time 115 pairs were in commission and
manned, many of them with old 'Number Ones', but the problems
of finding crews to operate those on order, of providing working
capital, and of paying debenture interest, appeared formidable. In
November it was decided to stop negotiations with S. E. Barlow,
to appoint John Miller managing director of the carrying company, and that 'it will be the Company's policy to work, for the
time being, only 100 pairs of boats and to lay up the remainder. . . .
All old boats to be withdrawn from commission and only those in
perfect working order to be used. As and when required, boats to
be brought back into service'.

The former manager, who had been appointed on 1 June 1934,
then resigned, followed in April 1937 by W. H. Curtis the chairman. In December a further £130,000 was raised in 6 per cent
debentures to pay for the boats on order, and, in addition to the
initial capital, 100,000 £1 ordinary shares were created and issued
to the Grand Union company, 2s 6d paid up. The sum paid up,
and further such sums called in future years, went to pay the
interest on the carrying company's debenture debt.

In the years that followed the figure for boats in commission
and manned (out of 184 pairs still owned after some weeding out),
never rose above 119 (in September 1937), and by July 1939 was
102, plus 9 motors and 8 butties on hire, mostly to the Erewash
Carrying Co. Even then, manning was a difficulty: in May 1937,
with 107 pairs manned, twelve were carrying trainees. Later,
during the war, both men and women[37] crews were trained.
Tonnage carried rose from 142,866 in 1936 to 211,959 in 1939. The
charges for debenture interest and depreciation on craft, many
laid up, were so high that for 1936 the carrying company's loss was
£25,576 (it had been £9,595 for the last ten months of 1935), and
for 1937, when the full weight of the charges was borne, £31,959.
Then the loss slowly fell, to £23,226 for 1939, and £14,501 (including a government subsidy of £7,613) for 1940. Thereafter
figures were much affected by the war and the subsidy, and it was
not until 1946 that a net profit of £2,333 was made by the carrying
company exclusive of subsidy. By this time, however, its finances
had been reorganized and debenture debt liquidated, and its fleet
was down to 79 pairs. Including the benefit of subsidies, the
carrying company's accumulated losses, which had reached a
maximum of £171,803 in 1944, fell to £130,743 in 1946, only to
rise to £141,178 in the last year of 1947.

Canal interchange traffic had almost ceased at Regent's Canal Dock. The new board considered that the dock must be made part of a complete water transport service offered to the public, if it were to bring much-needed traffic to the canal. Subsidiaries were therefore formed: Grand Union (Shipping) Ltd to operate a new Regent's Line of ships from the dock, Grand Union (Stevedoring and Wharfage) Co Ltd, to service the ships, take over some of the dock accommodation, and provide stevedoring services, and overseas, Grand Union Belge de Transports S.A. to act as agents at Antwerp, and arrange for Rhine barges in connection with Regent's Line sailings. In late 1937 the Regent's Line started operations with one small steamer, the *Marsworth*, running a weekly service to Antwerp; in 1938 a service to Rotterdam was begun with chartered craft; and in December 1939 a second and larger ship, the *Blisworth*, was bought. A third, the *Kilworth*, followed, and in 1945 two new ones, *Knebworth* and *Bosworth*, were launched. On the canal itself, warehousing was developed. Premises were built at Sampson Road, Birmingham and later at Tyseley, and improved at Brentford, Northampton and Leicester. The new policy had not time to prove itself before the war altered so much, though in the eighteen months before it broke out, the Regent's Line had brought 12,152 of new canal-borne traffic out of the 57,592 tons it had carried.

Some shipping companies had in 1939 started proceedings for *ultra vires* against the company for running its shipping subsidiary, and in 1943 the canal company sought and obtained an Act authorizing them to take a limited financial interest in sea, land or even air transport. In this they were helped by the persuasiveness of their Counsel, then Sir Walter Monckton. In 1943, also, they acquired a road transport firm, Cartwright & Paddock, in Brierley Hill and formed other subsidiaries, Grand Union Transport, Grand Union Warehousing, Grand Union Estates, and Grandion, the last to run the Ruislip lido, opened in May 1936, and develop recreational activities on canals and reservoirs. The revenue-earning potentiality of the policy of diversification can be seen from the figures. In 1939 revenue from tolls was £120,991 (including those paid by the carrying company) and a net £11,269 from other activities. In 1944 that from tolls had risen to £148,001, but from other activities to £76,293.

The company, which had paid no dividend on the £400,000 of 6 per cent preference stock since 1936, was sufficiently recovered to pay 3 per cent for 1942 and 1943, and the full dividend there-

15. Pegasus: The Grand Union Canal Bill, 1943—now awaiting the Royal assent—makes history by empowering the Company to take part in the operation of all forms of transport—by land, sea and air. The canal horse thus 'takes wings'. (Reprinted from *The Birmingham Mail*, Wednesday, 23 June 1943)

after. In 1945 it at last paid 1 per cent on the £2,159,542 of ordinary stock, and in 1946 2 per cent. In these two years also all the subsidiaries made profits, considerable in the case of shipping, stevedoring, Thomas Clayton, Grandion and Cartwright & Paddock. Water sales, too, had increased from £17,613 in 1937 to £31,970 in 1946. In 1948 the company's enterprises were incorporated in the British Transport Commission: Grand Union (Shipping) was soon afterwards sold for £180,000, and in 1951 the Ruislip/Northwood U.D.C. bought Ruislip reservoir and lido.

In 1948 Fellows, Morton & Clayton Ltd, whose fleet worked between the Midlands and London and between the Midlands and Manchester or Weston Point, decided to go into voluntary liquidation, the company having incurred a trading loss of £5,000 for the first half of that year. The British Transport Commission thereupon bought the company's assets, including its boats, road vehicles and properties, on 1 January 1949. Part of the fleet was transferred to the North Western Division, the rest being combined with the former Grand Union fleet in the south-east.

In 1962, the upper five miles of the former Erewash Canal, from Langley Mill to Ilkeston, was abandoned under a Commission Act. Commercial traffic had ended in 1952, when coal from the Barber Walker colliery at Langley Mill carried by water to Loughborough was transferred to road. The other waterways formerly controlled by the Grand Union are still open and carry some commercial craft, though in 1963 the British Waterways Board ceased to employ the remaining portion of the old Carrying Company's fleet, many of the craft being hired out under arrangements made with private carriers.

On 1 April 1968 a new channel linking Regent's Canal Dock to the Limehouse Cut was opened, so that Limehouse lock could be closed and filled in. Access to the Cut and so to the Lee Navigation is now, therefore, through the dock. Early in 1969 the British Waterways Board announced that all cargo-handling services at the dock would be ended during the year, as the necessary volume of traffic could not be obtained to make it an efficient unit in the long-term.

Conclusion

THE interesting thing about the canal network of the Midlands described in this book and its companion is that most of it has proved so durable. Lines like the Trent & Mersey, Staffordshire & Worcestershire, Coventry and Oxford have carried commercial traffic for nearly two hundred years; for longer, that is to say, than any significant railway line or most turnpike roads. And even now, though the commercial value of the smaller ones may be ending, they are finding new ways to usefulness.

Until the success of the locomotive railway, we can see in the figures below the quick expansion of the canal system in mileage and carrying facilities to cope with the needs of industry for the carriage of raw materials and finished goods, and to some extent those of agriculture also: not only the building of main lines, but the proliferation of branches to works and mines, or of tramroads where a branch was impracticable or too expensive.

*Canals and Navigations in the Midlands by type of waterway**

Date	*Ship Canal*	*Broad Canal*	*Narrow Canal*	*Tub-boat or Small Canal*	*River Nav.*	*Total*
	miles	*miles*	*miles*	*miles*	*miles*	*miles*
1760	—	—	—	—	249½	249½
1770	—	16½	37¾	6½	249½	310¼
1780	—	86½	276⅜	8½	258¾	630⅛
1790	—	86½	342¼	10¾	258¾	698¼
1800	—	312	493½	44¼	262½	1,112¼
1810	½	373⅛	576⅛	44¼	240¾	1,234¾
1820	½	351⅜	710¾	37⅞	240¾	1,341¼
1830	—	355⅛	717⅛	36	240¾	1,349
1840	—	355¼	822½	21½	240¾	1,440
1850	—	355¾	820¼	21½	240¾	1,438¼

* The canals and navigations included are those listed in Appendix I of this and its companion, *The Canals of the West Midlands*, that fall within the range of dates quoted. For classification purposes a ship canal is a canal that admitted sea-going

There was a moment when it seemed that railways might take the passengers and light goods, and canals the bulky and heavy traffics. But speed, larger units of organization, the ability of the companies to carry goods themselves, collection and delivery services, and the spreading of overheads over both passengers and goods, were among the advantages the railways had.

Some canal companies saw quickly enough the danger from railways—more quickly than some railway companies, anxious for a smooth passage of their bill through Parliament and no rate cutting afterwards, saw how little they really had to fear from the smaller waterways. So the quick sales, for instance the Cromford, Ashby and Macclesfield. Some railways tried to have second thoughts, but were not allowed to cancel their agreements by the Stratford, Nottingham or Grantham companies. A few small concerns were closed down—like the Oakham or the Newport Pagnell—but most continued, to develop in dissimilar ways.

The Shropshire Union, at first an independent attempt at some form of rail-canal integration, was soon leased by the L.N.W.R. and then discouraged from long-haul traffic to and from other canals, though welcome to develop within its own system certain specialized trades which supplemented those of the railway, and, in so doing, to build up the trade of Ellesmere Port. The Birmingham Canal Navigations, having the same master, developed similarly: discouragement of transfer traffic to other canals and intensive use of its own network, both for loads carried all the way by water, and for those transhipped to and from rail in the specialized interchange basins. The Trent & Mersey, owned by the smaller North Staffordshire Railway, developed in an opposite way, as a means by which the railway company could carry long-haul traffic to and from Liverpool, Runcorn, the Mersey and Manchester in one direction and the Trent in the other, so much so that in 1875 the independent Weaver trustees opened the Anderton lift to develop interchange traffic with it.

On other waterways, such as the Nottingham, Cromford and Ashby, railway ownership led at first to some neglect, and later to more. But this influence was always harmful to the future of water

---

ships; a broad canal one with locks at least 12 ft wide; a narrow canal one with locks less than 12 ft wide; and a tub-boat or small canal one taking boats carrying a few tons each. See my *British Canals*, 2nd ed., 1959, pp. 55–6, for a fuller description. For some branches I have had to conjecture the dates. Readers may like to compare these figures with those given in *The Canals of Southern England* and *The Canals of South Wales and the Border*.

transport because it kept the canals as they were, and hindered the negotiation of through tolls, amalgamation and modernization.

As the century moved on, we see the inability of the independent canal lines, however hard they tried, to maintain, let alone to increase, their share of an expanding market. The Warwick and Grand Junction route, well organized, powerful, with some ability to raise new money, a single carrying business and the enterprise to run power-driven craft, did best. The Leicester line, a sufferer from too many small companies managing too little canal, much worse. But the result was the same in the end.

The waterways reacted in two ways to their critical situation. One was to build up sources of income ancillary to tolls, from the sale of water to other canal companies, public authorities and industry; the development of property or interest derived from the proceeds of selling it; in the case of the Regent's from the use of their dock; and a little from fishing and pleasure-boat licences. By the end of the century some companies, the Leicester, Grand Junction and Coventry among them, derived a third to a half of their revenue from such sources.

The other was the reduction of compensation tolls, modernization and, sometimes, amalgamation. The Staffs & Worcs saw the value of improving the Severn, and put much money behind it. The Shropshire Union sought amalgamation and introduced (though temporarily) steam-hauled barge trains. In the nineties the Grand Junction bought the old Grand Union and the Union, and built the Foxton inclined plane in a gallant effort to open a broad waterway to revive the water-borne coal trade from Derbyshire to London. In the present century the enterprise of the Trent Navigation Co and the city of Nottingham transformed the River Trent.

Finally, these lines of development were brought together in the later Grand Union: amalgamation, modernization and diversification. Diversification was successful, amalgamation helped: but a great effort to rebuild narrow-boat carrying only demonstrated its limitations.

Date	Ship Canal	Broad Canal	Narrow Canal	Tub-boat or Small Canal	River Nav.	Total
	miles	miles	miles	miles	miles	miles
1900	—	334	$835\frac{3}{8}$	8	152	$1,329\frac{3}{8}$
1947	—	$253\frac{3}{4}$	$646\frac{3}{4}$	—	135	$1,035\frac{1}{2}$

Meanwhile the twentieth century had brought the motor-lorry, far more than the railway the enemy of the smaller canals. For both railway and canal were alike in this, that much of their traffic had to begin and end its journey by road. When it became possible to carry all the way by lorry, without transfer of cargo, the older ways had to seek new methods, or to succumb.

The lorry caused the canal network to contract, by the abandonment of rural or less useful industrial canals, such as much of the Shropshire Union, the Grantham, and the Droitwich. Yet much remained in existence. The bigger waterways still have a future as large-scale carriers of goods. Many of the smaller, those that run quietly through the countryside, see a new life opening in cruising, fishing, and the pleasure of those that walk beside them. Others, still useful to the community, will end their days as channels for storing and moving water wherever it may be wanted.

Much might have been different. All the same, it is not a bad record.

This 'Conclusion' is repeated in *The Canals of the West Midlands*. Generalizations are risky at the best of times, but they would be riskier still were they to be made about only a part of the Midlands.

Author's Notes
and Acknowledgements

IT is impossible for me individually to acknowledge the assistance I have had in writing this book—those who have sent me material, or whom I have consulted, are numbered in hundreds. I thank them all.

It could not have been written at all without the willing and efficient help of the staff of British Transport Historical Records and of the House of Lords Record Office, and the co-operation of many librarians and archivists. Again, without the friendships that link the members of the Railway & Canal Historical Society, and the aid they give each other, it would have been much the poorer. My fellow-members have answered questions, read sections of the text, and sought information for me, willingly and generously.

I would especially like to thank Mr C. P. Weaver for reading a file of *Aris's Birmingham Gazette*, and for doing much special research on the Birmingham Canal Navigations, and the Black Country and Newdigate canals; Mrs Mary Thomas for also reading *Aris*; Major Whitehead for reading the *Derby Mercury*, Mr J. C. Gillham for reading *Berrows' Worcester Journal*, Josiah Wedgwood & Sons Ltd for access to the Wedgwood Collection, Mr P. Stevenson for showing me his extracts from the Nutbrook Canal records and Stanton & Staveley Ltd for permission to use them, Mr C. R. Clinker for checking the references to railways in the text, and officials of the British Waterways Board, especially Mr W. L. Ives, Mr C. M. Marsh, Mr A. J. Brawn and Mr C. N. Hadlow, for answering questions.

I am most grateful for a grant towards the costs of research made by the Leverhulme trustees, and for the patient work of my secretary, Mrs Ann Simpkins, in typing the text.

My thanks are due to the following for permission to reproduce photographs and other illustrations: Waterways Museum, Stoke Bruerne: Plates 1(a) and (b), 3(b), 4(b), 10(a), 11(a) and (b), 12(a) and (b), 13(a), jacket picture, Figs. 5, 10, 11, 12; Oxford City Libraries, from the Taunt collection, by permission of the Library Committee, 2(a); C. Skellern, Esq., 3(a); P. Stevenson, Esq., 4(a), 5(a); M. I. Berrill, Esq., (6a) and (b); L. Hales, Esq., 7(a) and (b), 8(b), 9(b); London Midland Region, British Railways Board, 8(a); P. A. Stevens, Esq., 9(a); Mustograph Agency and Blue Line Cruisers Ltd., 13(b); British Transport Historical Records (from Laurie's map of London), 14(a) and (b); The Borough Librarian, London Borough of Camden, 15(a); C. P. Weaver, Esq., Fig. 1; County Archivist, Nottinghamshire, Fig. 2; Leicestershire Archaeological Society, Fig. 4; British Waterways Board for the material, and R. J. Dean Esq., for drawing the plan, Fig. 14; the *Birmingham Evening Mail*, Fig. 15.

Finally, no man can write in his spare time—as I did while most of this book was being drafted—unless he has the daily encouragement and support of his wife and the tolerance of his children. She and they have helped me more than words of mine can tell.

CHARLES HADFIELD

NOTES

Notes to Chapter I

1. Josiah Wedgwood to Thomas Bentley, 2 March 1767.
2. *Aris's Birmingham Gazette*, 27 July, 31 August 1767. For the Stratford project see Charles Hadfield and John Norris, *Waterways to Stratford*, 1962, p. 73.
3. *Derby Mercury*, 11 September 1767.
4. Josiah Wedgwood to Thomas Bentley, 17 December 1767.
5. Ibid., 24 December 1767.
6. 8 Geo III *c*. 36.
7. Coventry Canal Minute Book, 19 February 1768.
8. B. Poole, *Coventry; Its History and Antiquities*, 1870, p. 347.
9. Coventry Canal Minute Book, 3 January 1769.
10. Ibid., 29 August 1770.
11. *Aris's Birmingham Gazette*, 29 October 1770.
12. *Aris's Birmingham Gazette*, 31 October 1768.
13. Anon, *The History of Inland Navigations,* 2nd ed., 1769, p. 94.
14. 9 Geo III *c*. 70.
15. For Page and the Kennet, see Charles Hadfield, *The Canals of Southern England.*
16. Oxford Canal Minute Book, 6 June 1769.
17. Ibid., 2 October 1769.
18. Ibid., 6 September 1769.
19. Ibid., 26 July 1770.
20. Birmingham Ref. Lib., 177408.
21. Oxford Canal Minute Book, 4 October 1773. *Aris's Birmingham Gazette*, 18 October, 20 December 1773, 3, 10, 27 January, 4 April 1774.
22. Coventry Canal Minute Book, 9 May 1776.
23. Oxford Canal Committee Minute Book, 6 August 1777.
24. Ibid., 3 February 1779.
25. Oxford Canal Minute Book, 11 August 1774.
26. 15 Geo III *c*. 9.
27. *Oxfordshire Town & Country Magazine,* 4 April 1778. Also *Jackson's Oxford Journal,* 4 April 1778.
28. So Rees, *Cyclopaedia,* art 'Canal'; Bradshaw's map of 1830 gives 127 yd.
29. Oxford Canal Committee Minute Book, 24 January 1781.
30. Oxford Canal Minute Book, 20 June 1769.
31. Plan in Wedgwood Collection, Barlaston (55/30853).
32. Oxford Canal Minute Book, 8 February 1775.
33. Ibid., 26 April 1775.
34. Printed notice of 29 January 1829, B.T. Hist. Recs. OXC/4/110.
35. Oxford Canal Minute Book, 15 December 1773, 24 April 1776.
36. Coventry Canal Minute Book, 1 May 1781.
37. Ibid., 25 September 1781.
38. Coventry Canal Minute Book, 29 March 1785.
39. Printed *Case,* 27 May 1785, Wm. Salt Library, Stafford, Sneyd papers.
40. 25 Geo III *c*. 99.
41. *Aris's Birmingham Gazette*, 12 July 1790.
42. Coventry Canal Minute Book, 27 September 1791.
43. 26 Geo III *c*. 20.

44. See Charles Hadfield, *British Canals*, 2nd ed., p. 63.
45. *Aris's Birmingham Gazette*, 4 January 1790. The reference to New Year's Day probably ensures that this date is correct. The *Annual Register* for 1790 gives 2 January.
46. Oxford Canal Committee Minute Book, 16 December 1789.
47. Oxford Canal Committee Minute Book, 24 August 1790.
48. See Charles Hadfield, *British Canals*, 2nd ed., pp. 69–70.
49. *Derby Mercury*, 13 September 1792.
50. For the Duke's Cut, see H. J. Compton, 'The Link', *Journal* of the Railway & Canal Historical Society, July-September 1964.
51. Information from Mr Kingsley Belsten.
52. See Charles Hadfield, *The Canals of Southern England*, pp. 65–7.
53. This section is entirely based upon research by Mr Philip Weaver.
54. See L. T. C. Rolt, *Thomas Newcomen; the Prehistory of the Steam Engine*, 1963.

Notes to Chapter II

1. On the Idle generally, see Derek Holland, *Bawtry and the Idle River Trade* (Doncaster P. L), 1964.
2. Defoe, *Rural Rides*, ii, 181 (Everyman ed.).
3. T. S. Ashton, *Iron and Steel in the Industrial Revolution*, 1951, p. 245–6.
4. See T. S. Willan, *The English Coasting Trade*, 1938, p. 72.
5. 6 Geo I *c*. 30.
6. J. S. Piercy, *History of Retford*, 1828, p. 165.
7. Arthur Raistrick, *Two Centuries of Industrial Welfare; The London (Quaker) Lead Company*, 1692–1905, 1938, p. 85–6.
8. Piercy, *Retford*, 165.
9. H. M. Colville, 'Dale Abbey, Granges, Mills and other Buildings', *Derby Arch. Soc.*, 1936.
10. H. M. C. Cowper, MSS II, p. 180, quo A. C. Wood, *Trans. Thoroton Soc.*, op. cit.
11. John Houghton, *A Collection for improvement of Husbandry and Trade*, 1693.
12. 6 Geo I *c*. 27.
13. Derby City Library.
14. *The British Spy or The Derby Postman*, 18 January 1720–1.
15. *Derby Mercury*, 20 November 1752.
16. Ibid., 24 April 1755.
17. Ibid., 5 July 1771.
18. Ibid., 23 January 1783, and *Aris's Birmingham Gazette*, 29 January 1783.
19. Ibid., 18 January 1787.
20. A. C. Wood, *Trans. Thoroton Soc.*, op. cit.
21. *Derby Mercury*, 17, 31 July, 4 August 1788.
22. Ibid., 1 September 1769.
23. Raistrick, *Two Centuries of Industrial Welfare*, pp. 84–6.
24. 11 Geo III *c*. 75.
25. *Derby Mercury*, 5 April 1771.
26. Chesterfield Canal Minute Book, 25 June 1771.
27. Ibid., 24 January 1774.
28. *Derby Mercury*, 19 May 1775.
29. *Annual Register*, 1775, p. 116.
30. Chesterfield Canal Minute Book, 4 September 1777.
31. 6 Geo III *c*. 94.
32. T. S. Willan, *River Navigation in England* 1600–1750, 1936, p. 26.
33. Loughborough Navigation Minute Book, 24 June 1766.
34. Loughborough Navigation Minute Book, 23 September 1776.
35. 16 Geo III *c*. 65.
36. Loughborough Navigation Minute Book, 15 December 1777.

37. A. Temple Patterson, 'The Making of the Leicestershire Canals', quoting newspapers, p. 5.
38. Deposited plan, Nottingham Co. R.O.
39. *Derby Mercury*, 25 October 1776.
40. Ibid., 6 December 1776.
41. 17 Geo III *c*. 69.
42. *Derby Mercury*, 14 March 1777.
43. *Leicester & Nottingham Journal*, 18 December 1779.
44. *Derby Mercury*, 12 September 1782.
45. Ibid., 10 May 1787.
46. Ibid., 31 July 1788.
47. Ibid., 4 September 1788.
48. 29 Geo III *c*. 74.
49. Supplement to a Pamphlet entitled '*Seasonable Considerations*, etc', April 1766, B.T. Hist. Recs. HRP 6/12.
50. 13 Geo III *c*. 86.
51. *Derby Mercury*, 5 November 1773.
52. Ibid., 25 July 1782.
53. 'Navigator', *Observations on a 'Design for improving the Navigation of the River Severn'*, 1788 (Stoke P.L.).
54. 23 Geo III *c*. 48.
55. *Derby Mercury*, 27 November 1783, 8 April, 12 August 1784.

Notes to Chapter III

1. Cromford Canal Minute Book, 10 December 1793.
2. C. Woodham-Smith, *Florence Nightingale*, Penguin ed., pp. 11–12.
3. Cromford Canal Minute Book, 15 February 1803.
4. For this line, see J. A. Birks and P. Coxon, 'The Mansfield and Pinxton Railway', *Railway Magazine*, July-August 1949.
5. Cromford Canal Minute Book, 30 December 1834.
6. Ibid., 24 March 1841.
7. *Records of the Borough of Nottingham* VII, 21 September 1790 and *Nottingham Journal*, 22 September 1790.
8. Nottingham Canal Minute Book, 22 June 1791.
9. *Derby Mercury*, 3 November 1791.
10. Nottingham Canal Minute Book, December 1791.
11. 32 Geo III *c*. 100.
12. *Derby Mercury*, 17 May 1792.
13. J. F. Sutton, *The Date Book . . . Nottingham*, 1750 to 1865.
14. Nottingham Canal Minute Book, 8 October 1794.
15. *Nottingham Journal*, 14 February 1795.
16. T. W. Hammond, *Nottingham Past and Present*, 1926.
17. *Bradshaw's Canals and Navigable Rivers*, 1918 ed.
18. Nottingham Canal Minute Book, 24 March 1792.
19. F. S. Williams, *Midland Railway*, pp. 219–20. See also Peter Stevenson, 'The Bilborough Cut', *Journal* of the Railway & Canal Historical Society, 1966.
20. Loughborough Navigation Minute Book, 16 April 1798.
21. Nottingham Canal Minute Book, 17 December 1800.
22. Ibid., 6 October 1818.
23. *Annual Register*, 1818, p. 133.
24. Nottingham Canal Minute Book, 3 May 1825.
25. Ibid., 20 March 1832.
26. Act, 4 July 1839.
27. *Records* etc., 11 October 1860, 7 May 1866.
28. *Nottingham Journal*, 27 August 1791.

29. 33 Geo III *c.* 94.
30. *Nottingham Journal*, 18 May 1793.
31. Grantham Canal Minute Book, 18 April 1797.
32. 37 Geo III *c.* 30.
33. *Description of a plan for a Junction Canal between Grantham and Sleaford*, 1833. Institution of Civil Engineers Library. Tracts 8vo, Vol. 98.
34. Erewash Canal Minute Book, 7 May 1833.
35. Ibid., 12 March 1836.
36. *Derby Mercury*, 15 September 1791.
37. *Derby Mercury*, 16 August 1792.
38. 33 Geo III *c.* 102.
39. *Derby Mercury*, 14 May 1795.
40. Derby Canal Committee Minute Book, 9 June 1812
41. J. Farey, *A General View of the Agriculture of Derbyshire*, III, 357.
42. Derby Canal Committee Minute Book, 12 April 1814.
43. Erewash Canal Minute Book, 26 August 1791.
44. Erewash Canal Minute Book, 21 January 1793.
45. 33 Geo III *c.* 115.
46. Nutbrook Canal Proprietors' Minute Book, 1 June 1795.
47. Ibid., 17 September 1796.
48. I am indebted to Stanton & Staveley Ltd for permission to quote from the minute books, and to Mr P. Stevenson for access to his summary of them.
49. Farey, *Derbyshire* III, 451.
50. *Derby Mercury*, 16 August, 6 September, 8 November 1792.
51. Ibid., 13 December 1792.
52. Printed *Proposals* for the Grand Commercial Canal, 1824 (Author's collection).
53. *Aris's Birmingham Gazette*, 5 July 1824.
54. *Derby Mercury*, 22 August 1832.
55. B.T. Hist. Recs., HRP/6/15/64.
56. *Derby Mercury*, 10 October 1832.
57. P. Robinson, *The Smiths of Chesterfield*, 1957.
58. B.T. Hist. Recs., TRN/1/2.
59. 34 Geo III *c.* 95.
60. A. C. Wood, op. cit.
61. *Leicester Journal*, 2 April, 25 June 1830.
62. Leaflet of 1792, Institution of Civil Engineers Library, Tracts 8vo. Vol. 48.
63. Evidence on the Trent & Mersey bill of 1796. B.T. Hist. Recs., TMC 4/8.
64. *Aris's Birmingham Gazette*, 20 May, 3 June, 12 August 1805.
65. It seems likely that the Midland Railway first crossed the Bond End Canal on a drawbridge, for the engine and tender of a passenger train fell into the canal in October 1846 because it was not in place.
66. Trent Navigation Minute Book, 2 September 1823.

Notes to Chapter IV

1. I am greatly indebted to Mr A. Temple Patterson, not only for the excellent accounts of waterway development in his 'The Making of the Leicestershire Canals, 1766–1814', *Trans. Leics. Arch. Soc.* XXVII, 1951, and his *Radical Leicester*, 1954, but also for lending me his file of extracts from local newspapers. The reader should also see T. J. Chandler's article: 'The Canals of Leicestershire; their Development and Trade', *East Midlands Geographer*, No. 10.
2. Leicester Navigation draft Minute Book, 14 March 1791.
3. *Leicester Journal*, 14 September 1792.
4. Loughborough Navigation Minute Book, 24 November 1814.
5. Ibid., 28 October 1835.
6. Ibid., 16 April 1789.

R

7. Ibid., 13 April 1819.
8. Ibid., 11 April 1826.
9. Ibid., 19 April 1825.
10. Ibid., 23 December 1833.
11. *Derby Mercury*, 14 May 1834.
12. Loughborough Navigation Minute Book, 19 September 1834.
13. Ibid., 7 March 1836.
14. Leicester Canal draft Minute Book, 12 July 1790.
15. 31 Geo III *c*. 65.
16. Leicester Canal draft Minute Book, 24 October 1794.
17. Leicester Navigation draft Minute Book, 22 February 1799.
18. *Leicester Journal*, 28 February 1794.
19. P. Russell, *A Leicestershire Road*, 1934.
20. 37 Geo III *c*. 51.
21. See C. R. Clinker, 'The Leicester and Swannington Railway', *Trans. Leics. Arch. Soc.*, XXX, 1954.
22. Erewash Canal Minute Book, 13 October 1777.
23. *Leicester Journal*, 29 October 1785.
24. *Derby Mercury*, 29 July 1790.
25. 31 Geo III *c*. 77.
26. *Leicester Journal*, 31 October 1794.
27. *Leicester Herald*, 3 April 1795.
28. Tonnage Accounts of Leicester Navigation, Leicester Museum.
29. 40 Geo III *c*. 55.
30. *Leicester Journal*, 22 June 1804.
31. *Derby Mercury*, 2 March 1809.
32. *Leicester Journal*, 20 September 1833.
33. *Derby Mercury*, 29 September 1824.
34. Grantham Canal Minute Book, 4 May 1843.
35. For this account of the Oakham Canal I am greatly indebted to information provided by Mr David Tew.
36. *Leicester Journal*, 5 November 1785.
37. Ibid., 24 December 1785, 3 June 1786.
38. Ibid., 27 April 1792.
39. 33 Geo III *c*. 103.
40. 40 Geo III *c*. 56.
41. Rees, *Cyclopaedia*, art. 'Canal'.
42. *Leicester Journal*, 6 October 1815.
43. Union Canal Minute Book, 19 March 1792.
44. *Derby Mercury*, 14 June 1792.
45. Ibid., 16 August 1792.
46. Rees, *Cyclopaedia*, 1819, art. 'Canal', and *British Chronicle* (Hereford), 5 December 1792.
47. *Derby Mercury*, 16 August 1792.
48. 33 Geo III *c*. 98.
49. *Leicester Herald*, 1 February 1794.
50. Union Canal Minute Book, 25 October 1794.
51. Ibid., 16 August 1796.
52. Ibid., 19 April 1797.
53. *A Report and Estimate by James Barnes . . .* 26 July 1802, Inst. of Civil Engs. Lib., Tracts 4to, Vol. 7; *A Survey and Report of the proposed extension of the Union Canal*, Thomas Telford, 1803, loc. cit.
54. 45 Geo III *c*. 71.
55. Union Canal Minute Book, 18 November 1805.
56. Ibid., 16 November 1807.
57. Union Canal Minute Book, 16 May 1808.
58. Grand Union Canal Committee Minute Book, 25 July 1808.
59. Union Canal Minute Book, 21 November 1808.

60. Union Canal Minute Book, 19 November 1810.
61. Ibid., 21 November 1831.
62. Ibid., 20 May 1839.
63. Ibid., 17 May 1841.
64. Grand Union Canal Committee Minute Book, 11 June 1808.
65. The Peak canal schemes will be described in *The Canals of Northern England*, by Charles Hadfield and Gordon Biddle, now in preparation.
66. 50 Geo III *c*. 122.
67. Grand Union Canal Committee Minute Book, 1 December 1813.
68. *Derby Mercury*, 18 August 1814.

Notes to Chapter V

1. Oxford Canal Committee Minute Book, 11 January 1792.
2. For the Thames at this time, see Charles Hadfield, *The Canals of Southern England*.
3. A map issued by the London & Western shows this proposal, and compares distances.
4. See Charles Hadfield, *British Canals*, 2nd ed., 1959, p. 55.
5. *Derby Mercury*, 6 September 1792.
6. Ibid., 8 November 1792.
7. *Aris's Birmingham Gazette*, 30 July, 29 October 1792.
8. Report of 24 October 1792 in R. C. Sale's Notebook, in private hands.
9. 33 Geo III *c*. 80.
10. *Two Reports of the Commissioners of the Thames Navigation*, 1811.
11. *Aris's Birmingham Gazette*, 27 June 1796.
12. See Victor A. Hatley, 'The Blisworth Hill Railway, 1800–1805', *Reports & Papers of Northants Antiq. Soc.* 1962–3.
13. Rees, *Cyclopaedia*, 1819, art. 'Canal'.
14. *Glocester Journal*, 2 June 1800.
15. Because the original intention had been to cross the Ouse on the level, the first plan for the Buckingham branch was a canalization of the Ouse. (See A. H. Faulkner, 'The River Great Ouse and the Grand Junction Canal', *The Lock Gate*, October 1964.)
16. *A Design for bringing a Navigable river from Rickmansworth to St. Giles in the Fields*, 1641, with an *Answer*. Reprinted 1720 Inst. of Civil Engs. Lib., Tracts 8vo, Vol. 5.
17. Herbert Spencer, *London's Canal*, 1961, p. 15.
18. 35 Geo III *c*. 43.
19. *Derby Mercury*, 21 July 1803.
20. *Northampton Mercury*, 29 April 1815.
21. For this scheme see Bedford County Record Office, DX 37/29/1 and 2, GA/736/2 and 3, X 4/3, X 127/31.
22. For this scheme see Bedford County Record Office, GA 736/1.
23. *Bedford Mercury*, 30 March 1844.
24. Deposited plan, MR extension to Hitchin etc., November 1846.
25. *Railway Times*, 9 January 1892, p. 37.
26. Grand Junction Canal Minute Book, 17 November 1802.
27. For the Western Union and Western Junction Canal schemes, see also Charles Hadfield, *The Canals of Southern England*, 1955.
28. Grand Junction Canal Committee Minute Book, 11 May 1815.
29. Ibid., 3 June, 17 July 1793.
30. Ibid., 25 July 1805.
31. 51 Geo III *c*. 169.
32. For further information about the Waterworks company see H. W. Dickinson, *Water Supply of Greater London*, 1954.

33. The above figures are from R. C. Sale's notebook (in private hands) except the 1830 and 1840 figures for iron, which are from H. Scrivenor, *A Comprehensive History of the Iron Trade*, 1841.
34. Grand Junction Canal Minute Book, 23 July 1801.
35. Rees, *Cyclopaedia*, 1805, art. 'Canal'.
36. *Illustrated London News*, 11 August 1849.
37. Grand Junction Canal Committee Minute Book, 13 September 1808.
38. Ibid., 14 May 1811.
39. These noblemen did not favour boatmen. For some stories perhaps with a factual basis, see *Waterways*, September 1958, p. 10.
40. Grand Junction Canal Committee Minute Book, 10 March 1814.
41. Ibid., 8 August 1816.
42. Joan Evans, *The Endless Web*, 1955, pp. 12, 23–4. See also pp. 25, 91–2.
43. Grand Junction Canal Committee Minute Book, 16 November 1824.
44. Grand Junction Canal Proprietors' Minute Book, 10 March 1825.
45. Grand Junction Canal Committee Minute Book, 14 January 1830.
46. Oxford Canal Minute Book, 19 November 1827.
47. *Aris's Birmingham Gazette*, 12 April 1830, full report.
48. *Aris's Birmingham Gazette*, 2 January 1837.
49. *Northampton Mercury*, quo. A. H. Faulkner, 'A Forgotten Waterway', in *Journal of the Railway & Canal Historical Society*, May 1960, p. 50. This and the evidence given before the Select Committee of the House of Lords on the bill of 1862 are my main sources.
50. 54 Geo III *c*. 98.
51. John Willington's report of 7 January 1817 (Bedford County Records Office, GA 736/1) refers to it as 'lately . . . made but . . . not yet quite completed'. I am grateful to Mr F. W. Webb for making his material on the Bedford schemes available to me.

Notes to Chapter VI

1. Robert Whitworth, *A Report . . . of the Canal . . . from Waltham Abbey to Moorfields*, 1773. The route is reproduced in Herbert Spencer, *London's Canal*, 1961, p. 17.
2. Charles Hadfield, *The Canals of Southern England*, pp. 97–8.
3. Grand Junction Canal Committee Minute Book, 19 June 1802.
4. *Glocester Journal*, 12 July 1802.
5. I am indebted for the above account of John Nash's interest to Herbert Spencer's *London's Canal*, 1961, which contains much interesting information upon the planning and building of the Regent's Canal.
6. 52 Geo III *c*. 195.
7. Later Comptroller of the Royal Laboratory and superintendent of military machines.
8. Charles Hadfield, *The Canals of Southern England*.
9. Ibid.
10. Patent No. 3670 of 1813.
11. Regent's Canal Proprietors' Minute Book, 7 June 1815.
12. On the Bude Canal; see Charles Hadfield, *The Canals of Southern England*.
13. 53 Geo III *c*. 32.
14. See M. W. Flinn, 'The Poor Employment Act of 1817', *Economic History Review*, 1961, XIV, 82.
15. 2 Geo IV *c*. 43.
16. Regent's Canal Proprietors' Minute Book, 6 December 1820.
17. The half-tide restriction was removed by the Act of 1819, and a limit of 40,000 tons in 24 hours substituted.
18. Regent's Canal Proprietors' Minute Book 1 December 1819.

19. Ibid., 3 December 1823.
20. See Charles Hadfield, *British Canals*, 2nd ed., 1959, p. 78.
21. Regent's Canal Proprietors' Minute Book, 2 June 1830.
22. Ibid., 7 June 1826.
23. Ibid., 4 June 1828.
24. Ibid., 1 December 1824.
25. Ibid., 5 June 1833.
26. Regent's Canal Committee Minute Book, 30 January 1839.
27. *Aris's Birmingham Gazette*, 5 August, 7 October 1839.
28. Ibid., 19 March 1845.
29. 5 Geo IV *c*. 47.
30. Regent's Canal Committee Minute Book, 25 February 1835.
31. The above account is taken from Nicholas Barton, *The Lost Rivers of London*, 1962, pp. 76–8. The canal is included here and not in Part I for convenience.
32. *Derby Mercury*, 17 May 1771.
33. 39 Geo III *c*. 69.
34. *Aris's Birmingham Gazette*, 7 October 1799.
35. *Annual Register*, 1805, p. 407.
36. *Derby Mercury*, 22 April 1829.
37. All information upon this canal not otherwise acknowledged is from 'The Isle of Dogs Canal. A Study in early Investment', in *Economic History Review*, 2nd series, Vol. IV, 1951–52, pp. 359 ff.
38. 8 Geo I *c*. 26.
39. H. W. Dickinson, *Water Supply of Greater London*, 1954, p. 56.
40. Commemorative pamphlet issued by Westminster City Council, 3 July 1929.
41. 49 Geo III *c*. 117.
42. Charles E. Lee, 'Victoria Station, London, in the Nineteenth Century', *Railway Magazine*, September 1960, p. 615.
43. 5 Geo IV *c*. 65.
44. *Annual Register*, 1828.
45. Map, Phillimore Collection, Kensington P.L.
46. Preamble to the Act of 1859.

Notes to Chapter VII

1. Coventry Canal Minute Book, 8 December 1792.
2. Anon., Memorandum Book, 1810–25, Nuneaton Public Library.
3. Coventry Canal Minute Book, 22 January 1829.
4. Ibid., 22 April 1830.
5. Birmingham Canal Navigations Proprietors' Minute Book, 9 November 1838.
6. Ibid., 29 November 1844.
7. *Derby Mercury*, 8 September 1791.
8. Ibid., 20 September 1792, 24 January, 4 April 1793.
9. Ashby Canal Minute Book, 2 October 1792.
10. Ibid., 8 November 1792.
11. Ibid., 23 November 1792.
12. Ibid., 29 July 1794.
13. 34 Geo III *c*. 93.
14. Ashby Canal Minute Book, 15 January 1797.
15. *Derby Mercury*, 20 October 1796.
16. Ashby Canal Minute Book, 3 April 1797.
17. Ibid., 16 October 1797.
18. Ashby Canal Minute Book, 20 October 1800.
19. See C. R. Clinker and Charles Hadfield, 'The Ashby-de-la-Zouch Canal and its Railways', *Trans. Leics. Arch. & Hist. Soc.*, Vol. 34, 1958, for a full account.
20. Ashby Canal Minute Book, 2 April 1804.

21. Ibid., 1 October 1810.
22. P. Beaumont, *History of the Moira Collieries*, privately printed 1919, quoted from *The Times*, 20 September 1815.
23. Ashby Canal Minute Book, 1 October 1822.
24. Ibid., 7 January 1823.
25. The important Rawdon Pit had been sunk by Lord Moira in 1821.
26. P. Beaumont, op. cit., says 'about 1832', but the canal minutes for 2 April 1827 says that 1s was received as 'acknowledgement for pipes laid by the side of the Railway to convey Water to the Baths'.
27. P. Beaumont, op. cit.
28. *Derby Mercury*, 18 November 1840. The prospectus of this canal is in the William Salt Library, Stafford. D. 1734.
29. Information on Eynsham wharf from H. J. Compton, 'The Thames at Eynsham', *Journal* of the Railway & Canal Historical Society, July 1959, p. 70.
30. Information from Mr H. J. Compton.
31. For an account of this competition, see Charles Hadfield, *The Canals of Southern England*.
32. See Charles Hadfield, *The Canals of Southern England*.
33. Oxford Canal Committee Minute Book, 14 July 1811.
34. Ibid., 12 May 1813.
35. Ibid., 12 August 1795.
36. Ibid., 19 November 1829.
37. A. Rees, *Cyclopaedia*, 1819, art. 'Canal', written 1805.
38. 10 Geo IV *c*. 48.
39. *Rugby Advertiser*, 18 July 1857.
40. Oxford Canal Committee Minute Book, 4 November 1838.

Notes to Chapter VIII

1. In this book I have abbreviated my account of this canal, since its history has been fully told in *Waterways to Stratford*, by John Norris and myself.
2. Warwick & Birmingham Canal Committee Minute Book, 25 June 1793.
3. 33 Geo III *c*. 38.
4. Warwick & Birmingham Canal Committee Minute Book, 23 July 1793.
5. Ibid., 10 December 1793.
6. 36 Geo III *c*. 42.
7. Warwick & Birmingham Canal Proprietors' Minute Book, 2 January 1798.
8. For Thomas Sheasby see Charles Hadfield, *The Canals of South Wales and the Border*.
9. Warwick & Birmingham Canal Proprietors' Minute Book, 26 March 1805.
10. Warwick & Birmingham Canal Minute Book, 10 January 1825.
11. Ibid., 12 November 1827.
12. Warwick & Birmingham Canal Committee Minute Book, 25 June 1793.
13. Warwick & Napton Canal Committee Minute Book, 23 September 1793.
14. 34 Geo III *c*. 38.
15. Warwick & Napton Canal Proprietors' Minute Book, 28 September 1796.
16. Ibid., Committee Minute Book, 23 November 1795.
17. 36 Geo III *c*. 95.
18. Warwick & Napton Canal Proprietors' Minute Book, 17 April 1799.
19. Ibid., 25 September 1799.
20. Ibid., Committee Minute Book, 17 December 1799.
21. *Aris's Birmingham Gazette*, 10 March 1800.
22. Warwick & Napton Canal Proprietors' Minute Book, 16 April 1800.
23. See Charles Hadfield and John Norris, *Waterways to Stratford*, pp. 85–6.
24. Warwick & Napton Canal Proprietors' Minute Book, 21 January 1833.
25. Warwick & Napton Canal Committee Minute Book, 3 April 1832.

26. Ibid., 4 August 1834.
27. 3 & 4 Vic *c*. 57.
28. Warwick & Napton Canal Proprietors' Minute Book, 30 September 1840. A similar resolution had been passed the previous day by the Warwick & Birmingham.
29. I have here followed Canal Returns 1888, which seem clear. On the other hand, my own reading of the records lead me to think the Birmingham company raised some £73,000 and the Napton some £58,000 in loans in addition to the share capital, and that the cost was about £190,000. H. R. Hodgkinson, 'Notes on the History of Midland Waterways', *Birm. Arch. Soc. Trans.* xxxix, 1914, says £170,000.
30. For a fuller account see Charles Hadfield and John Norris, *Waterways to Stratford*, 1961.
31. 33 Geo III *c*. 112.
32. 35 Geo III *c*. 72.

Notes to Chapter IX

1. Erewash Canal Minute Book, 6 May 1845.
2. Ibid., 16 January 1855.
3. Ibid., 2 May 1853.
4. Victor Lewis, *The Iron Dale*, 1960.
5. Leicester Navigation Minute Book, 10 October 1863.
6. L & N. U.C. Minute Book, 19 May 1890.
7. Evidence on the 1845 bill.
8. 9 & 10 Vic *c*. 255.
9. Loughborough Navigation Minute Book, 27 June 1848.
10. Erewash Canal Minute Book, 9 October 1849.
11. Loughborough Navigation Minute Book, 24 April 1854.
12. Midland Railway Minute Book, 3 January 1877.
13. 40 & 41 Vic *c*. 78.
14. L & N.U.C. Minute Book, 15 May 1848.
15. Ibid., 18 November 1889.
16. Grand Union Canal Proprietors' Minute Book, 3 November 1851.
17. 8 & 9 Geo VI *c*. 2.
18. B. Baxter, 'Early Railways in Derbyshire', *Engineering*, 17 June 1949.
19. Nottingham Canal Minute Book, 6 May 1845.
20. *Derby Mercury*, 15 October 1845.
21. 9 & 10 Vic *c*. 358.
22. Manchester, Sheffield & Lincolnshire Railway Finance Committee Minute Book, 22, 29 October 1858, and Report, 1st half year 1848.
23. M.S. & L.R. Report, 1st half year, 1858.
24. Trent Navigation Minute Book, 30 September 1845.
25. Ibid., 22 July 1878.
26. See F. J. Meyer and W. Wernigh, *Steam Towing on Rivers and Canals*, 1876. Roger Pilkington's book, *Small Boat to Bavaria* (1962) contains interesting material on these systems on the Neckar and the Main.
27. 47 Vic *c*. 38.
28. 50 & 51 Vic *c*. 115.
29. 55 & 56 Vic *c*. 135.
30. See Charles Hadfield, *British Canals*, 2nd ed., p. 260.

Notes to Chapter X

1. For more information, see Charles Hadfield and John Norris, *Waterways to Stratford*, 1962.

2. Coventry Canal Minute Book, 11 September 1860.
3. See C. R. Clinker, 'The Leicester & Swannington Railway', 1954, and C. R. Clinker and Charles Hadfield, 'The Ashby-de-la-Zouch Canal and its Railways', 1958, *Trans. Leics. Arch. Soc.*
4. *Derby Mercury*, 11 June 1845.
5. Midland Railway Minute Book, 12 July 1845.
6. Oxford Canal Committee Minute Book, 10 June 1846.
7. For details of later tramroad and railway history, see Clinker and Hadfield, op. cit.
8. *Rugby Advertiser*, 18 August, 8 September, 15 September 1860.
9. RC 39065 and 39067 and related appendices.
10. RC 39045.
11. See Minutes of Evidence on the L.M.S.R. bill of 1944, which became 8 & 9 Geo VI c. 2.
12. Oxford Canal Committee Minute Book, 17 March 1852.
13. Ibid., 9 August 1865.

Notes to Chapter XI

1. Grand Junction Canal Minute Book, 28 May 1841.
2. Ibid., 16 July 1845.
3. Oxford Canal Committee Minute Book, 8 October 1845.
4. Grand Junction Canal Minute Book, 21 May 1846.
5. Oxford Canal Committee Minute Book, 27 January 1853.
6. Grand Junction Canal Minute Book, 7 January 1859.
7. The figures are taken from *An Epitome of the Progress of the Trade in Coal to London since* 1775, 1869 ed. (B.T. Hist. Recs. Gen 3/138). Until 1831 the duties were 1s 3d a ton, and subsequently 1s 1d till 1889, when they were partially, and 1890, wholly, abolished. Iron or stone obelisks to mark the limits of 20 miles from London, to enter which the duties were payable, were erected under an Act of 1851 along roads, railways, the Thames and the canal. That on the Grand Junction stood above Lot Mead lock, near Rickmansworth.
8. *Herapath's Railway Journal*, 19 August 1848.
9. Leicester Navigation Minute Book, 24 August 1864.
10. Ibid., 8 May 1867.
11. Erewash Canal Minute Book, 7 May 1867.
12. *Rugby Advertiser*, 14 September 1861.
13. C. N. Hadlow, 'Sweep's Paradise', *Waterways*, February 1961.
14. Regent's Canal Committee Minute Book, 27 February 1861.
15. Grand Junction Canal Minute Book, 28 August 1863.
16. Grand Junction Canal Select Committee Minute Book, 12 August 1891.
17. Grand Union Canal Committee Minute Book, 15 February 1893.
18. 57 & 58 Vic c. 85.
19. Grand Junction Canal sub-Committee Minute Book, 12 February 1896.
20. For the Foxton plane, see the illustrated account in *Engineering*, 25 January 1900, and the *Reports* by J. A. Saner and G. C. Thomas from the *Procs. IX Int. Congress on Navigation*, Sect. I, Dusseldorf, 1902.
21. Grand Junction Canal Select Committee Minute Book, 28 March 1900.
22. Ibid., 8 August 1900.
23. Erewash Canal Minute Book, 1 May 1901.
24. Ibid., 6 May 1902.
25. R.C. 19204–11, 19247.
26. Quo. Nicholas Barton, *The Lost Rivers of London*, 1962, p. 119.
27. *Daily Mail*, 7 October 1902.
28. 26 & 27 Vic c. 110.

29. A. H. Faulkner, 'A Forgotten Waterway', *Journal* of the Railway and Canal Historical Society, May 1960, p. 50.
30. Grand Junction Canal Select Committee Minute Book, 14 January 1903.
31. Regent's Canal Committee Minute Book, 23 July 1845.
32. Ibid., 27 October 1852.
33. Ibid., 29 October 1879.
34. 21 & 22 Vic *c.* 118.
35. 62 & 63 Vic *c.* 205.
36. 27 & 28 Vic *c.* 255.
37. See Susan Woolfitt, *Idle Women*, 1947, and Emma Smith, *Maidens' Trip*, 1948.

APPENDIX I

Summary of Facts about the Canals and Navigations of th
East Midlands

A. *Rivers Successfully Made Navigable*

River	Date of Act under which Work was begun	Date Wholly Opened	Approx. Cost at Opening	Terminal Points
Derwent (Derby)	1720	1721		R. Trent, Derwent Mouth–Derby
Fleet Canal	None	c. 1674	£50,000	R. Thames–Holborn Bridge
Idle	None			R. Trent, Stockwith–Bawtry
Loughborough (Soar)	1776	1778	£9,200	R. Trent, Redhill–Loughborough
Melton Mowbray (Wreak)	1791	c. 1797	c. £45,000	Leicester C.–Melton Mowbray
Soar (*see* Loughborough)				
Trent (Burton)	1699			Burton, Fleetstone Bridge–Wilden Ferry
Bond End branch		c. 1786[3] 1795[4]		Fleetstones Bridge–T. & M. C., Shobnall
Trent (Newark)	1772	1773		R. Trent, Averham–R. Trent, Crankley Point
Trent, towing paths and improvements	1783	1787	£13,000	Wilden Ferry–Gainsborough
Early locks	1794	1801	£20,000[6]	Wilden Ferry–Gainsborough[7]
Beeston Cut	1794	1796		Beeston–Nottingham C., Lenton
Later locks	1906	1926	c. £500,000	Nottingham–Cromwell
Wreak (*see* Melton Mowbray)				

[1] Perhaps two flash-locks.
[2] Originally 6. Kegworth flood-lock was added later.
[3] From the Trent to about 40 yd from the Trent & Mersey Canal.
[4] About 40 yd, from the end of the branch into the Trent & Mersey Canal.
[5] Originally. In 1926 Newark Nether lock was rebuilt to take craft 180 ft by 29 ft; Newark Town was similarly enlarged in 1952.

Length	Greatest Number of Locks	Size of Boats Taken	Date of Disuse for Commercial Traffic (N.B. 'used' means in 1947)	Date of Abandonment	Whether bought by Railway and Present Ownership
10 miles	1		c. 1795		Bought by Derby Canal Co.
⅜ mile			c. 1733		
10 miles	1		c. 1800		
9¼ miles	7²	72 ft 3 in. by 14 ft 3 in.	Used		Bought by Grand Union Canal, 1932. B.W.B.
14¾ miles	12	86 ft by 14 ft 6 in.	c. 1877	1877	
18¾ miles	2	85 ft 9 in. by 14 ft 9 in.	c. 1805 throughout		
1⅛ miles	1 & 1 stop-lock	85 ft 9 in. by 14 ft 9 in.³			
		72 ft by 7 ft⁴	c. 1870		
3⅞ miles	2	85 ft 9 in. by 14 ft 9 in.⁵	Used		Newark Navigation Comms; (leased to B.W.B.)
67⅛ miles					
	2 & 2 flood-locks⁸	85 ft 9 in. by 14 ft 9 in.	Used		B.W.B.
2½ miles	1 & 1 side-lock	83 ft by 14 ft 6 in.	Used		B.W.B.
	5⁹	180 ft by 29 ft	Used		B.W.B.

⁶ Including the Beeston Cut.
⁷ At first by Trent Bridge, later by the Beeston Cut and 2¾ miles of the Nottingham Canal.
⁸ The flood-lock at Holme was eliminated in 1954.
⁹ Cromwell lock had a tidal extension built in 1935 to form a semi-staircase lock; the extension was incorporated in the main lock in 1960.

B. *Rivers with Uncompleted Navigation Works*

None.

C. *Canals, the Main Lines of which were completed as Authorized*

Canal	Date of Act under which Work was begun	Date wholly Opened	Approx. Cost at Opening	Terminal Points	Branches Built
Adelphi	None	c. 1799		Adelphi works–Staveley road	
Birmingham & Warwick Junction	1840	1844	£112,600	Wk & B'ham C., Bordesley–B'ham & Fazeley C., Salford Bridge	
Cassington Cut	None	c. 1814		R. Thames–Cassington-Eynsham road	
Chesterfield	1771	1777 c. 1776	c. £150,000	R. Trent, Stockwith–Chesterfield	Norbriggs Lady Lee (private)
Coventry	1768	1790 1787	£91,000[5]	Coventry–T. & M. Canal, Fradley	Griff (private)
Cromford	1789	1794 1794 c. 1802	£78,900	Erewash C., Langley Mill–Cromford	Pinxton Lea Wood (private)[15]

[1] Above Retford. Below, 72 ft by 14 ft 6 in., and 72 ft by 17 ft 6 in. into Stockwith basin. Six of the locks were broad.

[2] Norwood tunnel and above.

[3] Worksop–Norwood tunnel.

[4] Lower portion.

[5] Excluding Fazeley–Whittington Brook, authorized as part of the Coventry Canal, but built by, and a part of, the Birmingham & Fazeley.

[6] Including ⅜ mile of former Parrott's Canal (see text), but excluding section from Fazeley to Whittington Brook.

[7] From Butterley tunnel east end to Cromford.

Length	*Greatest Number of Locks*	*Size of Boats Taken*	*Date of Disuse for Commercial Traffic (N.B. 'used' means in 1947)*	*Date of Abandonment*	*Whether bought by Railway, and Present Ownership*
mile	None	1½ tons	*c.* 1850		Built by J. & E. Smith & Co.
⅝ miles	6	72 ft by 7 ft	Used		Bought by Regent's C., 1929. B.W.B.
mile	1	100 ft by 14 ft	*c.* 1870		Built by Duke of Marlborough
46 miles	65	72 ft by 6 ft 11 in.[1]	1908[2] *c.* 1908[3] Used[4]	1962	Amalgamated with Manchester & Lincoln Union Rly 1847. To L.N.E.R. B.W.B.
mile	None				
mile	None				
2½ miles[6]	13 & stop-lock	72 ft by 7 ft 2 in.	Used		B.W.B.
mile			Used		Griff Colliery Co., later National Coal Board
4⅝ miles	14	78 ft by 7 in.[7] 78 ft by 14 ft[8]	1900[9] 1938[10] before 1943[11] 1952[12]	1944[13] 1962[14]	Bought by Manchester, Buxton etc. Rly., 1852. Eventually to Midland Rly & L.M.S.R. B.W.B.
⅜ miles	None	78 ft by 14 ft	Before 1943		
mile	None	78 ft by 7 ft	1936		

[8] Below Butterley tunnel.
[9] Butterley tunnel.
[10] Butterley–Cromford.
[11] Butterley–Brinsley colliery rly.
[12] Bottom half-mile.
[13] Except bottom half-mile.
[14] Bottom half-mile.
[15] There seem also to have been two early private branches, one ⅛ mile long on the west ide of the canal below Stoneyford, and another 1¼ miles long, behind locks 1–4.

Canal	Date of Act under which Work was begun	Date wholly Opened	Approx. Cost at Opening	Terminal Points	Branches Built
Derby	1793	1796	£100,000	Trent & Mersey C., Swarkestone– Erewash C., Sandiacre	
					T. & M. C.– R. Trent Little Eaton
					Darley Mills (Phoenix)
Erewash	1777	1779	£21,000	R. Trent–Langley Mill	
Grand Junction	1793	1805[2]	£1,646,000[3]	R. Thames, Brentford–Braunston	
	1795	1801			Paddington
	1879	1882			Slough
	1794	1799			Wendover[5]
	1794	1815			Aylesbury
	1793, 1794	1801			Old Stratford & Buckingham
	1793	1815			Northampton
		1804			Weedon (private)
		Not known c. 1818[8]			Rickmansworth Otter Dock Yiewsley[8] (private)[9]
Grand Union (old)	1810	1814	£292,000	L. & N.U., Foxton– G.J.C., Norton	
					Welford

[1] Langley Mill–Ilkeston.
[2] Open in 1800 except for Blisworth tunnel. Connection by tramroad.
[3] 1811 figure, including the cost of Wolverton embankment and the rebuilt aqueduct.
[4] There were nine more locks across the Ouse valley until the opening of the (second) Wolverton aqueduct. The original number was 101; King's Langley lock was made during the diversion there.
[5] Navigable feeder.
[6] Reopened for a short time in 1901. Still navigable to Little Tring lock.
[7] 1910 to Buckingham; 1931 to Leckhampstead; 1938 to Deanshanger.

Length	Greatest Number of Locks	Size of Boats Taken	Date of Disuse for Commercial Traffic (N.B. 'used' means in 1947)	Aban-donment Date of	Whether bought by Railway and Present Ownership
4½ miles	8 & 1 flood-lock	72 ft by 14 ft		1964	Derby Canal Co.
mile	4	72 ft by 14 ft	c. 1817		
⅛ miles	4	72 ft by 14 ft	c. 1908	1935	
mile	1	72 ft by 14 ft			
1¾ miles	14	78 ft by 14 ft 6 in.	1952	1962[1]	Bought by Grand Union, 1932. B.W.B.
3½ miles	102[4]	72 ft by 14 ft 3 in.	Used		Part of Grand Union, 1928. B.W.B.
3½ miles	None	72 ft by 14 ft 3 in.	Used		
⅞ miles	None	72 ft by 14 ft 3 in.	Used		
¾ miles	1 stop-lock	72 ft by 7 ft	1897[6]		
⅛ miles	16	72 ft by 7 ft	Used		
0½ miles	2	72 ft by 7 ft	1910[7]	1961	
miles	17	72 ft by 7 ft	Used		
mile	None	72 ft by 7 ft	c. 1920		
mile	1	72 ft by 14 ft 3 in.			
mile	None	72 ft by 7 ft			
3¼ miles	17	72 ft by 7 ft	Used		Bought by Grand Junction C., 1894. B.W.B.
⅝ miles	1		1938		

[8] Extended 1913.

[9] Other private branches in the same area include: Cowley Hall dock, opened c. 1811, mile long, disused c. 1893; Liddalls, extended 1881, 1913; Cooper's, Yiewsley, ⅛ mile long; tockley, Yiewsley, opened 1904–14, ⅛ mile long, disused 1960; Pocock's, West Drayton, pened 1811–22, extended 1880, 1895, ¼ mile long; Dawley, Yiewsley, ¼ mile long; Hanwell oop, North Hyde, opened 1818, extended 1895, ¼ mile long, disused 1936; Victoria dock, outhall, ⅓ mile long; Passmore's dock, Southall, ¼ mile long, disused c. 1895; Maypole ock, Southall, opened 1913, ⅙ mile long; and Clayton's dock, Hayes, opened 1860. Four ther small branches total ⅝ mile.

Canal	Date of Act under which Work was begun	Date wholly Opened	Approx. Cost at Opening	Terminal Points	Branches Built
Grantham	1793	1797	£118,500	R. Trent, Nottingham–Grantham	
Grosvenor	None	1824		R. Thames–Grosvenor basin	
Hertford Union	1824	1830	c. £50,000	R. Lea–Regent's C.	
Isle of Dogs	1799	1805	£168,000	To and from R. Thames across Isle of Dogs	
Kensington	1824	1828	£40,000	R. Thames–Warwick Road basin	
Leicester	1791	1794 1794	£80,000	Loughborough Nav. –Leicester	Charnwood Forest
Newdigate	None	1795		Coventry C., Griff–Seaswood lake	5
Newport Pagnell	1814	1817	£14,200	G.J.C., Linford–Newport Pagnell	

[1] Converted to a dock.
[2] Top portion.
[3] Originally nine; Limekiln lock added later.
[4] A combined canal and tramroad line. Loughborough–Nanpantan, 2½ miles, tramroad; Nanpantan–Thringstone Bridge, 7¾ miles, canal; Thringstone Bridge–Barrow Hill, 1 mile, canal; tramroads from Thringstone Bridge to Swannington and Coleorton. Projected tramroads from Barrow Hill.
[5] See text.
[6] Except Communication Canal, not known.

Length	Greatest Number of Locks	Size of Boats Taken	Date of Disuse for Commercial Traffic (N.B. 'used' means in 1947)	Abandonment Date of	Whether bought by Railway and Present Ownership
33 miles	18	75 ft by 14 ft		1936	Bought by Ambergate etc. Rly, 1854. To L.N.E.R. B.W.B.
¾ mile	1 tide-lock		c. 1859 and c. 1902. Part used	1858 and 1899	Bought by Victoria Station etc. Rly, 1858 and later. Westminster City Council
1¼ miles	3	84 ft by 14 ft 5 in.	Used		Bought by Regent's C., 1857. B.W.B.
½ mile	2 tide-locks		1829	1829[1]	Port of London Authority
1¾ miles	1 tide-lock	81 ft by 18 ft	1859[2]		Bought by West London Rly 1839. Part converted to rly. Lower ⅜ mile, B.W.B.
15¾ miles	10[3] & 1 flood-lock	83 ft by 14 ft 6 in.	Used		Bought by Grand Union C., 1932. B.W.B.
8¾ miles[4]	None		1799	1848	
5½ miles inc. br.	13 & 1 stop-lock	Locks 40 ft by 6 ft	1819[6]		Newdigate family
1¼ miles	7	72 ft by 7 ft	1863	1863	Bought by Newport Pagnell Rly and converted

[1] See text for details.

S

Canal	Date of Act under which Work was begun	Date wholly Opened	Approx. Cost at Opening	Terminal Points	Branches Built
Nottingham	1792	1796	£80,000	R. Trent–Cromford C., Langley Mill	
		c. 1794			Poplar Brewery Manvers (private) Bilborough (private) Greasley Robinetts Westcroft (private)
		c. 1836			
		1799			
		1800			
		1796			
		1842			
Nutbrook	1793	1795	£22,800	Erewash C., Stanton–Shipley wharf	
Oakham	1793	c. 1803	£65,000–£70,000	Melton Mowbray Nav.–Oakham	
Oxford	1769	1790[4]	£307,000	Coventry C., Long-ford–Oxford	Duke's Cut (private) Napton arm Wyken arm (private) Alexandra arm (private)[6]
Regent's	1812	1820	£710,000	Grand Junction C., Paddington–R. Thames	
	1813	1816			Cumberland City Road basin
	1819	c. 1820			

[1] Except Lenton-Trent lock.
[2] Except Lenton-Trent lock, transferred to Trent Navigation.
[3] The lowest portion was until recently kept open by the Stanton company.
[4] Except Isis lock, 1796.
[5] A branch to take coal to Napton back-pumping station.
[6] When the canal was straightened, various portions of the old canal became branches. The most important were: Clifton arm, ⅜ mile; Brownsover arm, 1¼ miles, a navigable feeder; Rugby arm, ¼ mile, disused 1958; Newbold arm, 1¼ miles; Fennis Field arm, ½ mile; Brinklow arm, ¼ mile, disused c. 1920; Stretton arm, ¼ mile; Wyken loop, ¾ mile.

Length	Greatest Number of Locks	Size of Boats Taken	Date of Disuse for Commercial Traffic (N.B. 'used' means in 1947)	Abandonment Date of	Whether bought by Railway and Present Ownership
4¾ miles	19 & 1 stop-lock	75 ft by 14 ft	1928[1]	1937[2]	Bought by Ambergate etc. Rly, 1855. To L.N.E.R. B.W.B.
mile					
mile					
mile					
⅝ miles			most c. 1813		
mile			c. 1875		
mile			1866		
½ mile					
4½ miles	13	73 ft by 14 ft 3 in.	1895[3]		Stanton & Staveley Ltd.
5¼ miles	19	72 ft by 14 ft 2 in.		1846	Bought by Midland Rly, 1846
91 miles sh. to 77½ miles	42	72 ft by 7 ft	Used		B.W.B.
mile	1				Leased to B.W.B.
mile			1948		
mile					
mile			1920s		
3⅝ miles	12	80 ft by 14 ft 6 in.	Used		Part of Grand Union, 1929. B.W.B.
mile			1937		
mile			Used		

Canal	Date of Act under which Work was begun	Date wholly Opened	Approx. Cost at Opening	Terminal Points	Branches Built
Stratford-upon-Avon	1793	1816 1802	£297,000	Worcs & B'ham C., King's Norton–Stratford	Kingswood
Warwick & Birmingham	1793	1800	£160,000	Birmingham C., Digbeth–Warwick	
Warwick & Napton	1794	1800	£75,000	Warwick & B'ham C. nr. Warwick–Oxford C., Napton[4]	Kaye's[5]
Woodeaves	None	c. 1802		Woodeaves brook–mills nr. Fenny Bentley	

D. Canals, the Main Lines of which were not Completed

Canal	Date of Act under which Work was begun	Date Opened	Approx. Cost at Opening	Authorized Terminal Points	Terminal Points as Built
Ashby-de-la-Zouch	1794	1804	£166,300[7]	Coventry C., Marston–Ashby	Coventry C., Marston–Moira
Leicestershire & Northamptonshire Union	1793	1797[11] 1809[12]	£205,000	Leicester C., Leicester–Northampton	Leicester C., Leicester–Market Harborough

[1] One less after 1932–4.
[2] As built. Increased in 1932–4 to 83 ft 6 in. by 15 ft except for the 6 locks at Camp Hill.
[3] Except for section from junction with Warwick & Napton to Warwick (Saltisford), disused 1934.
[4] Originally to the Oxford Canal at Braunston; line changed 1796.
[5] This branch originally crossed the canal from quarries on the north side to cement works on the south. The northern arm, ⅜ mile, was shut off during 1931–5. The southern is open.

Length	Greatest Number of Locks	Size of Boats Taken	Date of Disuse for Commercial Traffic (N.B. 'used' means in 1947)	Abandonment Date of	Whether bought by Railway and Present Ownership
5⅝ miles mile	55 & 1 stop-lock 1	72 ft by 7 ft	Part used		Bought by O.W.W.R. 1856. Now King's Norton–Kingswood–B.W.B.; Kingswood–Stratford, National Trust
2⅝ miles	33[1] & 1 stop-lock	72 ft by 7 ft[2]	Used[3]		Bought by Regent's C., 1929. B.W.B.
4¼ miles	25	72 ft by 7 ft[6]	Used		Bought by Regent's C., 1929. B.W.B.
mile	None		Used		
¼ miles	None				

Branches Built	Length	Greatest Number of Locks	Size of Boats Taken	Date of Disuse for Commercial Traffic ('used' means in 1947)	Date of Abandonment	Whether bought by Railway, and Present Ownership
	30 miles	1 stop-lock	74 ft 4 in. by 7 ft[8]	Used (part)	1944[9] 1957[10]	Bought by Midland Railway. 1846. To L.M.S.R. B.W.B.
	23¾ miles	25[13]	72 ft by 14 ft	Used		Bought by Grand Junction C., 1894. B.W.B.

[6] Increased in 1932–4 to 83 ft 6 in. by 15 ft.
[7] Including tramroads.
[8] Originally 14 ft wide, later narrowed.
[9] Moira–Donisthorpe.
[10] Donisthorpe–Ilott wharf.
[11] To Gumley Debdale.
[12] To Market Harborough.
[13] Later 24; one at Leicester eliminated 1890.

E. *Canals Partly Built but not Opened*
   None.

F. *Canals Authorized but not Begun*
   None.

APPENDIX II

Principal Engineering Works

A. *Inclined Planes*

Canal	Name of Plane	Vertical Rise	Dates Working	Notes
Grand Junction	Foxton	75 ft 2 in.	1901–10	Double-track, boats carried sideways in caissons, worked by steam engine

B. *Lifts*

Canal	Name of Lift	Vertical Rise	Dates Working	Notes
Regent's	Camden Town	6 ft 8 in.	Trials 1815–16	A boat floated in one of two tanks suspended by chains from carrying wheels, and balancing each other. Motive power manual, helped by the movement of compressed air

C. *Tunnels over 500 yards*

Chesterfield Canal	Norwood	2,850 yd[1]
Cromford Canal	Butterley	3,063 yd[2]
Grand Junction Canal	Blisworth	3,056 yd
Grand Junction Canal	Braunston	2,042 yd
Grand Union Canal	Crick	1,528 yd
Grand Union Canal	Husbands Bosworth	1,166 yd
Regent's Canal	Islington	960 yd
Leicestershire & Northamptonshire Union Canal	Saddington	880 yd
Oxford Canal	Fenny Compton	788 yd[3]

[1] See note to p. 35.
[2] As built, 2,966 yd.
[3] In two sections, 336 yd and 452 yd, separated by an opening of 155 yd. Later both sections were opened out.

D. *Outstanding Aqueducts*

Birmingham & Warwick Junction Canal	Tame
Coventry Canal	Tame
Cromford Canal	Derwent
Grand Junction Canal	Wolverton (Ouse)
Oxford Canal	Brinklow[1]
Stratford-upon-Avon Canal	Bearley
Warwick & Napton Canal	Avon

[1] Now partly an embankment.

INDEX

*The principal references to canals and river navigations
are indicated in bold type*

Abingdon, 115, 158, 175
Adelphi Canal, 36, **74**, 268-9
Agricultural produce, carried on canals, etc., 50, 63. *See also* Corn, Flour, Wool, Cheese, Beans, Flax, Hay, Straw, Vegetables, Cattle
Aldenham, 132, 236
Alderwasley, 42
Alexandra Arm, 274-5
Alfreton, 41-2, 70
Allport, J. J., railway manager, 194
Amber River, 33, 41, 51
Ambergate, 51, 186, 195
Ambergate, Nottingham etc. Railway, 195-6
Anderton, 249
Andover Canal, 158
Anker River, 23, 43
Anson, Lord, 146
Ansty, 123-4, 144, 161
Apsley, 122
Aqueducts, canal, Amber, 51; Arbury, 27; Avon, 173, 280; Bearley, 180, 280; Blyth, 167; Brinklow, 21, 160, 280; Charnwood Forest, 88; Cole, 180; Derwent, 51-3, 280; Holmes, 68; Rugby-Lutterworth road, 160; Tame (Coventry), 17, 22-4, 280; Tame (B. & W. J.), 280; Wolverton, 113, 280; Wootton Wawen, 180; Yarningale, 180
Arbury, 26-9
Arkwright, Sir Richard, 41-2
Ashbourne, 72
Ashby-de-la-Zouch, 142, 147-8, 150, 156, 212
Ashby-de-la-Zouch Canal, 42, 67, 77, 79-81, 85-6, 88, 117, 126, 141, **146-56**, 187, 209, **211-13**, 249, 276-7
Ashby Woulds, 80, 147-51, 154
Ashes, carried on canals, etc., 119
Ashover, 33
Ashton-under-Lyne Canal, 50
Ashted, 174, 176
Associated Canal Carriers Ltd., 242
Aston (Birmingham), 176, 178
Atherstone, 16-17, 19, 22-4, 42, 213
Atherstone, Ashby & Burton Railway, 211
Autherley, 123
Averham, 204
Avon River, 123-4, 173, 280
Avon, Upper, Navigation, 15, 164-5, 179-81

Aylesbury, 109, 133, 220
Aylesbury branch, 110 n., 114-16, 188, 270-1
Aylestone, 80, 99
Aynho, 25, 108

Bakewell Canal, 52
Ballast, carried on canals, etc., 40, 53
Baltic goods, carried on canals, etc., 98
Banbury, 15, 17-18, 20-1, 24-5, 158, 214
Banks, and canal companies, 192, 229
Baring, Sir Thomas, Bt, committeeman, 129
Barlow, S. E., carriers, 243-4
Barnes, James, engineer, 25, 90, 100-1, 104, 109-11, 116, 126
Barnsley Canal, 74
Barrow-upon-Soar, 91
Barrow Hill, 79, 86
Bawtry, 30-4
Bascote, 172, 241
Baxendale, Joseph, shareholder, 134
Baynes, Sir Christopher, promoter, 128
Bean, William, engineer, 29
Beans, carried on canals, etc., 63
Bearley, 180, 280
Beaumont, Sir George, coalowner, 88, 92
Bedford, 98, 114, 126
Bedford-Grand Junction canal projects, 114, 126
Bedford Railway, 114
Bedworth, 15-16, 19-20, 25, 144, 161
Beer, carried on canals, etc., 76, 146, 162
Beeston, 55, 58, 65, 75, 205
Beeston Cut, 45 n., 55-8, 64, 74-6, 196, 266-7
Belgium, 235, 243, 245
Belper, 42, 71
Beresford, Francis, ironmaster, 42
Berkhampstead, 241
Bernard, Sir Thomas, Bt., committeeman, 129
Bevan, Benjamin, engineer, 97, 104-5, 126
Bilborough, 49, 58
Bilborough Cut, 57, 274-5
Bingham, 61
Birmingham, 19, 22, 40, 82, 108, 116, 119, 122-3, 134, 141-3, 152-3, 156, 159, 163-7, 169, 171, 186, 212, 214, 217-8, 221, 228, 230, 236-7, 240-3, 245

T